COUNTRY WISDOM ALMANAC

COUNTRY WISDOM ALMANAC

373 Tips, Crafts, Home Improvements, Recipes, and Homemade Remedies

Excerpted from Storey Publishing's
* Country Wisdom Library *

BLACK DOG
& LEVENTHAL
PUBLISHERS
NEW YORK

Published by
Black Dog & Leventhal Publishers, Inc.
151 West 19th Street
New York, NY 10011

Distributed by
Workman Publishing Company
225 Varick Street
New York, NY 10014

Portions of the material contained in this book were originally published
by Storey Publishing LLC as part of its Country Wisdom Bulletin series.

Manufactured in the United States of America
Cover and interior design by Elizabeth Driesbach

ISBN-13: 978-1-57912-774-9

hgfedcba

Library of Congress Cataloging-in-Publication Data available on file.

CONTENTS

Spring

CRAFTS

GARDENING

Summer

Summer Solstices, 2008–2020
Summer Holidays (United States and Canada)

ANIMALS

COOKING

Autumn

Autumnal Equinoxes, 2008–2020
Autumn Holidays (United States and Canada)

ANIMALS

COOKING

Winter

Winter Solstices, 2008–2020
Winter Holidays (United States and Canada)

ANIMALS

COOKING

CRAFTS

GARDENING

Spring

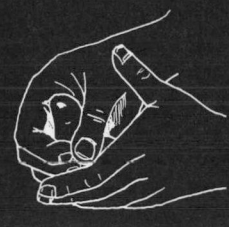

VERNAL EQUINOXES, 2008–2020
Times given are Eastern Standard Time (EST)

2008	Thursday	March 20	1:48 a.m.
2009	Friday	March 20	7:44 a.m.
2010	Saturday	March 20	1:32 p.m.
2011	Sunday	March 20	7:21 p.m.
2012	Tuesday	March 20	11:14 a.m.
2013	Wednesday	March 20	7:02 a.m.
2014	Thursday	March 20	12:57 a.m.
2015	Friday	March 20	6:45 p.m.
2016	Sunday	March 20	1:30 a.m.
2017	Monday	March 20	6:28 a.m.
2018	Tuesday	March 20	12:15 p.m.
2019	Wednesday	March 20	5:58 p.m.
2020	Thursday	March 19	11:49 p.m.

SPRING HOLIDAYS

(United States and Canada)

ST. PATRICK'S DAY • *March 17*
DAYLIGHT SAVING TIME BEGINS • *second Sunday in March*
APRIL FOOLS' DAY • *April 1*
GOOD FRIDAY* • *Friday before Easter Sunday*
EASTER SUNDAY • *first Sunday after first full moon after vernal equinox*
EASTER MONDAY* • *Monday after Easter Sunday*
EARTH DAY • *April 22*
NATIONAL ARBOR DAY • *last Friday in April*
MOTHER'S DAY • *second Sunday in May*
VICTORIA DAY • *Monday preceding May 25*
MEMORIAL DAY • *last Monday in May*
FLAG DAY • *June 14*

*CANADIAN FEDERAL HOLIDAY

Animals

001

PROVIDING NESTING MATERIALS

To make the nest-building process easier (and possibly make your birdhouse more attractive to potential nest builders), you can offer birds nesting materials. Robins and barn swallows need mud. Songbirds use twigs, feathers, straw, grasses, and leaves to build their nests but will be thankful for short threads, string, yarn, tissues, hair (human or horse), lint from the clothes dryer, and bits of cloth. Long threads or wads of cotton may be more dangerous than useful; they can become tangled in a bird's claws.

002

NESTING PLATFORM FOR ROBINS, EASTERN PHOEBES, AND BARN SWALLOWS, PART 1 OF 3

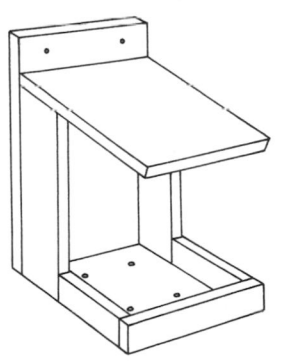

Robins, phoebes, and barn swallows will not use an enclosed birdhouse; they prefer a shelter with one or more open sides.

Materials
Back and roof: *3/4 x 7 1/2 x 23—inch (1.9 x 19 x 63.5 cm) piece of wood*
Bottom: *3/4 x 8 x 6—inch (1.9 x 20.3 x 15.2 cm) piece of wood*
Sides: *3/4 x 6 x 11 1/2—inch (1.9 x 15.2 x 29.2 cm) piece of wood*

Closure Strips: *3/4 x 1 1/2 x 17 1/2–inch (1.9 x 3.8 x 44.4 cm) piece of wood*
Eighteen 1 5/8–inch (4.1 cm) stainless-steel drywall screws or 6d galvanized
   ring-shank nails
Two brass or galvanized 6 x 2–inch (5.1 cm) wood screws and washers to fit
Glue

Tools

Tape measure
Carpenter's square
Pencil
Circular saw or handsaw and miter box
Hand or power drill and drill bits: 1/4 inch (6.35 cm), 3/8 inch (9.53 cm)
Phillips-head screwdriver or power drill filled with screwdriver bit

Cutting diagram

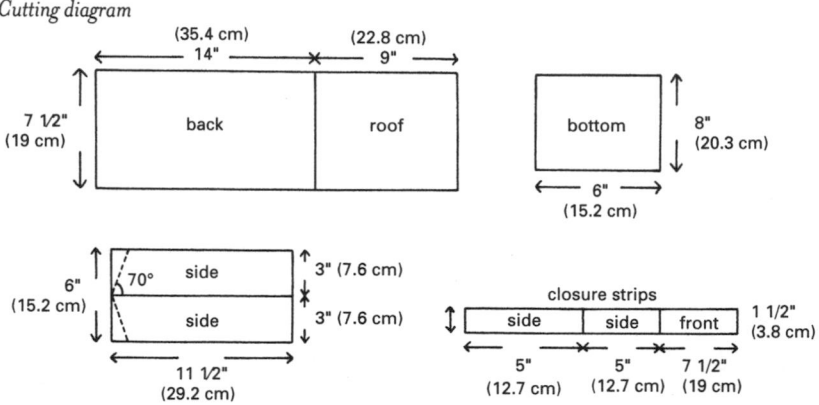

Cutting note: For barn swallows and phoebes, the bottom should be cut to 6 x 6 inches (15.2 x 15.2 cm) and the side closure strips should be measured off at 3 inches (7.6 cm).

NESTING PLATFORM FOR ROBINS, EASTERN PHOEBES, AND BARN SWALLOWS, PART 2 OF 3

Directions

1. Cut one end of each **side** at a 70-degree angle.
2. In the **bottom**, drill four 1/4-inch (0.6 cm) drainage holes. Then

align each **side** with the back of the **bottom**, glue both faces, and nail or screw together.

3. If you will be mounting the platform, predrill two 3/8-inch (1 cm) holes 1 inch (2.5 cm) down from the top and 2 inches (5.1 cm) in from either side of the **back**. Align the **back** with the **sides** and **bottom**; glue and screw or nail together.

4. Bevel-cut the **roof** at 70 degrees along one of the 7 1/2-inch (19 cm) edges. Glue and screw or nail the **roof** to the **sides** and the **back** to the **roof**.

5. Glue and screw or nail 1 x 2–inch (2.5 x 5.1 cm) front and side **closure strips** around the edge of the **bottom**.

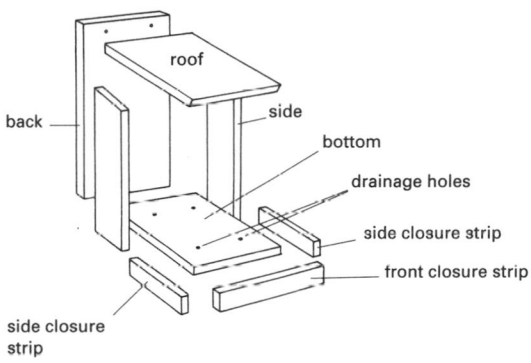

004

NESTING PLATFORM FOR ROBINS, EASTERN PHOEBES, AND BARN SWALLOWS, PART 3 OF 3

Mounting

If you're going to attach the platform to a tree, building, or post, secure it through the back with 2-inch (5.1 cm) screws and washers.

For robins: Mount platform 6 to 15 feet (1.8 to 4.6 m) above the ground.

For phoebes and barn swallows: Mount platform 8 to 12 feet (2.4 to 3.7 m) above the ground.

Hanging

Hang the platform in partial shade, either from the main branch of a tree or under a shed or porch overhang.

RESCUING A FALLEN BABY BIRD

If you find a baby bird that's fallen from its nest, your first priority should be warmth, because young nestlings have no control over their body temperature. If the nestling feels warm to the touch and the nest it fell from is within fairly easy reach, simply climb up (carefully!) and replace the nestling. (Don't worry about that old myth that a bird will reject its young if the baby has been touched by a human—with the exception of vultures, birds barely have a sense of smell.) If, however, the baby bird feels cool, you'll need to gently warm it in your cupped hands first. So long as the bird doesn't seem extremely lethargic or weak, it's safe to replace it in the nest once it feels warm.

If the baby bird's nest has been knocked down as well, you'll need to pick up the nest and replace it in the tree in the spot from which it fell (or reasonably close to it). Secure the nest with heavy twine or some wire if necessary. (Avoid thin string, which birds can get tangled in.) If you need both hands to climb up, enlist a friend to hold and warm the bird. When the nest has been safely secured, replace the bird and monitor the scene for a while to make sure there is parental activity.

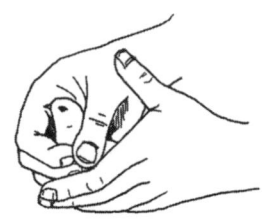

Baby birds can easily become hypothermic, so if a downed nestling feels cool, warm it in your hands before replacing it in the nest.

RECOGNIZING A HEALTHY RABBIT

When you're considering purchasing a rabbit as a pet (or a trio of rabbits as an initial investment), good health is the most important quality to consider. Look for the following features to determine whether a rabbit is healthy:

- **Eyes.** The eyes are bright, with no discharge, no spots, and no cloudiness.

- **Ears.** The ears look clean inside. A brown, crusty appearance could indicate ear mites.
- **Nose.** The nose is clean and dry, with no discharge that might indicate a cold.
- **Front feet.** These are clean. A crusty matting on the inside of the front paws indicates that the rabbit has been wiping a runny nose and, thus, may have a cold.
- **Hind feet.** The bottoms of the hind feet are well furred. Bare or sore-looking spots can indicate the beginning of sore hocks.
- **Teeth.** The front teeth line up correctly, and the two top front teeth slightly overlap the bottom ones.
- **General condition.** The rabbit's fur is clean. Its body feels smooth and firm, not bony.
- **Rear end.** The area at the base of the rabbit's tail should be clean, with no manure sticking to the fur.

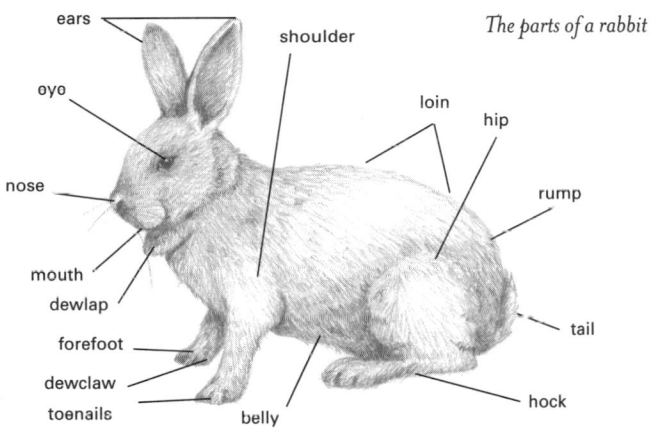

The parts of a rabbit

ears, shoulder, eye, loin, hip, nose, rump, mouth, dewlap, forefoot, tail, dewclaw, toenails, belly, hock

GETTING ACQUAINTED WITH A NEW RABBIT

Get to know your rabbit in a setting where both of you can be comfortable. A good place to get acquainted is at a picnic table covered with a rug, towel, or some other covering that will give the rabbit secure, not slippery, footing. Your rabbit will be able to move around safely on the table, and you can safely visit and pet your rabbit without having to lift it. Rabbits will usually not jump off a table. In spite of this, *never leave a rabbit unattended when it is out of its cage.*

Once your rabbit seems comfortable on the table, practice picking it up. Because the table offers a handy surface to set the rabbit safely back onto, this setting is much better than risking a possible fall to the ground.

See tip 100 for advice on how to pick up your rabbit.

CLEAN FLOORS EQUAL HEALTHY HORSES

Horse owners take heed: *never* feed a horse on the floor of a dirty stall. If he is exposed to filth, you may well have a recurring internal parasite problem. If you don't want to use an elevated hay feeder, be sure that the floor of the stall is clean before leaving hay there for your horse to feed on.

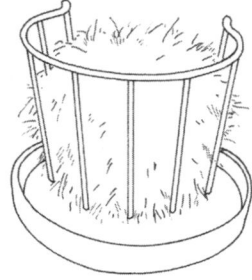

A wall-mounted hay feeder

SOLVING COMMON DOG BEHAVIOR PROBLEMS: BARKING

Dogs bark for several reasons:

- They sense danger.
- They want something they can't get by themselves: food, water, a toy, a cat in the neighbor's yard, another dog.
- They're annoyed or bored.
- They're joining other dogs in song.

Solution: The first two reasons for barking can be corrected by changing the situation. In the case of the last two reasons, don't allow the dog to bark for so long that it becomes a habit. These are usually problems of an outside dog that has little interaction with his family. Such barking is irritating to anyone who hears it and can cause problems between your family and your neighbors. A barking dog wants attention. Give him plenty of attention. Play fetch or take him for a healthy jogging expedition before you go to bed. Both of you will sleep more soundly.

010

QUIETING A WHINING PUP

Puppies are adorable, but their whining can become an irritating habit if it isn't corrected immediately. Spending too much time with your puppy can cause him to be overly dependent on you. He needs to learn to accept being alone or being without your attention, even if you're home or in the same room. Your dog may also whine when he needs to go out or when he's hungry.

Solution: If it's near the time the puppy needs to relieve himself, take him right out to the potty area. Return him to the same spot when he's finished.

If the dog is in his crate, be sure he has some toys to keep his interest. You don't want the puppy to think he's banished or being punished when he's in the crate.

If the puppy isn't in the crate, watch his body language when he whines. Is he trying to get your attention because he needs your help? Maybe his chew toy was taken by another dog or is behind a closed door.

If you can't find any reason for the whining, ignore it completely. When it stops, you can take the puppy out of the crate and play with him. Never remove the puppy when he's whining, or you will reinforce the whining, and it will continue—only stronger next time.

011

NATURAL FLEA PROTECTION FOR DOGS

An easy way to protect your dog from fleas is to apply a drop or two of eucalyptus essential oil on top of her head and ears, down her spine, and on her tail.

Aromatic Homemade Flea Collar

This flea collar discourages fleas from taking up residence on your dog.

1 part chamomile flowers
1 part pennyroyal leaves
1 part rosemary herb
1 part rue leaves
1 part southernwood leaves
1 part wormwood leaves
3–5 drops eucalyptus essential oil

Combine all the ingredients and spread across the length of a scarf or bandana. Roll up the scarf around the herbs and tie it around your dog's neck.

Regular application of a flea rinse or powder will rid your dog of these pests and discourage them from returning.

012

FLEAS-FLEE POWDER

This powder is great for keeping fleas away. If, however, your pet already has fleas, you'll need to purchase a commercial flea killer.

1 part powdered rosemary
1 part powdered pennyroyal leaves
1 part powdered rue leaves
1 part powdered southernwood leaves
1 part powdered wormwood leaves

Combine all the herbs. Apply liberally to your pet's fur, remembering to get underneath the tail, the inner thighs, the "armpits," and the genital area. You may want to undertake this task outdoors so the powder does not end up all over your house.

PLANTS THAT ARE POISONOUS FOR CATS

You don't need to be a horticulturist to have cats, but knowing safe plants from dangerous ones can save your cat's life. Here's a list of some of the more popular—but poisonous—houseplants that all cat owners should banish from their homes and yards:

- American mistletoe
- Azalea
- Buttercup
- Ficus
- Foxglove
- Horse chestnut
- Hyacinth
- Hydrangea
- Iris
- Jack-in-the-pulpit
- Lily
- Lily of the valley

- Morning glory
- Nightshade
- Onions and chives
- Ornamental tobacco
- Poinsettia
- Poison hemlock
- Poppy
- Rhubarb
- Rubber plant
- Sweet pea
- Tomato vines
- Tulip

If your cat displays any of the following symptoms of poisoning, take her to the vet right away:

- No appetite
- Acute diarrhea
- Repeated vomiting

- Swollen tongue
- Tender or painful abdomen
- Convulsions

HOUSEPLANTS VERSUS CAT PLANTS

To teach your cat which plants are a no-no and which are okay, you'll first need to make your houseplants unavailable. Hang them from ceiling hooks or situate them on high shelves your cat can't access. Then offer a green alternative such as cat grass or dill. Place the new grass or herb where the favored houseplant used to be. If a houseplant *still* attracts your cat, spray the plant with a cayenne-pepper- or citrus-based repellent, which should turn off your plant hunter in no time.

Many cats love to chew, especially on houseplants. Be sure that none of your houseplants is poisonous to cats. To satisfy your cat's chewing obsession, you might consider setting out a cat-friendly plant or two for her to munch on.

015

BEYOND CATNIP: OTHER GREENS YOUR CAT WILL ENJOY

Most cats enjoy munching on plants, and they don't distinguish between outdoor and indoor plants. To accommodate your foliage-seeking feline and save your houseplants, consider growing a couple of plants especially for your cat.

Cat Grass
Cat grass is especially suited for feline digestion. You can purchase preseeded cat-grass beds at most pet- and garden-supply stores. Just follow the sprouting instructions. You can also make your own cat-grass bed. Fill an aluminum brownie pan with organic seed-starting mix and scatter wheatgrass berries over the surface. Cover with about 1/4 inch (6 mm) of soil and set the tray in a warm, sunny location. The grass will be ready in about a week.

Herbs for Cats
Dill and catnip are excellent herbs to offer fresh to your cat. Purchase a few seedlings of each; once they've matured to a sturdy height, set them out in a high-cat-traffic area.

Cooking

016

HOMEMADE BALLPARK MUSTARD

This is the mustard for hot dogs and other sausages. It can also be used in potato salads.

2 tablespoons (30 ml) powdered mustard
1 tablespoon (15 ml) turmeric
1/4 teaspoon (1 ml) salt
1 teaspoon (5 ml) sugar
Water or mixture of water and white vinegar to mix

Put the mustard, turmeric, salt, and sugar into a small bowl. Gradually add water or water and vinegar, stirring to make a smooth paste of the consistency you want.

Tip
An English brand of yellow powdered mustard, Coleman's, is widely available, and it now also comes in a coarse-ground form. You may also find powdered mustard in bulk in health and other specialty food shops.

017

MAKE YOUR OWN BEAN SPROUTS

It's easy to sprout beans. Wash I cup (237 ml) of dried beans and pick out any that are broken. Soak them overnight in warm water. Drain. Place the beans in a glass jar and cover the mouth with a screen or cheesecloth. Keep the jar in a warm, dark place for 3 to 5 days. Rinse the beans gently with warm water, draining them thoroughly each time, at least 3 times a day, more often if the weather is very warm.

Sprouts are ready when they are I or 2 inches (2.5 or 5 cm) long. Rinse them thoroughly in cold water, drain well, and store in a covered container in the refrigerator. The sprouts will keep about 4 days. One cup (237 ml) of dried beans yields 4 cups (946 ml) of sprouts.

THE BEST BLOSSOMS FOR EATING

If your only criterion is that they be nonpoisonous, then many flowers are edible—but not all of them are yummy. Following are the best-known, most delicious edible flowers:

- Basil
- Chamomile
- Chives
- Dill
- Hibiscus
- Lavender
- Marigolds
- Nasturtiums
- Roses
- Sweet peas
  (Note: Other parts of the sweet pea plant are poisonous —only the flower is edible!)
- Violas (pansies, Johnny-jump-ups, and violets)

SNOW-PEA SALAD WITH SWEET-PEA FLOWERS

8 ounces (225 g) fresh snow peas in their pods
1 teaspoon (5 ml) sesame oil
1 teaspoon (5 ml) tamari
1 teaspoon (5 ml) balsamic vinegar
8 sweet-pea flowers

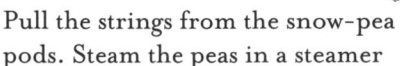

Pull the strings from the snow-pea pods. Steam the peas in a steamer basket until they turn bright green, about 1 minute. Immediately plunge the peas into a bowl of ice water or rinse them under very cold water until they are cool. (If you don't stop the cooking this way, they will continue to cook and turn olive drab.) Dry the snow peas.

Combine the oil, tamari, and vinegar in a small bowl; whisk until well combined. Pour the dressing over the snow peas.

Just before serving, decorate the salad with the sweet-pea flowers.

Yield: 4 servings

SPRING FLING TEA

This is a light, refreshing tea. To maximize the fresh, lively taste, it's best to use fresh herbs rather than dried.

2 parts violet leaves and flowers
2 parts sweet-cicely leaves
1 part nettle leaves
1 part raspberry leaves
1 part mint leaves

Mix 10 to 12 tablespoons (150 to 180 ml) of fresh herbs, or 5 to 6 tablespoons (75 to 90 ml) of dried, in 2 to 3 cups (473 to 710 ml) of cold water and let sit for several hours. Drink warm or cool.

STAND-UP STEAMING FOR SPRING ASPARAGUS

Break off the lower part of the stalk at the point where it snaps easily. Clean stalks well. Now gather them into a bundle and secure it with string or a rubber band. Stand the bundle upright in a tall pan in about one inch of water. Cover, or invert a bowl over, the pan to form a tall steam chamber (or use a tall coffeepot). Bring the water to a boil and steam for 3 to 4 minutes or until the stalks are tender. Now remove the string or rubber band and serve the asparagus with a little salt, pepper, and butter.

WHAT MAKES HOT PEPPERS SIZZLE?

Researchers at New Mexico State University have identified at least six compounds in hot peppers that pour on the heat, but the chief chemical ingredient is capsaicin, a crystalline alkaloid that acts as an irritant.

The degree of heat in hot peppers can be measured on a scale using Scoville units. Created by William Scoville in 1912, the scale refers to the parts per million of capsaicin in a pepper variety. Scoville discovered that the human tongue can detect as little as 1 part per million of the substance.

How Hot Is Hot?

Pepper Variety	Scoville Heat Units
Anaheim Chile	250–1,400
Jalapeño	4,000–6,000
Serrano Chile	7,000–25,000
Cayenne	30,000–35,000
Chile Pequin	35,000–40,000
Tabasco	30,000–50,000
Habañero	200,000–350,000

SAFE PEPPER HANDLING

When handling hot peppers, be sure to
wear rubber or latex gloves. Take care not
to touch your face—especially your eyes—and
wash your hands thoroughly with soap and water afterward.

TWO SALSAS

One of these is hotter-than-Hades spicy, the other is much milder.

Xnipec, or Dog's Nose Salsa

1 red onion, diced
1/3 cup (2.75 fl oz/75 ml) freshly squeezed lime juice
5 habañeros, stems and seeds removed, diced (for greater hotness, don't remove the seeds)
2 Roma or plum tomatoes, diced
Salt to taste

Soak the diced onion in the lime juice for at least 30 minutes.
Add the other ingredients and run in a food processor or blender,
adding a little water if desired. This salsa is best when used within an
hour or two of being made.

Yield: About 1 1/2 cups (355 ml)

Tomatillo Salsa Verde

8 medium tomatillos, husked, rinsed, and quartered
3 tablespoons (45 ml) fresh cilantro, chopped
1/2 cup (2.75 oz/75 g) green Anaheim or New Mexico chiles, chopped
  (or use a 4-ounce [113 g] can of peeled green chiles)
1 teaspoon (5 ml) garlic, minced
2 tablespoons (30 ml) onion, chopped

Run all of the ingredients together in a food processor or blender—or mince everything very finely by hand and combine. Refrigerate, covered, for at least an hour.

Yield: About 1 1/2 cups (355 ml)

NUTRITION NOTES: GETTING THE MOST FROM COOKED VEGETABLES

To conserve the nutritional value of cooked vegetables, use only a small amount of water (or none) and cook until just tender. Stir-fried vegetables should be tender yet crisp. Save the cooking liquid, if any, to use in soups, stews, and sauces. Or drink it!

SPINACH SQUARES

4 cups uncooked fresh spinach, chopped (about 10 ounces)
2–3 tablespoons (31–47g) butter or margarine
3 eggs
1 cup (237 ml) flour
1 cup (237 ml) milk
1/2 teaspoon (2.5 ml) salt
1 teaspoon (5 ml) baking powder
3/4–1 pound (83–110 g) Monterey Jack or Cheddar cheese, grated

Preheat the oven to 350°F (180°C).

Wash the spinach well and pat or spin it dry. Melt the butter in a 9 x 13–inch (22.9 x 33 cm) pan in oven. Meanwhile, beat the eggs in a large bowl. Add the flour, milk, salt, and baking powder. Stir in the cheese and spinach. Mix well and pour into the buttered pan. Smooth the surface and bake for about 35 minutes. Cool for 20 minutes before cutting into 1-inch (2.5 cm) squares.

If you want to freeze these, arrange them on a cookie sheet and place in the freezer. Once they're frozen, put them into a plastic bag. Reheat on a cookie sheet for about 20 minutes at 350°F (180°C), or if at room temperature, 20 to 35 seconds in a microwave oven.

Yield: About fifty 1-inch squares as an appetizer or 8 servings as an entrée.

RAS AL HANOUT

This North African spice mix can be used the way curry is used in Indian cooking; just like curry, its fragrance and flavor are nearly indescribable. It is excellent as a rub for lamb.

1 tablespoon (15 ml) cinnamon
1 teaspoon (5 ml) ground cardamom
1 teaspoon (5 ml) ground nutmeg
1 teaspoon (5 ml) ground cumin
1/2 teaspoon (2.5 ml) freshly ground black pepper
1/4 teaspoon (1.3 ml) turmeric
1/4 teaspoon (1.3 ml) mace
1/4 teaspoon (1.3 ml) ground coriander
1 cup (237 ml) dried rose petals

Sift together all of the spices to remove any little stems and pieces. Toss with the rose petals and store in an airtight jar.

Yield: About 1 cup (237 ml)

SWEET SUGAR SUBSTITUTES

If you're making something sweet that calls for sugar, but you don't have any of the stuff around, keep in mind that I cup (8 oz/225 g) of white sugar is equal to each of the following:

1/2 cup (4 oz/118 ml) honey
1/2 cup (4 oz/118 ml) molasses
2/3 cup (5 fl oz/158 ml) maple syrup
1/3 cup (1.5 oz/42 g) crystalline fructose
1 1/2 cups (18 oz/510 g) maltose
1/2 cup (6 oz/175 g) sorghum
1 cup (6 oz/175 g) brown sugar, lightly packed

HONEY CHOCOLATE BROWNIES

Make this sweet treat for your honey (or for yourself).

1 cup (8 oz/227 g) butter, softened
1 1/2 cups (18 oz/350 g) honey
3 eggs, beaten
1 teaspoon (5 ml) vanilla
1/2 teaspoon (2.5 ml) salt
4 ounces (110 g) unsweetened chocolate, melted and cooled
1 cup (5 oz/150 g) unbleached white flour
1 cup (4–6 oz/110–175 g) chopped walnuts

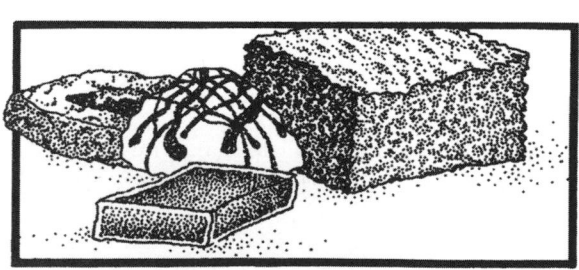

Beat the butter with an electric mixer until creamy. Slowly add the honey in a steady stream, mixing constantly. Add the eggs, vanilla, and salt. Add the melted chocolate alternately with the flour. Stir in the nuts. Pour the batter into a well-greased 9 x 12 x 2–inch (23 x 30 x 5 cm) pan and bake at 350°F (180°C) for 20 to 25 minutes. Watch for burning, turning down the oven if the brownies darken too quickly.

COUNTRY INN GRANOLA

The currants in this recipe are made from dried Zante grapes, native to Greece. They are quite different from the tiny berry called a currant.

10 cups (900 g) rolled oats (not instant oatmeal)
1/4 cup (78 ml) pure Vermont maple syrup
3/4 cup (150 g) dried blueberries
3/4 cup (150 g) dried cranberries
1/2 cup (100 g) dried apples, chopped
1/2 cup (75 g) slivered almonds
1/2 cup (75 g) Zante currants
1/2 cup (75 g) chopped pecans
1 tablespoon (14 g) kosher salt
1 cup (200 g) granulated sugar
1 cup (180 g) light brown sugar, firmly packed
1 cup (240 ml) apple cider or apple juice
1/4 cup (1/2 stick/55 g) butter

1. In a large mixing bowl, combine the oats, syrup, blueberries, cranberries, apples, almonds, currants, pecans, and salt.
2. In a saucepan over low heat, dissolve the granulated and brown sugars in the cider and bring to a simmer. Continue simmering until the amount is reduced by one third, then add the butter in small pieces, stirring with a wire whisk.
3. Drizzle the cider syrup over the oat mixture, stirring well to prevent clumping.
4. Spread the mixture on a baking sheet and cool at room temperature for 30 minutes. Store in an airtight container or freeze.

Yield: 14–16 servings

SALT

Because sodium, a necessary nutrient, occurs naturally in adequate amounts in foods (including vegetables), we don't really need to use salt in our cooking. Babies who don't get salt in their food don't miss it, but those of us who have acquired a taste for salt seem to think that it makes foods, especially vegetables and eggs, taste better. Because some people, primarily older persons, find that salt and salty foods cause fluid retention, and because sodium is associated with high blood pressure, many cooks are choosing to leave it out.

A sensible approach is to moderate our use of salt, in the same way we moderate our intake of fats and sugars. Salt in modest amounts is found in some of the recipes in this book. Feel free to cut it down or leave it out if you wish or if your doctor recommends that you do so.

Swapping Herbs for Salt

If you want to cut back on your dietary salt, try using herbs as flavorings. Here are time-tested guidelines for cooking with herbs.

- Add most herbs about 30 minutes before the end of cooking time. Simmer them slowly with the food to release the flavor and retain the volatile oils.
- Dried herbs are more potent than fresh—1 teaspoon (5 ml) dried equals 1 tablespoon (15 ml) fresh.
- Experiment! Try herbs in old recipes, taste new ones, try new combinations.
- Use moderation. Some herbs may be overpowering if too much is used. Familiarize yourself with the strongly flavored ones—sage, rosemary, thyme, and tarragon.

Thyme (Thymus vulgaris)

FROZEN TARRAGON CUBES

When you have a supply of these little cubes in your freezer, you will never suffer from a lack of minced "fresh" tarragon. If the tarragon sprigs you use are supple and tender, the stems can be used right along with the leaves. If the stems are woody, it's best to strip off and use only the leaves.

4 cups (946 ml) packed tarragon sprigs (see above)
1/2 cup (4 fl oz/118 ml) olive oil
Garlic, optional (see below)

Tarragon

1. Put the tarragon in a food processor. Start the machine and add the olive oil gradually until the mixture reaches a pastelike consistency. (You may not have to add all the oil.) If you want to add the garlic, do so now.
2. Put the tarragon paste into ice cube trays and place in your freezer.
3. When the paste is frozen, put the cubes into one or more plastic bags, label, and store in the freezer.
4. Use whenever fresh tarragon is called for and wherever it sounds like a good idea. (A few "good ideas": add a cube or two to scrambled eggs or any rice dish, or on top of any vegetable.)

Variation: If you don't want to add garlic, you can add other herbs. Make sure you label your cubes as plain, garlic, or mixed herb.

CHIVED GREEN BEANS

What chives can do for food! Their fresh, sharp bite adds zest to many dishes.

1 pound (454 g) fresh green beans, washed, stems snapped off
2 tablespoons (30 ml) butter

1/4 cup (60 ml) chives, chopped
1 teaspoon (5 ml) white wine vinegar
Salt and freshly ground black pepper

I. Steam or boil the green beans until just tender, then drain.
2. In a saucepan, melt the butter over medium-low heat and add the chives. Stir for I minute, then add the green beans and continue stirring for another 2 minutes.
3. Add the vinegar and salt and pepper to taste, then remove from the heat and serve immediately.

Yield: Serves 4 as a side dish

Chive (Allium schoenoprasum)

CREATIVE USES FOR CELERY LEAVES

The outer, darker green leaves of celery are strong tasting and are good for flavoring or for adding to green salads. The inner, lighter leaves are delicate and are nice chopped and added to sandwich fillings, salads, and soups. You can easily make cream of celery soup by cooking the chopped leaves and outer stalks in chicken broth until tender. Add an equal amount of medium cream sauce and season to taste. Blend until somewhat smooth.

COOKING WITH BLUEBERRIES

Fresh Versus Frozen

There is little difference between cooking with fresh and cooking with frozen blueberries. Nutritionally, while the calories remain the same—90 calories and 0.7 grams of fat per cup—other nutritional values per cup are somewhat different.

Nutrient	Fresh	Frozen
Calcium	22 mg	17 mg
Vitamin A	150 units	120 units
Ascorbic acid	20 mg	12 mg
Iron	1.5 mg	1.3 mg
Potassium	117 mg	134 mg

Wild Versus Cultivated

For cooking purposes, there is a slight difference between the small, intensely flavored wild blueberries and the larger, milder-flavored cultivated ones. If you are fortunate enough to have a choice, go for the smaller wild berries for bread recipes that use batters, and the larger, cultivated ones for recipes in which the blueberries blend into a sauce or thick filling.

BLUEBERRY SYRUP

2 cups (8 oz/225 g) blueberries, washed and patted dry
1 cup water (8 fl oz/237 g)
1/2 cup sugar (4 oz/100g)
1 tablespoon (15 ml) cornstarch
1 teaspoon lemon juice (1/2 fl oz/15 ml)
1 teaspoon (5 ml) cinnamon
1/2 teaspoon ginger (2.5 ml)

1. In a small saucepan, combine all of the ingredients. Turn heat on low and bring to a simmer. Simmer for 5 minutes.
2. Use a potato masher to mash the berries, then simmer for another 5 minutes.
3. Remove from heat. Cool before serving.

Yield: About 1 pint

BLUEBERRY BETTY

Here's a great way to use up bread that's just starting to turn stale.

2 cups (8 oz/225 g) blueberries
2 tablespoons (1 fl oz/30 ml) lemon juice
3/4 cup (4.5 oz/128 g) brown sugar
4 cups (6.5 oz/182 g) bread cubes without crusts
1/4 cup (2 oz/56 g) sugar
1 teaspoon (5 ml) cinnamon

Preheat the oven to 350°F (180°C).

Mix together the berries, lemon juice, and brown sugar. Put half the blueberry mix into a greased 9-inch (23 cm) square baking dish.

Mix together bread cubes, sugar, and cinnamon. Put half the bread mixture over the berries in the baking dish.

Spoon the remaining blueberry mixture over the bread mixture. Top with the remaining bread mixture.

Bake for 25 minutes. Serve with ice cream or whipped cream.

Yield: 8 servings

Crafts

DECORATED GIFT SOAPS

To make your own beautifully decorated gift soaps, start with a bar of either homemade or purchased soap and some small dried flowers or leaves. Simply moisten the surface of the bar and apply the dried flowers. If your design consists of multiple flowers that overlap, melt a little paraffin or beeswax and brush gently onto the underside of each botanical. Press into place on the soap according to the design. Let the bar dry completely, then cover with plastic wrap.

CREPE PAPER EASTER EGG DECORATIONS

With bits of colored paper and blown eggshells, you can make these great Easter egg decorations.

What You Will Need

Tissue paper in bright or pastel colors
White glue
Shallow container
Small paintbrush
Clean, dry, blown white eggshells
Spray finish

1. If working a pattern, keep the shapes simple and geometric. Cut tissue paper shapes by folding paper over itself (up to 8 thicknesses) and cutting out all the pieces at once. For a random or crazy-quilt look, cut or tear the pieces into small, irregular shapes.
2. Place the tiny pieces in a dish or bowl.

Spring Crafts

3. Pour a little glue into a shallow dish. Thin with water to the consistency of milk.

4. Brush the thinned glue onto a piece of tissue paper and place it, glue-side down, on the egg. Lightly press into place. Continue gluing, placing, and pressing until the entire egg surface is covered. Overlapping pieces will blend to create new shades. Torn pieces will blend more subtly than the sharp, distinct lines of cut pieces.

5. If you're working a pattern with open spots, cover the whole egg first with torn bits of white (or light-colored) tissue, let dry a few minutes, then apply the pattern pieces.

6. When dry, apply a coat of spray finish to prevent the dye in the paper from bleeding.

MAKING A BASIC FLOWER PRESS

A flower press is a simple tool used to flatten and dry flowers and foliage. The following plans are for a reasonably large and very sturdy flower press:

Materials

Two 12 x 12 x 5/8–inch (30 x 30 x 1.6 cm) pieces of plywood
Four 6 x 1/4–inch (15.2 cm x 6 mm) carriage bolts
  (rounded head for flush mounting)
Four 1-inch (2.5 cm) flat washers with 1/4-inch (6 mm) hole
Five 1/4-inch (6 mm) wing nuts (large wings for easy tightening)
Two 1 x 2 x 12–inch (2.5 x 5 x 30 cm) boards

Tools

Pencil
Straightedge or metal ruler
Drill
Hammer
Nails or screws
Small brush
Polyurethane

1. On one of the pieces of plywood, measure out 1 3/4 inches (4.4 cm) along each side and mark with a pencil. Using a straightedge, draw a line along each side of the board at the markings.

2. Align the marked board on top of the other plywood board. Drill a 5/16-inch (8 mm) hole at each of the four intersections of your drawn lines. Drill through both boards, then set aside the unmarked one.

3. Insert two of the bolts through the holes in the marked board. When only the head of the bolt is visible, use a hammer to drive the head into the wood until it is flush with the board. Repeat with the other two bolts.

4. Nail or screw (predrill the holes for screws) the 1 x 2–inch (2.5 x 5 cm) pieces of wood over these bolts to hold them in place. This will serve as the base of the flower press.

5. Turn over the baseboard so the bolts are facing up and place the unmarked 12 x 12–inch (30 x 30 cm) board over the holes. Put on the flat washers and wing nuts, and brush on a coat of polyurethane. Let dry before using.

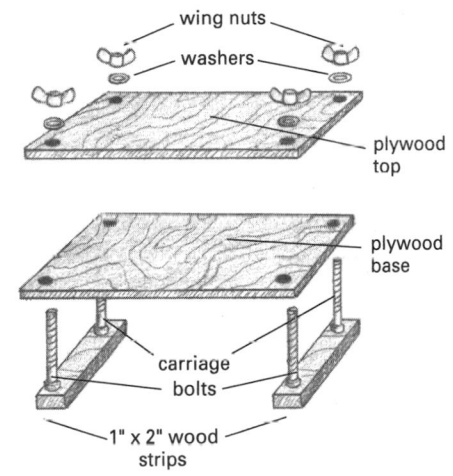

MAKING A PORTABLE FIELD FLOWER PRESS

Because it's best to press flowers as soon as they are picked, consider making a portable field press to use until you can get your plants home to the big model.

- A large telephone book or an outdated encyclopedia will suffice as a temporary press. Simply place the botanical materials in the book and secure with string or elastic bands. Add weight by stacking other books on top.
- For smaller pressing projects, you can use a pair of paperback books with their covers removed. Place your flowers between the books and secure with strong elastic bands. If the books are thick, place materials every 20 to 30 pages inside the books as well as between them.
- A handy portable press can be made from four pieces of cardboard cut to the size of standard printer paper (or smaller, if you prefer). Place several sheets of blotting paper or some paper from an old telephone book between the cardboard pieces. Wrap twine around the outside length and width of the cardboard, and tie firmly in a bow.

042

FORAGING FOR FIELD SPECIMENS

Whether you are collecting botanicals to press, print from, or draw, it's useful to keep the following items close at hand in your car or in your backpack:

- Notebook, self-stick notepads, self-stick labels for bags, and waterproof marker
- Scissors and/or hand pruner for cutting stems, twigs, and woody plants (if you have an interest in collecting leaves and flowers from trees, you may also need to purchase a long-handled pruner)
- Trowel for digging up plant specimens
- Zip-seal plastic bags to store specimens
- Spray bottle of water to keep specimens from wilting
- Lightweight plant press, or if you're traveling by car, newspapers

and some weights (delicate plants, especially, should be pressed quickly)

- Container of water for transporting cut flowers or whole plants that you want to print fresh, not pressed
- Field guide(s) describing the wild plants found in your region of the country

USING YOUR FLOWER PRESS

With a few tips to help you get started and some basic supplies, you can begin using your new flower press immediately.

What You Will Need:

A good pair of tweezers for handling fragile, often small plant materials
Blotting paper or blank newsprint
Four to six rectangles of cardboard cut to the dimensions of your flower press
Boxes and paper for storage (lay flowers on construction paper or newsprint in flat boxes or shallow drawers. You can stack dried flowers and foliage, separating each layer with paper. Flowers should retain their color for two years.)

1. Using tweezers, gently place your flowers, leaves, or stems into the press, directly on the newsprint. Do not let them touch or overlap. Place items with like thicknesses on the same sheet. For bulky flowers, remove the petals from the centers and press separately— you can reassemble them before using them in a project. Be sure to clearly pencil in the name and date beside each item.
2. After one sheet of paper has been filled, lay two sheets of paper on top. If the flowers are relatively thin, just add more flowers and put two more sheets of paper on top. If they are thicker, cover them with a sheet or two of paper and a piece of cardboard before layering on another sheet of paper and more flowers. Always place paper between the flowers and the cardboard, and always place cardboard against the wooden base and top of the press.
3. Check your flowers the day after pressing them and replace any damp paper; do the same the next day. (If the paper is not absolutely dry, the flowers may mold.) Press botanicals for 4 to 6 weeks before removing them to boxes for storage.

THE THICK AND THIN OF PRESSING

If you do not want to separate the thinner parts of your plant from the thicker parts, here are a couple of ideas to help you press the entire plant successfully.

Place pads of blotting paper over the thinner parts of your flower to even up the pressure in the press.

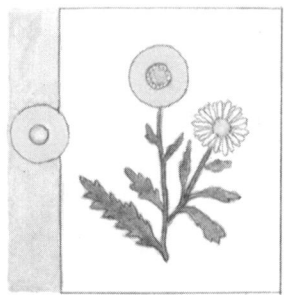

Cut pieces of foam slightly larger than the thin part of your plant. If you have a flower with a thicker center, cut a hole in the foam and lay it over the flower.

PERFECTLY PRESSED ROSEBUDS

There's a secret to pressing lovely rosebuds. Detach each bud from the stem and press it separately. You may also choose to remove the leaves and press them separately. If the leaves on your stem are not all perfect, simply pick perfect leaves of similar sizes and press them instead. Discard those with brown spots or holes. Press only the freshest and closest to perfect. When you decorate something with the rosebud, you will simply reconstruct it from the best leaves and stems you pressed.

Using a sharp pair of scissors or a utility knife, cut the rosebud in half vertically. Then lay the two halves in your press, cut-side down. This reduces the thickness and moisture of a bud and, at the same time, doubles the number of rosebuds available for your projects.

PRESSED FLOWER BOOKMARKS

The flattest of foliage and flowers are necessary for this project. When a protective film covering is applied, bulky materials will cause uneven lumps on the surface. Bookmarks can be made on ribbon or stationery paper or a combination. Choose a width of ribbon to complement the flowers you will be working with, but generally, a bookmark should not exceed 2 inches in width and 8 inches in length.

To make a bookmark, select a 1- to 1 1/2-inch-wide satin ribbon and cut to a length of 16 inches. Fold in half. At the bottom of the ribbon, opposite the folded end, cut an upside-down V no more than 1 inch deep. Apply a thin bead of glue across the notched bottom to hold the two ends together. Decorate with delicate dried botanicals like ferns and Queen Anne's lace, gluing these to the ribbon. Seal with clear contact paper or laminate.

Or you can use paper instead of ribbon. Decorate stiff paper or poster board with dried flowers and seal. Tie a complementary yarn string to the top to dangle out of the book.

DECORATING CANDLES
WITH PRESSED BOTANICALS

It's a simple matter to embellish tapered or pillar-style candles with pressed flowers. Choose the candles you wish to work with and select pressed materials compatible with the candle colors. Arrange the materials into a design, such as a simple flower and a couple of leaves for a taper, or a band of daisies or pansies for a chunky pillar.

Pour a little glue into a bottle cap or jar lid. Using a toothpick or a very fine artist's paintbrush, apply glue to the entire back of each botanical. Press onto the candle. Wipe away any extra glue with a damp sponge or cotton swab, making sure not to wet the flowers. When working with tapered candles, you can seal the flowers with paraffin if you wish.

Use care when burning flower-decorated candles, especially narrow tapers—make sure the flame does not touch the dried flowers. It is always best to decorate only the base of tapered candles. For pillars and wide tapers, the flame does not come close to the outside of the candle, so fire danger is minimal.

048

CLASSIC ROSE POTPOURRI

Homemade potpourri is a wonderful gift. This rich blend has hints of garden and woods mingled with a strong rose scent.

Combine in a gallon jar:

1 quart (946 ml) rose petals
1–2 cups (237–473 ml) lavender flowers
1–2 cups (237–473 ml) rose geranium leaves
1/2 cup (118 ml) patchouli leaves
1/4 cup (59 ml) sandalwood chips
1/4 cup (59 ml) vetiver
1 cup (237 ml) rosemary

Mix, then add:

2 teaspoons (10 ml) cracked frankincense
1 teaspoon (5 ml) coarsely ground cloves
1 teaspoon (5 ml) myrrh
1 teaspoon (5 ml) crushed Ceylon cinnamon
2 tonka beans, ground or broken

Mix, then add:

1 cup (237 ml) orrisroot
30 drops rose oil

Stir thoroughly and age for 3 weeks.

049

STENCILING SAVVY

Stenciling is suitable for any kind of room, in both new and older homes. Designs can be applied on rough plaster walls, where larger designs are usually more effective, and on smooth walls or wallboard, wood, or plaster. Stenciling can be applied to floors or paneling and also is impressive on brick. Old wallpaper can be painted over and then stenciled, and if the wallpaper has a texture, the finished product is all the more interesting.

Almost any paint can be used for the background. It can be flat, satin finish, semigloss, latex, or oil based. Stenciling can also be done over wood stains, varnishes, polyurethanes, or shellacs. But slippery materials such as glass, glossy paints, waxed surfaces, and vinyl will resist paint and for that reason shouldn't be used as a base for stenciling.

The paint you use to stencil is easier to work with if it is oil based. Latex paint dries too quickly and builds up on the stencil.

050

TRACING AND CUTTING A STENCIL

You can enlarge or make smaller the designs below using a copy machine, or use them as they are. Place a sheet of heavy waxed stencil paper over the design (at whatever size you choose) and trace the outline with a pencil, bearing down hard enough to cut through the wax. Place the waxed paper on a piece of plywood, glass, or other smooth, hard material and, holding the stencil firmly with one hand, cut out the lines of the design with an X-Acto knife. Lift out the parts of the design you wish to paint through, and you've got your stencil ready to go!

051

USING A STENCIL TO PRINT A CONTINUOUS DESIGN

If you want to create a running design (one without an end, such as a vine), make sure the beginning and ending holes on the stencil are identical. For the first design, place the edge of the stencil along the ceiling or along the horizontal that you have drawn with a level, and print the design. Then, lift the stencil and place the first holes of the design over the last part of the design you have just printed at the point where they match. Repeat the printing process. Continue until you have gone all around the room. Since it is unlikely that the first printed design and the last one will work out exactly, begin your printing in the least conspicuous part of the room so the mismatch will show up the least.

Here are some designs to try in a continuous line:

Gardening

052

PLANTING DATES IN RELATION TO FROST

Hardy	Semihardy	Tender	Very Tender
Plant as soon as ground can be prepared.	*Plant 1 to 2 weeks before average date of last frost.*	*Plant 2 weeks after date of last frost.*	*Plant 2 weeks after average date of last frost.*
Asparagus	Cauliflower	New Zealand	Cucumber
Beet	Potato	spinach	Eggplant
Broccoli		Snap bean	Lima bean
Cabbage		Sweet corn	Musk melon
Carrot		Tomato	Pepper
Chard			Pumpkin
Kale			Squash
Lettuce			Watermelon
Onion			
Parsnip			
Pea			
Radish			
Spinach			
Turnip			

053

PLANTING SPRING POTATOES

The Irish potato, like other annual vegetables, will be best during certain seasons. Being primarily a cool-weather crop, it does best when planted in early spring or in the fall.

To determine your sowing date, establish the last killing-frost date in your area, then back up about 20 days. Since the potato takes about 20 days to sprout, the danger of frost should have passed by sprouting time. If frost is predicted after the potatoes have sprouted, cover the young sprouts with soil to prevent damage in the event the frost is severe. A light frost may burn the top leaves but will not damage the entire plant.

See tip 248 for information on fall potato sowing.

054

ASPARAGUS: AN IDEAL EARLY-SPRING VEGETABLE

In the early spring, when other fresh vegetables are unavailable, how pleasant it is to have one of the tastiest vegetables ready to harvest. And it is reassuring to know that the harvest will continue each spring for years to come. A well-prepared asparagus bed in good soil should produce abundantly for up to 25 years. If you can be patient in the beginning, you will be rewarded by a wonderful return for your labor.

A gourmet treat, expensive when purchased (and never as fresh), asparagus can be grown in almost any garden where there is a cold or dry season to provide it with a dormant period. As a vegetable, the versatile asparagus can be cooked in many ways and dried, canned, or frozen for off-season eating. Low in calories, high in flavor, each serving of four spears (60 g) contains only ten calories, with two grams of carbohydrates and one gram of protein. Asparagus is a very good source of thiamin and a good source of vitamin A and riboflavin.

The asparagus plant is a beautiful addition to any location. Few garden sights are more attractive than early dew glistening in the feathery, dark green foliage of the summer plants. In the fall, the asparagus fern turns a bright yellow, and when snow is on the ground, the light brown brush bends high over the white.

055

SELECTING A SITE FOR STRAWBERRY PLANTING

When the time comes to select a site for strawberry planting, consider air and water drainage, the slope of the land, and the direction of land exposure.

If late spring frosts are frequent in your area, choose a site on ground slightly higher than the surrounding areas. A site that slopes gradually and is less susceptible to soil runoff is better than one that slopes steeply.

For an early crop, select a site that slopes toward the south (or the north, if you live in the southern hemisphere). Select one that slopes in the opposite direction if you wish to delay ripening.

056

GROWING YOUR BEST CARROTS

The trick to growing carrots is selecting varieties that will produce best in your garden's soil conditions. The long, slender carrots sold commercially require a soil so deep, friable, and smooth that they're virtually impossible for most home gardeners to grow. Unless you have a deep, loose soil free of obstructions, it's best to plant shorter varieties like Nantes Half Long, Goldinhart, and the Chantenay types. A new variety, A-Plus, is recommended for its higher vitamin A content.

If your soil is extremely heavy, try the beet-shaped carrots, like Gold Nugget, Kundulus, Oxheart, and Planet. Beet-shaped carrots offer high yields in a small space. These are the best carrots for the patio garden. Because they can be grown close together and have short roots, they can be planted in window boxes or any container at least 6 inches deep.

057

THE BENEFITS OF WIDE-ROW PLANTING

Wide-row planting is simply a matter of broadcasting seeds in bands anywhere from 10 inches (25 cm) to 3 or more feet (90 cm or more) wide. Although it might seem odd, it can actually be easier and involve less work than conventional gardening methods. Here are some other great reasons to give it a try:

Wide-row planting . . .
1. Increases yield
2. Saves time
3. Saves space
4. Saves mulching
5. Makes harvesting easier
6. Permits cool-weather crops in heat
7. Improves quality of crops
8. Reduces insect damage
9. Makes companion planting easier
10. Frees gardener for vacation
11. Keeps plants cleaner
12. Makes the garden more beautiful

058

CROPS THAT DO WELL IN WIDE ROWS

Here is a list of vegetables and herbs that can be grown in wide rows:

"Small" Seeds	"Larger" Seeds and Transplants
Anise	Beans of all kinds
Beets	Cabbage
Caraway	Garlic
Carrots	Onion plants (sets)
Chard	Peas (English, crowder, field, Southern)
Chives	Shallots
Collards	
Cress	
Dill	
Endives	
Kale	
Kohlrabi	
Leeks	
Lettuce	
Mustard	
Onions	
Oregano	
Parsley	
Parsnips	
Peppermint	
Radishes	
Rutabagas	
Salsify	
Spearmint	
Spinach	
Summer savory	
Sweet marjoram	
Turnips	

See tip 164 for advice on harvesting from wide rows.

Spring Gardening

spring peas followed by Chinese cabbage

New Zealand spinach

spring scallions followed by fall turnip greens

spring peas followed by summer amaranth

early spring spinach followed by summer snap beans followed by fall radishes

early beets followed by late cabbage transplants

early radishes followed by fall kale

leaf lettuce interplanted with pumpkins

spinach interplanted with melons

By using succession planting and intercropping, you can grow an extensive variety of greens in a small space.

INTERCROPPING FOR SUPER SALAD GREENS

A great way to fit more greens into your garden is to tuck a quick-maturing leafy vegetable, such as spinach or leaf lettuce, in the wide space between your tomato, melon, or squash transplants. By the time the spreading vegetable needs all the room you have allowed for it, the leafy vegetable will have been picked and eaten. Shade from larger vegetables nearby sometimes helps to keep some spring vegetables, such as spinach, producing for an additional week before going to seed in the summer warmth and longer days.

SUCCESSFUL SUCCESSION PLANTING

With some planning, you can pick your own fresh greens from spring through winter. The secret of a continuous harvest is succession planting. You might, for example, plant early-spring spinach, followed by green beans bearing in August, with a quick crop of radishes put in after the beans finish. Your summer greens can be grown in the rows where spring peas or scallions have finished. For a fall harvest, you can transplant kale, cabbage, and other good fall greens into spaces left by early radishes or beets. Fall spinach and escarole can follow summer-harvested onions.

RAISING ROOT CROPS IN RAISED BEDS

Experienced gardeners agree: root crops produce best in raised beds, planted in blocks rather than single-file rows. If you have a heavy clay or shallow soil, growing long root crops like carrots, parsnips, and salsify is next to impossible without a raised bed.

Why Grow Root Crops in Raised Beds?

1. Root crops are cool-weather vegetables. The earlier you can plant them in the spring, the better. A raised bed warms and dries faster than surrounding ground, permitting earlier sowings. This is particularly beneficial in areas that receive much spring rain. Raised beds drain well and seldom puddle after a downpour.
2. A raised bed has deeper, looser topsoil and more concentrated nutrients than the surrounding ground, allowing for better root development. The beds are easier to prepare, and you have better control over the soil's friability and fertility.
3. Because you can walk in the pathways between the beds, rather than on the beds themselves, soil compaction is eliminated.
4. Raised beds are easier to weed and harvest because they are 6 to 12 inches higher than the ground. Root crops must be sown and thinned, a back-breaking chore without a raised bed!

Perimeter Problems

The perimeter of a raised bed dries out faster than the rest of the bed. If not watered regularly, plants near the edge of the bed can bolt and produce tough, bitter roots. A mulch often prevents this problem.

062

MAKING A RAISED BED

Dimensions: 3 feet (91 cm) by 6 feet (1.8 m).

1. Dig a 6-foot (1.8 m) trench, 1 foot wide (30 cm) and 1 foot (30 cm) deep. Remove the dirt to a garden cart.
2. Widen the trench by digging up additional soil.
3. Continually throw the loosened soil well ahead of where you are digging.
4. Add 2 or 3 bushels of compost or manure.
5. Pat the raised sides of the bed smooth and rake the top.

063

ADD ORGANIC MATTER TO IMPROVE DIFFICULT SOILS

It may sound like an oversimplification, but it bears repeating over and over again. When in doubt about the quality or workability of a soil, add organic matter such as compost. You can't go wrong.

Good Sources of Organic Material

Alfalfa meal
Coffee grounds
Compost (commercial or homemade)
Corncobs (ground or chopped) and corn husks
Grass clippings
Green manures (cover crops)
Hulls from buckwheat, oats, cocoa, and rice
Leaf mold
Leaves (chop with lawn mower)
Manure (cow, sheep, goat, or rabbit)
Oilseed meals (cottonseed, linseed)
Pea and bean pods and vines
Peanut shells
Peat moss and sphagnum moss
Pomace from apples, grapes, or cranberries
Rotted wood
Sawdust
Sewage sludge (composted)
Shredded brush trimmings
Spent hops (brewery waste)
Straw
Tea leaves
Vegetable parings
Weeds (preferably without seeds)
Wood chips and shavings

Spring Gardening

PUTTING GRASS CLIPPINGS TO USE

Grass clippings are great for improving garden soil. There are several ways to use them:

- Add them to your compost pile. They'll give you the nitrogen you need to make the pile "cook." Mix them well with other materials, such as weeds, leaves, or hay.
- Spread them around the garden area, then till them in. They're an excellent green manure.
- Let them dry, then spread them in the garden, or spread them in thin layers when green. They are one of the best mulches you can find.

THE PROS AND CONS OF DIFFERENT MULCHING MATERIALS

Here's a simple list of the pluses and minuses of various mulching materials. Weigh the pros and cons when choosing which is right for your garden.

Straw/Hay
Pros: Cheap; generally available; adds organic matter
Con: Can contain weed seed, insects, and/or disease

Leaves
Pros: Readily available; generally free; rich in nutrients
Con: Can mat down or be too acid for some plants

Grass clippings
Pros: Easy to get and apply; good source of nitrogen
Cons: Can burn plants; may contain weed seeds

Pine needles
Pros: Attractive; easy to apply
Cons: Large quantities hard to collect; may be too acid

Wood shavings

Pros: Weed and disease free; easy to apply; available
Cons: Can be acid; tends to tie up nitrogen in soil

Manure

Pro: Great source of fertility and organic matter
Cons: Should be well rotted; expensive to buy; usually contains weeds

Newspaper

Pros: Easy to get and apply; earthworms thrive in it
Cons: Decomposes very fast; must be weighted down

Plastic

Pros: Total weed control if opaque is used; warms soil for early start; heavy plastic can be used more than one season
Cons: Expensive, unattractive; adds nothing to soil; must be weighted down and cleaned up in the fall

066

GROW YOUR OWN MULCH

Don't overlook the possibility of cutting a green manure crop and using it as mulch in another part of your garden. By doing so you

can transfer the benefits of the green manure crop immediately to that part of the garden where you are growing food crops. The mulch will conserve, smother weeds, encourage soil life, improve soil structure, and prevent erosion.

For more on green manures, see tips 239 to 241.

DIVIDING SUMMER BULBS

If your summer bulbs need dividing, do it in spring just prior to planting. Cut roots and tubers with a sharp knife, making sure that each division contains at least one growing shoot or eye. True bulbs and corms produce offsets called bulblets or cormels, which can be pulled from the parent and planted separately. They may not bloom during their first year of growth, but in time they will mature to full size.

For information on winter care of summer bulbs, see tip 247.

GROWING YOUR OWN DILL

If you've never grown annual herbs before, dill might be a good one to start with. You can choose particular dill plants for their fragrant, feathery fronds or others for their seeds, which are a mainstay in pickle recipes. Either way, dill will thrive in spite of almost everything you might do to it!

You should grow your dill from seeds sown right where you want the plants to be, rather than either buying plants and transplanting them or starting the seeds indoors early in the spring, then moving them outdoors. Despite the fact that dill really is a cinch to grow, it does

Dill (Anethum graveolens)

have fragile stems that could easily be crunched in the course of being transplanted.

Because dill grows to be up to 3 feet (90 cm) tall, it should be planted in a sunny patch at the back of your garden—among flowers and vegetables is fine—so it doesn't overshadow other plants. To determine when to plant your seeds, follow the directions on the back of the seed packet, which will give specific information about when to plant in your particular zone. Plant the seeds 1/8 to 1/4 inch (3 to 6 mm) deep and spaced no more than 1 foot (30 cm) apart; press down the seeds gently. Keep the seeds well watered until the little plants pop their heads out of the soil.

VEGETABLE RESPONSES TO TRANSPLANTING

Transplanting checks growth. The severity of the checking depends on the vegetable planted; the number of times the vegetable is moved, causing roots and root hairs to break; and the plant size. The larger the plant, the greater is the check in growth. The following chart will give you a good sense of how different veggies respond to being transplanted:

Easily Survive Transplanting	Require Care in the Operation	Not Successfully Transplanted by the Usual Methods
Beet	Carrot	Bean
Broccoli	Celery	Corn
Brussels sprouts	Eggplant	Cucumber
Cabbage	Onion	Lima bean
Cauliflower	Pepper	Musk melon
Chard	Salsify	Pea
Lettuce		Turnip
Tomato		Watermelon

The crops of the last group will usually suffer a very serious check if the roots are disturbed. The cucurbit members of this group can be seeded in a row and then placed in containers before the first true leaves have appeared.

NECTAR PLANTS FOR HUMMINGBIRDS, BUTTERFLIES, AND BEES

Asters, Zones 2–9, depending on the species
Azaleas, Zones 3–9, depending on the species
Bee balms, Zones 3–8
Butterfly bushes, Zones 5–9
Butterfly weed, Zones 3–9
California fuschia, Zones 9–10
Columbines, Zones 3–8
Coneflowers, Zones 3–9
Coralbells, Zones 3–9
Delphiniums, Zones 4–8
Jewelweed, Zones 3–9
Lobelias, Zones 2–9
Penstemon, Zones 3–9
Phlox, Zones 2–9
Salvias, Zones 4–9

Bee balm

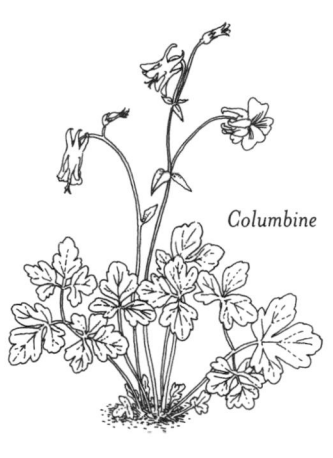

Columbine

Penstemon

FERTILIZER BY THE NUMBERS

If the big numbers on a package of commercial fertilizer say "10-6-4," it means that the fertilizer contains 10 percent nitrogen (N), 6 percent phosphate (P), and 4 percent potash (K). Different fertilizers contain different NPK ratios. Fertilizers such as 10-6-4 that contain all three of the heavy-hitter nutrients are called "complete" fertilizers. Superphosphate (0-20-0) is called "incomplete" because it only contains phosphate and no significant percentage of either nitrogen or potash.

"Complete" is an odd term for these fertilizers because they don't contain all the essential nutrients. Manufacturers rarely tell you much about the sulfur, magnesium, or calcium content; you have to check the fine print. Synthetic fertilizers contain few if any micronutrients; you need to use them in conjunction with sources of organic matter such as compost to keep plants supplied with micronutrients.

Most organic fertilizers contain a good supply of micronutrients. In addition, one of the biggest advantages of organic fertilizers is that they don't release all their nitrogen at once but keep supplying small amounts over a much longer time. Standard, concentrated synthetic fertilizers supply nitrogen in its most mobile form; while this means it's available quickly, it also means it can wash away quickly.

APPROXIMATE COMPOSITION
OF NATURAL FERTILIZER MATERIALS

Material	Nitrogen (N)	Phosphorus (P)	Potassium (K)
Manures			
Bat guano	10.0	4.5	2.0
Cow manure, dried	1.3	0.9	0.8
Cow manure, fresh	0.5	0.2	0.5
Hen manure, dried, with littler	2.8	2.8	1.5
Hen manure, fresh	1.1	0.9	0.5
Horse manure, fresh	0.6	0.3	0.5
Pig manure, fresh	0.6	0.5	0.4
Sheep manure, dried	1.4	1.0	3.0
Sheep manure, fresh	0.9	0.5	0.8
Vegetative and Animal Concentrates			
Bonemeal, steamed	2.0	22.0	–
Castor pomace	6.0	1.9	0.5
Cocoa shell meal	2.5	1.5	2.5
Cottonseed meal	6.0	3.0	1.0
Dried blood meal	13.0	1.5	0.8
Fish meal	10.0	6.0	–
Fish scrap	5.0	3.0	–
Garbage tankage	1.5	2.0	0.7
Hoof and horn meal	12.0	2.0	–
Sewerage sludge	2.0	1.4	0.8
Sewerage sludge, activated	6.0	3.0	0.1
Soybean meal	7.0	1.2	1.5
Wood ashes	–	1.8	5.0

Health and Wellness

073

10 ESSENTIAL HEALING HERBS

In today's marketplace, there are many "popular" herbs renowned for their medicinal qualities. The 10 herbs discussed here are among those that are particularly well known. Because they are also easy to use, widely available, and recommended for treating an amazingly wide range of ailments, they are well suited for presenting a basic overview and introduction to the ways herbs can help create health, happiness, and harmony in your life.

Although each herb can be used in many different ways, here is a quick summary of their primary uses.

Herb	Primary Use
Calendula	*Applied externally in the form of salves and ointments for treating skin irritations.*
Chamomile	*Taken as a tea that calms and relaxes; also good for stomachaches.*
Echinacea	*Taken in tincture or capsule form to boost the immune system and help fight off colds and flu.*
Garlic	*Eaten or applied raw as an antibacterial and antiviral and for cardiovascular benefits; eaten cooked, retains only cardiovascular benefits.*
Ginger	*Eaten raw or in capsule form to combat motion sickness, nausea, indigestion, and inflammation.*
Lavender	*The herb and essential oil are used in baths and compresses to treat insomnia, headaches, and burns.*
Lemon balm	*Taken as a tea that acts to calm, soothe, and uplift.*
Peppermint	*Taken as a tea that soothes stomachaches and headaches and eases symptoms of colds and flu.*
St. John's wort	*Taken as a tea or in tincture or capsule form to treat mild to moderate depression or anxiety.*
Valerian	*Taken in tincture or capsule form to relieve anxiety and nervous tension.*

CALENDULA-INFUSED OIL

You can use the infused oil for topical healing of minor skin irritations.

2 parts extra-virgin olive oil
1 part dried calendula blossoms

1. Combine the olive oil and calendula blossoms in the top of a double boiler. Simmer gently for approximately 1 hour.
2. Strain the cooled mixture through a double layer of cheesecloth. Store in a cool, dark location, where it will keep for 3 to 6 months.

Calendula (Calendula officinalis)

For more information on making infused oils, see tips 174 and 175.

Chamomile (Matricaria recutita)

CALMING CHAMOMILE BATH BAGS

A warm bath with these fragrant sachets provides a gentle way to wind down from a stressful day. This recipe will make enough for eight baths.

2 cups (473 ml) dried chamomile flowers
1 cup (237 ml) dried lavender flowers
1/2 cup (118 ml) dried hops flowers
1/2 cup (118 ml) dried passionflower

Combine all ingredients. Place 1/2 cup (118 ml) of the mixture in the middle of a piece of permeable fabric and tie it closed. When running the bath, loop the tie over the faucet so that the water runs through the bag as the tub fills.

ECHINACEA-ROOT TEA

Start drinking this tea at the first sign of a cold or flu. You'll know it's potent when your tongue feels a bit tingly after downing a mugful.

1 teaspoon (5 ml) dried echinacea root, or 1 tablespoon (15 ml) fresh
1 cup (237 ml) water
Honey (optional)

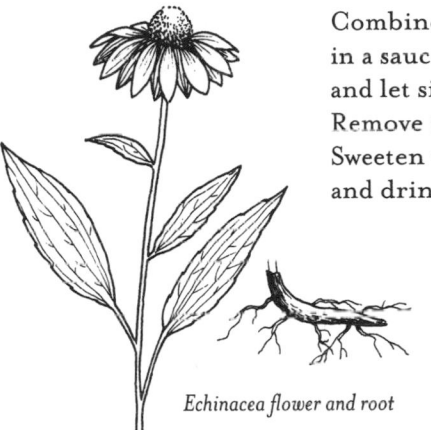

Combine the echinacea and water in a saucepan. Bring to a boil, cover, and let simmer 20 to 30 minutes. Remove from heat and strain. Sweeten with honey, if desired, and drink.

Echinacea flower and root

BAKED GARLIC

Baking a whole head of garlic softens its texture and taste. Individual cloves spread on bread or baked potatoes are delicious, may help stave off a cold, and are a tasty way to include garlic's cancer-fighting and cholesterol-lowering qualities into your diet.

1 full head of garlic
Olive oil

Trim the top of the bulb slightly and cut the bottom so that it sits flat. (Do not peel off the papery sheath.) Place on a baking dish and drizzle with olive oil. Cover with aluminum foil and bake at 350°F (180°C) for 1 hour, or until soft.

After the garlic has cooled, remove the foil. The roasted cloves will pop out easily when squeezed.

Garlic (Allium sativum*)*

078

GINGER TEA

This pungent remedy will help ease the symptoms of nausea or indigestion.

1 cup (237 ml) water
1 teaspoon (5 ml) grated or powdered ginger

1. Bring the water to a boil. Remove from heat, add the ginger, and cover. Let steep for at least 10 minutes.
2. Strain and enjoy!

Variations

- Grate up to 1 tablespoon (15 ml) fresh ginger into a cup of brewed black or green tea.
- For a homemade ginger ale, mix a cup of strongly brewed ginger tea with carbonated water and lemon.

Ginger (Zingiber officinale*)*

079

LAVENDER TOILET WATER FOR EASING HEADACHES

1 1/2 cups *(355 ml)* dried lavender flowers
1 pint *(16 fl oz/473 ml)* cider vinegar
1 cup *(8 fl oz/237 ml)* rosewater

Place lavender in a glass jar, pour in vinegar, cover, and leave for a week in a cool, dry place, shaking each day.

After a week, strain through muslin and stir in rosewater. Apply to temples to give relief from headaches caused by fatigue.

Lavender (Lavandula officinalis)

080

LOVELY LEMON-LAVENDER SLEEP PILLOW

Lemon balm makes a great herbal remedy for insomnia. Its calming qualities are put to good use in bath bags and sleep pillows.

2 parts dried lemon–balm leaves
1 part dried lavender flowers
1 part hops strobiles

Combine the herbs. Put the mixture in a small drawstring bag or sew into a flat pillow and place between your pillow and pillowcase.

Lemon balm (Melissa officinalis)

PEPPERMINT INHALATION

When suffering from congestion due to a cold and/or a sinus condition, peppermint can be helpful simmered in water as an inhalation.

1 quart (1.67 pts/946 ml) water
1/2 cup (118 ml) or 1 cup (237 ml) fresh peppermint

Combine the water and peppermint in an enamel or stainless-steel saucepan. Bring to a boil, reduce heat, and let simmer, uncovered, on the stovetop; this will release benefits if you are in the same room as the mixture.

An alternative way to prepare the inhalation is in a small simmering potpourri pot, which can be placed in any room you choose. Do not allow the mixture to boil dry; add more water if needed.

Peppermint (Mentha piperita*)*

GOOD NIGHT TEA

For all the days when you're overworked, overstressed, and overly tired and can't get to sleep despite the fact that you're exhausted, this tea is a gentle way to relax the nerves and ensure a good night's rest.

1 part St. John's wort flowers
1 part catnip leaves
1 part lemon-balm leaves
1 part linden blossoms
1 part oat straw
1 part passionflower leaves

St. John's wort (Hypericum perforatum*)*

Pour 1 cup (237 ml) boiling water over 1 to 2 teaspoons (5 to 10 ml) dried or 2 to 4 teaspoons (10 to 20 ml) fresh herbs. Cover, let steep 10 to 15 minutes, and strain well. Drink 1 cup (237 ml), and you'll be off in dreamland by the last sip!

083

HOW TO USE VALERIAN

Valerian's primary drawback is its strong, unpleasant odor, often compared to the smell of dirty socks. To overcome this real aesthetic disadvantage, take valerian in its more palatable forms, either as a capsule or as a tincture, and not as a tea. Although the strong taste is still evident in the tincture, this form may be chosen for its strength. Combining it with tastier herbs like chamomile, catnip, peppermint, and lemon balm is a good alternative. As a secondary ingredient blended with other, sweeter-scented herbs, valerian can also be used effectively in soothing herbal baths.

Valerian (Valeriana officinalis)

Home

SANDSTONE AND QUARTZITE: GREAT STARTER STONES

When building your own stone walls for the first time, keep in mind that sandstones and quartzites are the most versatile building stones to work with. They range from coarse, soft, crumbly rocks to dense, fine-grained creek quartzites so hard they ring when struck.

Sandstone is a good stone to learn on because it cuts well, occurs in layers, and is porous enough to age quickly after shaping. It comes in as many colors as sand itself—grays, browns, whites, roses, and blues (the most common are grays and browns)—and is composed of fine sand particles that were fused together under great pressure. Many types of sandstone have a definite grain that they can be easily split along. Therefore, sandstone is best laid flat, the way it was formed. Set on edge, it may weather in such a way that the layers separate. The sandstone you have access to could be soft or hard, weak or strong. In mortared work, the stone should be at least as hard as the mortar.

Sandstone usually splits into even thicknesses in nature, so the critical top and bottom surfaces are already formed. If any shaping is necessary, it may be nothing more than a bit of nudging on the face of each stone to give it an acceptable appearance. When making your selection, of course, try to find stones that are already well shaped, thereby keeping any necessary shaping to a minimum. Any sandstone can be worked to the shape you desire, but there's a logical limit—if you spend all your available time shaping, then efficiency plummets.

FINDING A SOURCE FOR GOOD STONE

When building your own stone walls, you'll want to find great materials. And where you get them depends a lot on where you happen to be. However, whether you plan on buying stone from a stone lot or collecting loose rock from the back woods of your own property, there are four points to remember that will simplify your task:

- Because one criterion for good stone is that it be as native to the environment as possible, start your search close to home.
- Especially when you're prospecting, look for usable shapes, such as a flat top and bottom, with the appearance you're looking for on what will be the stone's face. When you find some, there'll usually be more of the same nearby, because stone tends to fracture naturally along the same lines in a given area.
- If a stone looks doubtful for laying, pass it up. Bring home only the very best—you'll still have lots of rejects.
- If you're looking for a particular type of stone, seek the help of your state geology or mineral resource headquarters. Field geologists map stone underlayment and can tell you where certain stones occur.

STONE-COLLECTING ETIQUETTE FOR PRIVATE LANDS

When searching for stones to use in walls and other structures, there are many sources on private lands. However, there are also some important standards of etiquette that you must be aware of before venturing out into the countryside on a stone-collecting mission.

1. Don't trespass. Ask the landowners for permission to explore the property.
2. Communicate with the landowners. Share with them what you are doing. The more they know, the more apt they will be to let you onto their property.

3. Leave the site in better shape than you found it. For example, repair your ruts.
4. Never take more than you need.
5. Do not mark stone with spray paint; use a chalk or removable marker, such as ribbon.
6. Be careful not to remove stones that could initiate or exacerbate an erosion problem.
7. Pay a fair price for the stones. This will vary by region and stone availability. You can find out what's a fair price by checking in with a local stone center, pit, or stone broker (a person who buys stone for redistribution to masons, stone centers, and landscape contractors).

Adapted from *Natural Stonescapes* by Richard L. Dubé and Frederick C. Campbell

When dismantling an old stone wall, to the greatest extent possible, watch out for and try to avoid disturbing its inhabitants.

MOVING AND LIFTING STONE

It's hard to overemphasize the importance of lifting stone properly. Learn to squat and lift with your legs.

The procedure is simple. Grab the stone in what would be a normal position, and drop your rear another 2 feet (60 cm). When lifting, hug the stone close. It's a lot easier on your back and arms.

Incorrect lifting

Correct lifting

The wheelbarrow is your handiest tool for moving small- to medium-size stones. You can lay it on its side, slide a stone in, and stand the wheelbarrow up by yourself to move the stone. On rocky or steep ground, load the wheelbarrow back near the handles. You'll lift more, but the wheel will go over obstacles better. With the weight on the wheel, it's harder to push; even a pebble can stop you.

To load a large stone, lay the wheelbarrow on its side, slide the stone in, and pull the wheelbarrow upright.

You can also use simple plank "slides" to push heavy stones from the ground up to truck beds or the top of a wall. Just make sure the bottom of the plank is well anchored, set the top of the plank on the desired destination at a relatively low angle, and push the stone up the plank, flipping it end over end. For large stones with flat bases, you can place rollers between the stone and the plank, which will allow you to slide the stone up the plank.

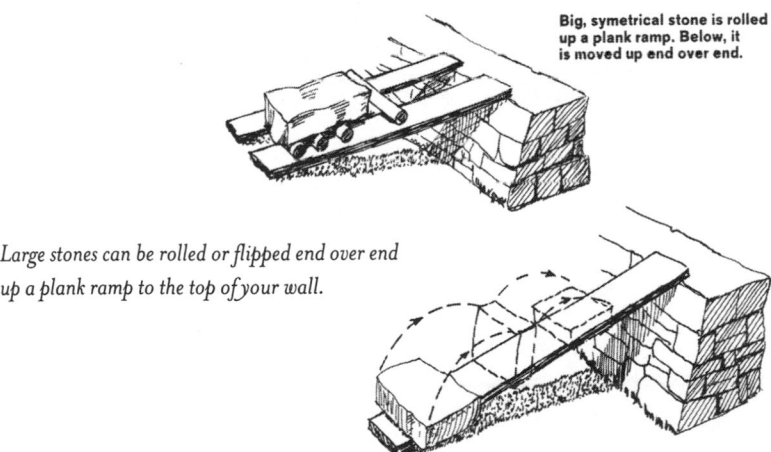

Big, symetrical stone is rolled up a plank ramp. Below, it is moved up end over end.

Large stones can be rolled or flipped end over end up a plank ramp to the top of your wall.

FIVE SECRETS FOR SUCCESS WITH A DRYSTONE WALL

1. **Establish an even plane.** The surface of a stone wall is never even, but if you establish a plane that you go back to often, the stone in the wall can jut out or be recessed without appearing sloppy.
2. **Use step patterns on sloping ground.** When building a drystone wall that runs downhill, keep the stones level by removing the topsoil at the base of the wall in a stepped pattern and repeating this pattern with the capstones.
3. **Lay stone with their best edges out.** If that leaves gaps in the center of the wall, fill these with rubble—that is, any scrap stone not usable otherwise. More than likely, your supply of neat stone with nice edges will be limited, so you'll have to shape at least one end for a face. (See tip 89 for more on how to do this.)
4. **Work with thin stones.** It's simpler to build a drystone wall with thin stones, because they're easier to handle and can be shaped more easily.
5. **Avoid vertical running joints.** Always lay stones side by side with the top edges parallel to the ground, and make sure to cover the crack between them with a stone on the next course.

When working with a stepped base, the top of the wall must be stepped as well.

Good wall | Too much run

Vertical running joints will compromise the strength and durability of your wall and should be avoided at all costs.

THE ELUSIVE "PERFECT FIT"— HOW TO SHAPE STONES FOR WALLS

To cut a corner off a stone, lay the stone on something soft to absorb the shock. Sand in a box is good, or use a table padded with old rugs. Elevate the area to counter height, if possible.

Mark the cut you want by making a series of light hits with a striking hammer on a stone chisel, then go over this line again, striking harder. After about the third pass, turn the stone over and mark the other side. Repeat the procedure, using more force with each repetition. If you're working near the edge of the stone, lean the chisel out a bit to direct it into the mass of the stone.

Remember that a light tap will tend to chip the stone out toward the edge; a heavier hit will crack it deeper, usually closer to where you want it. Slope the chisel sharply, just enough for it to bite into the surface, striking into the mass near the ridge. Take off small chips from both sides this way until you have dressed the surfaces sufficiently. Ideally, the stone will break all the way through from marked line to marked line (but don't count on it).

A large stone-breaking maul, which has an edge to it, will create small stones from big ones. Use a 12-pound maul (5.4 kg) for this if there's no way to utilize big stones as they are. As with the chisel, hit the line lightly first, then more heavily. You'll have to smooth your breaks afterward with the hammer and chisel because the maul only gives approximates.

WORKING WITH TIE-STONES

In the cross section of a freestanding wall, you will see two walls leaning into each other. Because this is a precarious balance in which the two walls can come apart, masons tie across the wall whenever possible with a tie-stone, a stone that spans the width of the wall and provides stability and support.

Tie-stones must be laid completely flat or they will creep downhill with freezes and thaws. They're especially important for capping the wall (in which case they're called *capstones*), for they hold it together and keep out rain, which will freeze and push the wall apart. Capstones also make it more difficult for dust, leaves, and other debris to blow into the wall, where they can nurture into tree seeds; allowing tree roots to sprout in your wall is guaranteed to force it apart.

Tie-stones placed along the courses span the width of the wall.

Capstones are tie-stones placed on the top of the wall.

SEVEN SECRETS FOR SUCCESS WITH MORTAR

When building a mortared wall, the following tips will be very helpful:

1. **Lock the ends.** If your wall has a freestanding vertical end—if it doesn't end against a building or fade into the ground—alternate short and long stones so that the end is even and each course is locked together. Cover the crack between two stones with the stone above.
2. **Keep the wall straight.** You can use a guide string to do this. Just tie the string to tall stakes driven into the ground and elevate the string if necessary (*fig. 1*).

Fig. 1

3. **Test before mortaring.** Dry-fit a few stones to see how they look before you mortar them. Then set this half dozen or so and rake the excess mortar from the joints.

4. **Fill wide joints with stone chips.** Fill any wide mortar joints with appropriately shaped chips (there will be a lot of bits from your shaping). Lay an almost-good stone, and count on a shim to take up the slack.

5. **Avoid vertical running joints.** Cover the crack between adjacent stones with a stone on the next course. If you don't, you'll have a running joint or vertical crack, which will weaken the wall.

6. **Prepare for the next day's work.** When you stop for the day, leave stone in steps so it's easier to tie onto the next time.

7. **Keep the mortar wet.** Moisture is important to curing mortar, which is a chemical process that goes on for several days. Wet it thoroughly about four times during the day after you lay mortared stone (although after two days, the process slows naturally). In very hot weather, drape plastic sheeting over it to hold in the moisture.

092

HOW TO BUILD A HOT SMOKE PIT

A hot smoke pit—an extremely simple contraption made from a hole in the ground—turns out delicious hot-smoked chickens, roasts, and fish ideal for toting on a picnic.

The grill used in a hot smoke pit should not be galvanized or chromed. Half an old picnic grill or the grill from a hibachi is ideal.

Materials and Tools

shovel
flat rocks
nongalvanized grill

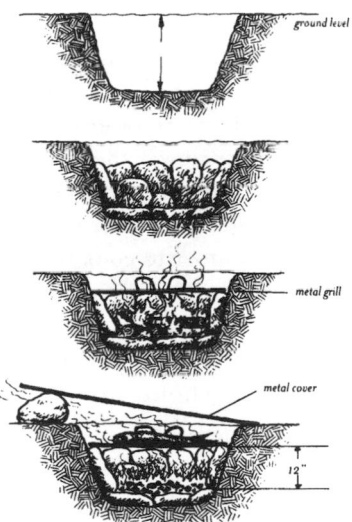

A hot smoke pit, dug 2 feet below ground level, lined with stone, and covered with a metal lid makes an ideal temporary smoker.

1. Dig a fire pit about 2 feet deep (60 cm) and wide enough to accommodate the grill.
2. Line the hole with flat rocks so that the grill is supported about 12 to 15 inches (30 to 37.6 cm) above the level of the coals.

(Be sure to surround the hole with a circle of temporary fencing to prevent anyone from accidentally stepping into it.)

USING A HOT SMOKE PIT

Half an hour before starting the hot-smoke process, build a good hardwood fire in the fire pit and let it form a bed of red-hot coals. Cover the coals with several handfuls of dampened hickory or other chips or small, green hardwood twigs from apple, pear, maple, oak, or birch trees. Set the grill in place and arrange the food to be smoked on the grill. (Chickens will cook much more rapidly if halved or quartered, but they will be much less juicy.)

Use a piece of nongalvanized sheet metal for a cover. Put on the cover, then position a vent rock under it to allow some smoke to escape. The narrower the vent opening, the smokier the flavor will be and the slower the meat will cook. The wider the opening, the more subtle the smoke flavor, the more rapid the combustion of the wood, and the higher the cooking temperatures. It will take the meat slightly longer to cook than in a kitchen oven—an additional 15 to 20 minutes for every hour.

You can put the food to be smoked on the grill with no preparation; sweet corn in the husk is also very fine. Or you can marinate meat 4 to 6 hours in your favorite marinade.

Summer

SUMMER SOLSTICES, 2008–2020

Times given are Eastern Daylight Saving Time (EDT)

2008	Friday	June 20	7:59 p.m.
2009	Sunday	June 21	1:45 a.m.
2010	Monday	June 21	7:28 a.m.
2011	Tuesday	June 21	1:16 p.m.
2012	Wednesday	June 20	7:09 p.m.
2013	Friday	June 21	1:04 a.m.
2014	Saturday	June 21	6:51 a.m.
2015	Sunday	June 21	12:38 p.m.
2016	Monday	June 20	6:34 p.m.
2017	Wednesday	June 21	12:24 a.m.
2018	Thursday	June 21	6:07 a.m.
2019	Friday	June 21	11:54 a.m.
2020	Saturday	June 20	5:43 p.m.

SUMMER HOLIDAYS

(United States and Canada)

FATHER'S DAY • *third Sunday in June*
CANADA DAY • *July 1*
U.S. INDEPENDENCE DAY • *July 4*
LABOR DAY/LABOUR DAY • *first Monday in September*

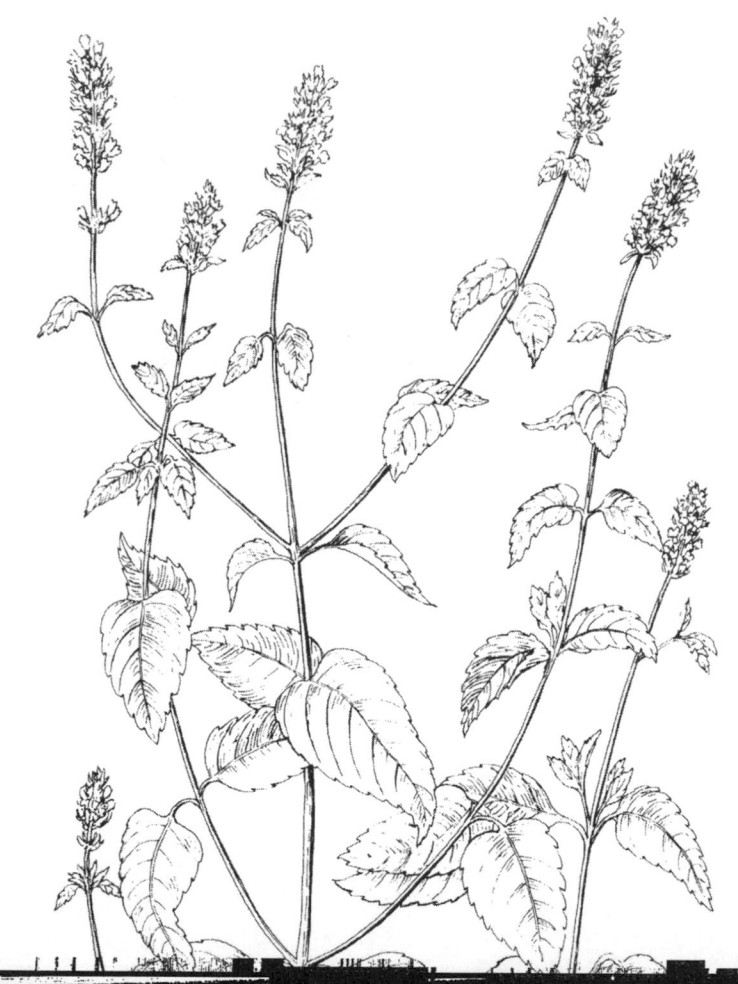

Animals

094

FEEDERS FOR ALL

Having a variety of foods and feeders reduces friction among various birds. To address the feeding needs of all the birds that frequent your backyard, you will need to supply water and four types of feeders:

- A ground or platform feeding tray
- A suet feeder
- A hanging feeder stocked with sunflower and other seeds
- A hummingbird feeder

Tip
Stock a few feeders so birds can move to another if frightened by a predator.

095

BIRD FEEDER PLACEMENT TIPS

Here are some tips to help make your bird feeders successful:

- Place feeders so they are easily visible, both by you and the birds. Birds won't eat what they can't see.
- Birds prefer to eat in the sun, but out of direct wind and weather.
- Avoid placing feeders directly in front of windows; to the side is better. Birds can be warned away from otherwise invisible glass by closing curtains or putting stickers on windows.
- Put feeders near shrubs or trees, so birds can perch there to check out the situation before they feed.

CUSTOM BIRD-SEED MIXES

Most commercial mixes contain a large amount of "filler" seed, such as milo or wheat. While not totally lacking in nutrition, these seeds are not of much value because many birds scratch them aside. Good commercial mixes contain sunflower, safflower, white or red proso millet, cracked corn, and even peanuts. If you can't find a mix to suit your particular clientele, whip up a batch of your own.

50/50

A simple combination sure to draw a crowd.

Black oil–type sunflower seed
Cracked corn

Combine equal parts and set out at ground level or in elevated feeders.

Come One, Come All

A healthy mix with vast appeal.

3 parts sunflower seed
3 parts millet
1 part finely cracked corn
3 parts hemp seed
1 part canary seed
Grit

Combine ingredients and offer at ground level. Be sure there is nearby cover to allow shy birds a chance to retreat if they feel threatened.

CREATIVE BIRD FEEDING

First prepare the dining table. Drive several large nails through an old plank or mill end. Old, weathered wood blends into the surroundings better, both in scent and sight, and is less startling to shy ground-feeding birds. Grease each spike with shortening or salad oil and push an ear of corn (fresh or dried) over each. Set out at ground level near cover.

PEANUT-BUTTER LOG FOR BIRDS

This quick and easy bird feeder can be made by young children and their parents. You may also want to sprinkle some wild-bird seed on the peanut butter for an added bird treat. Then hang up the log and go sit on your back porch to watch the crowd arrive!

What You Will Need
One 12-inch (30-cm) length of 2 x 2—inch rough wood
Small screw eye
Peanut butter
Nylon cord

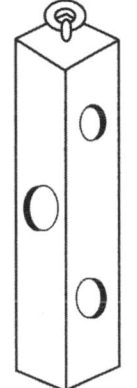

1. Measure and cut the wood to the necessary length. Do not sand it—the rougher it is, the better.
2. Using a 1-inch (2.5 cm) bit, drill a hole through the center of one side. Drill additional holes in the tip and bottom about 4 inches (10 cm) from each end of the other side.
3. Attach a small screw eye at the top.
4. Fill the holes with peanut butter and go find a branch to hang the project from. Use nylon cord to attach the project.

Adapted from *Birdfeeders, Shelters & Baths* by Edward A. Baldwin

REPLENISHING TROUGH CHICKEN FEEDERS

If you use a trough feeder to serve your chickens their meals, never fill it more than two-thirds full. Chickens waste approximately 30 percent of the feed in a full trough, 10 percent in a two-thirds-full trough, and 3 percent in a trough that's only one-third full. Obviously, you'll save a lot of money by using more troughs and putting less feed in each one.

Since you fill a trough from the top and chickens eat from the top, trough feeders tend to collect stale or wet feed at the bottom. Never add fresh feed on top of feed already in the trough. Instead, rake or push the old feed to one side, and empty and scrub the trough at least once a week.

THE PROPER WAY TO PICK UP YOUR RABBIT

The best way to pick up a pet rabbit is to first place one hand under it, just behind its front legs. Place your other hand under the animal's rump. Lift with the hand that is by the front legs and support the animal's weight with your other hand. Place the animal next to your body, with its head directed toward the corner formed by your elbow—just like tucking a football against you. Your lifting arm and your body now support the rabbit. Your other hand is free and can rest on the rabbit's back for extra security.

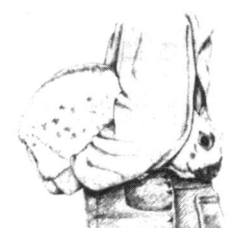

A "football hold" is a secure way to carry your rabbit.

To help your rabbit become comfortable with being carried, practice handling skills often, but for short periods of time—about 10 to 15 minutes at a stretch.

Sometimes an overactive or frightened bunny will struggle and get out of control. When this happens, drop to one knee as you work to quiet your animal. Lowering yourself to one knee shortens the distance the rabbit has to fall and provides a more secure base for a frightened bunny. You can also easily set the animal on the ground from this position.

If your rabbit starts to struggle while you are holding it, drop to one knee.

THE IMPORTANCE OF PADDOCKS AND PASTURES

To keep your horse healthy, it's crucial that his barn have access to a good pasture or large paddock for daily exercise and grazing. Horses are open-space creatures, and to lock one up in a stall, day in and day out, is cruel. It nearly always causes mental and physical problems, no matter how expensive the barn or how good the care. Bad habits like cribbing, wind sucking, weaving, and pawing are nearly always caused by boredom.

IS YOUR PUPPY AFRAID OF THE STAIRS?

Many young dogs are eager to gallop up the stairs, but then stand at the top and refuse to come down. Puppies are rarely afraid to go upstairs because their balance seems to be fine in that direction. But when their head and front feet are facing down, they feel off balance, as if they're going to tumble down.

Solution: Put the puppy just two stairs from the bottom. Call him to you or show him one of his favorite toys or a tiny piece of his favorite treat. The puppy should easily master this short distance. Praise him with great zest. Gradually, over a period of many days, increase the number of steps until he has mastered them all. Be very careful, however, because stairs can be dangerous to puppies if they tumble.

Pups love climbing upstairs, but they may need training to learn how to come down.

TESTING YOUR DOG FOR FOOD ALLERGIES

Just like humans, dogs can have food allergies. If your dog has never been exposed to an ingredient in a recipe or store-bought treat you want to try, introduce the treat very slowly. Start with a simple recipe that has few ingredients. (If you introduce many new ingredients at one time and your dog has a bad reaction, it will be hard to pinpoint which of them caused it.)

1. Give your dog a small piece of the treat—less than half—and wait a few hours, watching the dog for any sign of allergic reaction. This can be as simple as scratching more than usual or as dramatic as vomiting, swelling of the face and/or throat, or diarrhea. If any of these more dramatic symptoms develop, contact your vet immediately.

2. If no reaction occurs, give your dog the rest of the treat and wait a few hours, watching for a reaction. If one does occur, do not give your dog any more of that particular treat. Make note of which ingredients were used in the treat, and try making and testing different versions, keeping track of which ingredients are used in each case and which recipes cause your dog to have a negative response. With time and patience, you should be able to isolate the ingredients to which your dog is allergic.

GIVING PILLS AND OTHER MEDICINES TO YOUR POOCH

To administer pills to your dog, first pry open his mouth and place the pill on the tongue in the back of the mouth (1). Then hold your dog's mouth shut while gently massaging his throat until he swallows (2).

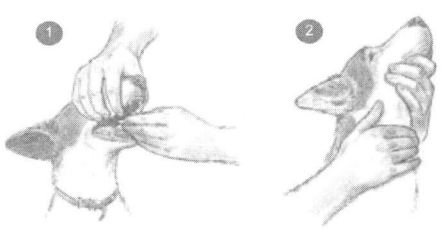

To give your dog liquid medication, squirt the prescribed amount along his lower back teeth using a plastic dropper.

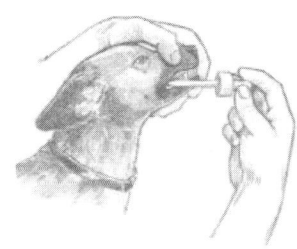

For ear drops, simply drip the prescribed number of drops in your dog's afflicted ear, tilt his head back, and hold the ear closed, massaging gently.

105

TOP 12 RULES FOR TRAINING CATS

1. Always say your cat's name to get her attention before giving any command.
2. Be consistent with your verbal and hand-signal commands.
3. Pay attention to your cat's moods. Train when your cat is receptive to learning.
4. Select a quiet time and room where you can be one-on-one with your cat.
5. Be positive, patient, and encouraging.
6. Provide food rewards and enthusiastic praise and petting immediately after for each success, no matter how small.
7. Start with the basic commands: come, sit, and stay.

8. Gradually introduce advanced commands, such as "Go fetch your mouse" or "Go to the kitchen door if you want to go for a walk outside."
9. Take advantage of your cat's natural curiosity and love for attention. Let him sniff out new toys and training tools, and always approach training sessions as if they were the ultimate opportunity for pampering your pet.
10. Be flexible; recognize that sometimes your cat just isn't in the mood to perform a trick. Don't try to force training on your feline; she's likely to decide she doesn't want to be trained ever again.
11. Be sure your cat understands each training step before going to the next. If the cat isn't performing the desired behavior, chances are you are moving too quickly.
12. Teach your cat only one new behavior at a time. Cats are not multitaskers. Keep it simple and short—no more than 10 or 15 minutes at a time.

Use a treat to teach your cat a command.

106

TEACHING YOUR CAT TO FETCH

Cats are born predators. They love to chase, stalk, and capture. Tap into these instinctive drives to teach your cat how to fetch. Select a large, uncluttered room or a long hallway for this trick.

1. Take a piece of paper and ball it into a wad about the size of a cherry, a tempting size for most cats. Make sure your cat sees you create this paper wad and hears it crinkle between your fingertips.
2. Show your cat the paper wad, toss it over her head, and say "Fetch."
3. Praise your cat as she chases after the paper ball, bats it around, and grabs it in her paws or mouth. Use your hand to motion your cat to come to you as you say, "Come here."
4. If the cat brings the paper wad to within a foot (30 cm) or so of your feet, reward her with a treat and lavish praise. You may need to retrieve the paper wad a few times until your cat understands how to play this game.

SILENT HELLO

Cats have a natural instinct for this trick, and you may find that it becomes your cat's preferred method of greeting. It's also a great trick to teach cats that are slightly skittish—making the initial contact on their terms helps them feel more at ease when they are petted or picked up. For the first few training sessions, be sure that your cat is in a calm, contented mood before approaching him.

1. Kneel down within arm's length of your cat. Curl the fingers of one of your hands into a soft fist. Slowly raise your arm until it is extended in front of you and your fist is at your cat's eye level.
2. Be patient while waiting for the cat to approach you. If and when he gives your fist a rub or a head butt, give him a scratch behind the ears and then get up.
3. Repeat steps 1 and 2 several times a day as a form of greeting your cat. He will soon learn to come quickly to your hand.

Cooking

108

VEGETABLES ON THE GRILL

When you're cooking outside on the grill or hibachi, it's easy to cook your vegetables along with your meat. Simply place sliced vegetables such as carrots, onions, squash, cauliflower, and peas on a square of heavy-duty foil. Add a few teaspoons of water (but not to summer squash), a little butter or margarine, and slightly salt if you wish. Fold the packet, overlapping the foil to make a sealed envelope. Place it on the grill and cook until the vegetables are tender. To shorten cooking time, cut less-tender vegetables, such as carrots, into thinner pieces.

Vegetables placed directly on the grill take on a barbecued flavor and cook in less time than in foil. Some vegetables, such as onions and carrots, need to be partially cooked beforehand, especially if they are to join other vegetables on skewers, as in vegetable kabobs. Mushrooms, green peppers, cherry tomatoes, onions, and chunks of zucchini are especially good this way and can be enhanced by brushing them with Italian dressing or a marinade.

109

STORING BASIL

Fresh basil should not be placed in the refrigerator; it is too cold in there for the tender leaves. Instead, place the cut stems in water, and the basil will sit happily on the windowsill—perfuming the air, to boot—for a week.

Sweet basil

POTATO AND BASIL GRATIN

1 cup cold water
1 cup milk
1 pound red potatoes, thinly sliced
1 bay leaf
1 clove garlic, peeled
4 tablespoons butter
1 cup chopped fresh basil
1/2 cup grated Cheddar cheese
1 cup cream

Preheat oven to 375°F (190°C).

Pour the water and milk into a saucepan, then add in the sliced potatoes, bay leaf, and garlic. Boil for 10 minutes, just until tender. Drain.

Grease a 10-inch baking dish with 1 tablespoon of the butter. Layer the potatoes and basil in the baking dish. Sprinkle with grated cheese, then pour on the cream. Dot with the remaining butter. Bake for 45 minutes, or until the top is golden brown.

Yield: 4–6 servings

BOURSIN AT HOME

That delectably fragrant spread known as Boursin cheese is quite easy to make at home—which will impress your guests and save you some money at the grocery store!

1 clove garlic, peeled
1/2 cup (118 ml) fresh basil leaves
1/4 cup (59 ml) chives
One 8-ounce (226 g) package cream cheese
1/4 cup (6 oz/170 g) black olives, pitted

In a food processor, chop the garlic and herbs. Add the cream cheese and blend until smooth. Add the olives and chop briefly. Transfer the mixture to a small bowl. Serve with crackers or spread on pieces of French bread, topped with thin slices of roast beef.

Yield: 1 cup (237 ml)

SUGAR VERSUS HONEY

Honey is generally considered to be more nutritious than white sugar. This is because the refining process removes all the trace minerals and vitamins in the sugar cane. Honey does contain minerals, but both honey and sugar have insignificant vitamin content. Brown sugar, which can be made in your kitchen just by combining white sugar and molasses, compares more favorably to honey in terms of food value.

HONEY LEMONADE

1/2 cup (4 fl oz/118 ml) honey
1/2 cup (4 fl oz/118 ml) hot water
Juice of 4 lemons
4 cups (32 fl oz/946 ml) cold water

Blend honey with hot water to make a syrup and pour it into a pitcher. Add lemon juice. Pour in cold water and stir. Serve icy cold.

Yield: 6 servings

COOKING WITH ROSEMARY

Some easy tips:

- Start with a small amount until you develop a taste for this adventurous flower.
- Remember the rule—1 teaspoon dried equals 1 tablespoon fresh.
- Use rosemary to transform cauliflower into company fare.
- Cream chopped fresh rosemary into softened butter or cream cheese for a hot bread treat.
- Garnish orange slices with rosemary.
- Try rosemary on spinach, eggplant, peas, or squash.
- Serve the flowers as an attractive edible garnish.
- Skewer shish kebabs on 12-inch (30 cm) lengths of rosemary.
- Enhance a variety of Mediterranean dishes with just a pinch of rosemary.
- Use several sprigs of rosemary, tied together, as a flavor-enhancing brush for sauces.
- Add a few leaves to any marinade.
- Try using rosemary in your fruit salad—you'll be amazed!

Rosemary (Rosemarinus officinalis*)*

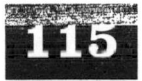

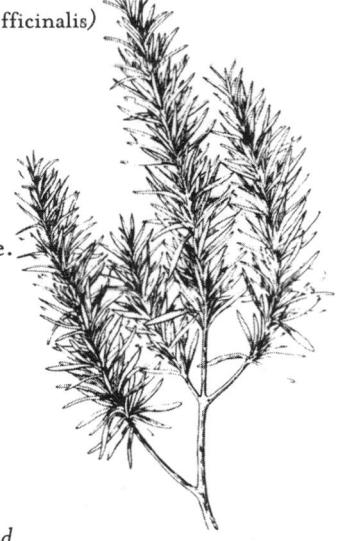

ROSEMARY–LEMON VERBENA TEA CAKE

This recipe transforms a convenient mix into a moist cake you can serve with pride.

1 package yellow cake mix
4 eggs
1 cup (8 fl oz/237 ml) water
1 package instant vanilla pudding mix
1/2 cup (4 fl oz/118 ml) oil
2 tablespoons (30 ml) lemon juice
1 tablespoon (15 ml) fresh rosemary, finely chopped
2 tablespoons (30 ml) lemon verbena, finely chopped

Mix all ingredients for 2 1/2 minutes. Put in lightly greased Bundt pan. Bake at 350°F (180°C) for 40 minutes. Cool 15 minutes in pan. Remove.

Glaze

1 cup (4.5 oz/128 g) powdered sugar
2 tablespoons (30 ml) lemon juice

Combine and drizzle over warm cake.

Yield: 12–20 servings

WHAT TO DO WITH THAT EXTRA ZUCCHINI

- Brush an electric skillet or heavy frying pan with vegetable oil (not olive oil). Heat to 350°F (180°C) or medium-high heat until the pan is piping hot. While it's heating up, cut the zucchini into 1/2-inch slices and quickly place in skillet in single layer. Cook slices, turning once until they're crisp and golden brown. Sprinkle them lightly with salt. Serve hot.
- Stir-fry thinly sliced zucchini and onions in a minimum of hot oil (start with a teaspoon and add more if you need it), using very high heat and stirring frequently until the vegetables are tender crisp. Sprinkle with a little salt or soy sauce.
- Stir-fry chunks of green pepper, onions, and zucchini until just tender. Add some tomato sauce or spaghetti sauce and stir. Cook some ramen noodles, drain, and cover with a slice of Swiss, Monterey Jack, or other cheese and top with the tomato-vegetable sauce.
- Young zucchini can be split lengthwise and brushed with oil to which seasoned salt or a combination of onion powder, garlic powder, salt, pepper, and paprika have been added. Grill, turning occasionally, until just tender and slightly brown—10 to 20 minutes or more, depending on the size and the heat of the grill. Delicious!

SHORTCUT PICKLES

This is a "nonrecipe" recipe just for fun!

Buy a jar of your favorite pickles. When they're all gone, or even as you're still using them, put fresh cucumber or zucchini slices, quarters, or spears into the jar with the pickle juice. Refrigerate. After a few days or a week, your new pickles will have absorbed the flavor of the pickle juice and be similar to the pickles you purchased.

FOR THE BEST QUICK BREADS

The cardinal rule about quick breads is: *Do not overmix.* Overmixing results in tough breads. Mix batters with a wooden spoon or rubber spatula just enough to combine the wet and dry ingredients. A few lumps are all right. Electric mixers, food processors, and blenders do not produce good quick breads.

For more quick-bread tips, see tip 214.

BEER QUICK BREAD

Someone once said of this recipe that it is so simple they were embarrassed to tell anyone. It really is that simple and it's equally delicious. Beer gives the loaf a robust, yeasty flavor. It's wonderful eaten soon after it emerges fragrant from the oven, and it makes toast like no other.

3 cups (375 g) self-rising flour
3 tablespoons (38 g) sugar
One 12-ounce can (1 1/2 cup or 338 ml) beer
4 tablespoons (2 oz/28 g) butter or margarine, melted

Combine the flour, sugar, and beer in a small bowl. Scrape it into a well-greased loaf pan or 1-quart soufflé dish. Bake at 375°F (190°C) for about 50 minutes. Pour the melted butter over the top and bake 10 minutes longer. Cool on a rack.

Variation I
Add 1/2 (2 1/2 oz/75 g)cup minced herbs and parsley.

Variation II
Use brown instead of white sugar, add 1 tablespoon (15 ml) cinnamon, 1/2 teaspoon (3 ml) nutmeg, and 1/2 cup (2 1/2 oz/75 g) walnuts, chopped.

SUMMER VEGETABLE SOUP

The soup:
1 leek, chopped
1 onion, diced
2 cups (10.75 oz/303 g) carrots, diced
8 small new potatoes, chopped
1 medium tomato, chopped
1 pound (454 g) fresh cranberry beans or broad beans, shelled
6 sprigs fresh common sage
10 cups (80 fl oz/2.4 l) water
1/2 pound (227 g) string beans
1 zucchini, cubed
1/4 pound (113 g) linguine, broken into short pieces

The pistou:
4 garlic cloves, smashed
1/3 cup (75 ml) fresh basil, chopped
1/2 cup (2 oz/55 g) freshly grated Parmesan cheese
1/4 cup (2 fl oz/59 ml) olive oil
1 medium tomato

Over medium-low heat, sauté the leek and onion until they're just turning brown. Add the carrots, potatoes, tomato, and beans. Add the sage and the water. Bring to a boil, then lower the heat and simmer, covered, for 45 minutes or until the vegetables are soft.

About 25 minutes before serving, add the string beans, zucchini, and linguine. Add more water if needed. Mix well and continue cooking.

While the soup finishes, make the pistou. Place the garlic, basil, and Parmesan cheese in a food processor and blend until grainy. Continue processing while adding the oil slowly until the mixture is smooth. Mince the tomato finely and drain in a sieve. Add to the sauce.

Add a ladleful of hot soup to the sauce, mix well, then pour the sauce back into the rest of the soup and combine. Serve right away.

Yield: 6 servings

PATRIOT'S PUNCH

This superb recipe for herbal tea was devised during the U.S. bicentennial celebration. Depending upon the occasion, you can divide it into two punch bowls, half according to this recipe and the other with dry white wine added.

5 tablespoons (75 ml) dried peppermint, whole
3 tablespoons (45 ml) dried sage, whole
2 tablespoons (30 ml) dried rosemary, whole
1 quart (1.67 pts/946 ml) water, boiled briskly
1 cup (8 oz/225 g) sugar (or to taste)
1 small can frozen lemonade concentrate
4 tablespoons (.5 oz/14 g) instant tea
2–3 gallons (13.33–20 pts/7.5–11.4 l) cold water
Lemon slices, whole cloves, and rosemary for garnish

Steep herbs in boiled water for 5 to 10 minutes until well flavored. Strain out herbs and discard them; add remaining ingredients to the tea. Serve iced with lemon slices stuck with whole cloves. Garnish with rosemary.

Yield: 50 servings

MICROWAVE MINT

Have some extra fresh mint that you don't know what to do with? Try drying it in the microwave. Put a double layer of white paper towels on the floor of the microwave. On this, spread out a handful or two of fresh mint in one layer. Make sure you have removed any hard, woody stems; soft, new stems can be dried right along with the leaves. Do not cover.

Microwave on high for 4 minutes, and that's it! You now have absolutely perfect dried mint. Store in an airtight bag or container in a dark place, and it will give you many months of cooking pleasure.

Peppermint

STORAGE GUIDE FOR FRESH VEGETABLES

Store in a cool room away from bright light
Mature onions, potatoes, sweet potatoes, waxed turnips, winter squash

Store at room temperature
Tomatoes

Refrigerate uncovered
Corn in husks, lima beans, peas in pods

Refrigerate covered (or keep in vegetable crisper)

Asparagus, beans (snap or wax), beets, broccoli, cabbage, carrots, cauliflower, celery, corn (if husked), cucumbers, leafy greens, leeks and scallions, parsnips, peas (if shelled), green peppers, radishes, summer squash, turnips (unless waxed)

Vegetables kept in a refrigerator vegetable crisper will keep well for seven days or longer. If you don't have a crisper, a closed plastic bag is a good substitute.

124

COUNTRY DILL PICKLES

These resemble the country-store pickles our grandparents enjoyed, the ones they fished out of big barrels or crocks.

Those were (and are) "cold-pack pickles," the theory being that the vinegar and salt in the brine would prevent the development of any toxins. But now that most of us are so afraid of food poisoning, we're giving you another version, one where the vinegar and water are boiled and the jars are sealed.

1 tablespoon (15 ml) mixed pickling spices
4 heads and stems of dill
4 cloves garlic
4 quarts (6.25 lbs/4 l) Kirby pickling cucumbers
2 quarts (4 pts/2 l) vinegar
1 quart (1.67 pts/946 ml) water
1 cup (8 oz/225 g) kosher or other coarse salt

Sterilize four 1-quart jars. (Try to find and use wide-mouthed jars.)

Divide the pickling spices among the jars. Put one head of dill, complete with its stem, into each jar. Peel the garlic cloves and put one into each jar.

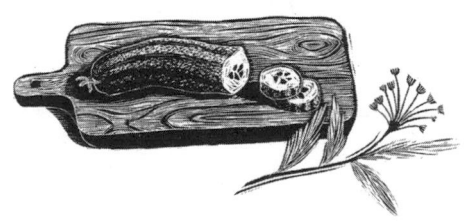

Scrub the cucumbers well, then place in the jars, cramming them in as best you can.

Put the vinegar, water, and salt in a medium-size nonreactive saucepan and bring to a boil. Pour over the cucumbers, filling jars to within 1/2 inch (12 mm) of the top. Seal.

Restrain yourself. Try not to eat the pickles for at least a week!

Yield: 4 quarts (7.75 pt/4 l)

PICKLE PROBLEM SOLVING

Problem	Cause
Soft or slippery pickles	*Scum not skimmed from surface daily (slow brining)*
	Pickles not well covered by brine
	Jars did not seal properly
Shriveled pickles	*Brine too strong*
	Syrup too sweet
	Vinegar too strong
	Cucumbers not fresh
Dark pickles	*Water too hard*
	Used copper, brass, galvanized metal, or iron equipment
	Canning lids corroded
Hollow pickles	*Cucumbers overmature or sunburned*
Lids didn't seal	*Proper headspace not maintained*
	Nonstandard jars or lids used
	Jars not sufficiently processed
	Jar rim not wiped well

RED POTATO SALAD WITH
KIELBASA AND YOGURT DRESSING

Tiny, red new potatoes in their jackets make this the perfect late-summer luncheon salad, but larger red potatoes cut into cubes work just as well.

2 pounds (908 g) tiny, red new potatoes, or about 5–6 large potatoes
8 ounces (226 g) plain yogurt
1/4 cup (2 fl oz/59 ml) white vinegar
1 teaspoon (5 ml) Dijon-style mustard
1 tablespoon (15 ml) sugar
4 cloves garlic, finely minced
1 teaspoon (5 ml) summer savory
1 teaspoon (5 ml) basil
1 teaspoon (5 ml) thyme
1/4 cup (1/2 oz/14 g) green onions, sliced
1/4 cup (1 oz/28 g) celery, finely chopped
1 tablespoon (1/4 oz/7 g) carrot, finely shredded
1 pound (454 g) fully cooked kielbasa, thinly sliced
2 tablespoons (30 ml) fresh parsley, minced, for garnish

Wash the potatoes and cook them in a large pot of simmering water for approximately 15 to 25 minutes (depending on size). Drain and rinse under cold water. If larger potatoes are used, cut them into 1/2-inch (12 mm) cubes. Set aside.

In a large mixing bowl, combine the yogurt, vinegar, mustard, sugar, garlic, savory, basil, and thyme. Add the onions, celery, and carrot and mix thoroughly. Add the kielbasa and the reserved potatoes and stir through. Cover and chill thoroughly before serving.

Yield: 6–8 servings

CRYSTALLIZED VIOLETS

These violets are beautiful adornments for cakes and cookies and are packed with vitamin C.

10–20 violet flowers
Powdered egg-white mix
Fine castor (granulated) sugar

Gently wash the violet flowers, then lay them on paper towels to dry.

Prepare the egg white according to the package directions so that you have about 1 egg white, beaten.

Using a fine brush, coat each flower with the egg white. Dust with sugar. Snip the stems and set aside in a warm place (but not in direct sunlight) until dry, usually about 24 hours.

Store the violets in a sealed jar between layers of paper. Keep the jar in a cool, dark location.

HOW TO CLEAN AND FILLET A FISH

1. Scrape off scales.
2. Insert knife at vent and slit up to head.
3. Remove entrails.
4. Cut off head, fins, and tail.
5. Cut the fillet from head to tail.
6. Cut along backbone from tail to head to remove fillet.

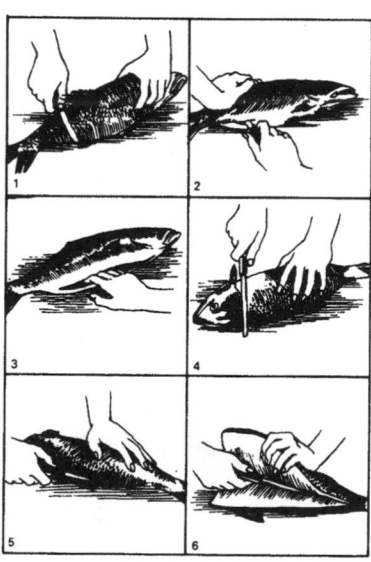

FISH COOKING TIPS

Small fish usually are cooked whole, with the tail on, but larger fish may be cut crosswise into steaks or lengthwise into fillets.

Cook fish quickly but gently. All fish, regardless of age, are tender and may be baked, poached (never stewed), fried, or broiled. Fish should be cooked over low heat just until the flesh flakes easily with a fork.

FISH BAKED IN MILK

6 whole fish, cleaned and scaled
3 cups hot milk
salt and pepper
3 tablespoons flour
4 tablespoons butter or margarine

Wash fish and wipe dry. Place in a baking pan and cover with hot milk. Bake at 350°F (180°C) for 20 to 30 minutes, depending on the thickness of the fish. Remove fish to platter, sprinkle with salt and pepper. Thicken milk in pan with flour and season with butter and salt and pepper. Pour sauce over fish.

Yield: 6 servings

Crafts

USES FOR AROMATIC DRIED HERBS

The fragrance of many aromatic herbs can spice up and perfume your daily existence. Here are a few ideas:

Breath fresheners: Chew on a sprig of mint.
Herbal bathing waters: Add angelica, mint, rosemary, and thyme directly to the water or place them in a small piece of cheesecloth. Use very hot water and let the herbs steep for ten minutes. Hop in and enjoy.
Sachets and potpourris: Combine mint, thyme, rosemary, sage, dill, and savory. Let them sit in a closed container for the scents to marry.

- **For sachets**: Grind the herbs into powder and place in a small fabric bag or pillow. Place in drawers for fragrance.
- **For potpourris**: Place the herbal mixture in an open-topped container to scent the room.
- **Catnip mice**: Crush freshly dried catnip and sew into little pillows or merry mice. A feline favorite!

Angelica (Angelica archangelica)

SIMPLE, EFFECTIVE MOTH-CHASER SACHETS

1 cup (237 ml) rosemary leaves, dried
1 cup (237 ml) lavender blossoms, dried
1 cup (237 ml) cinnamon bark, crushed

Mix well and divide into small, breathable cloth bags to make half a dozen lovely drawer sachets. Use patterned or colorful bags and ribbon closures to make wonderful favors or small gifts.

LEAF-STAMPED STATIONERY

Leaf stamping is an easy way to create beautiful gift packets of stationery for letters, memos, postcards, and envelopes.

What You Will Need

Stamp pads (colors of your choice)
Tweezers
Variety of small leaves
Typing paper, copier paper, or stationery
  of your choice
Envelopes to fit selected paper

1. Using a stamp pad and tweezers, ink both sides of several small leaves. Turn over each leaf once or twice while pressing it on the stamp pad to ensure enough ink has adhered. (Note: Stamp-pad-embossing inks and powders create glossy, raised designs that look very professional. However, some printers and fax machines may not accept paper with glossy, raised designs.)

2. Arrange the inked leaves on a piece of stationery as you would like them to print.

3. Position an envelope facedown over the leaves on the stationery as you would like it to be printed, and press with the heel of your hand. Inking the stationery and the envelope at the same time will allow you to design a matching set.

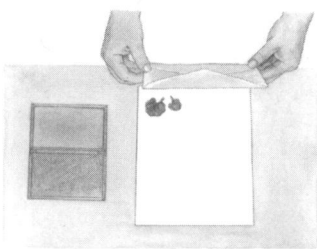

4. Remove envelope and leaves carefully and allow printed paper to dry before packaging as a gift.

Variation: To create 2 prints at once, simply place a second sheet of paper facedown over leaves in step 2.

Adapted from *Nature Printing with Herbs, Fruits & Flowers* by Laura Donnelly Bethmann

134

BASIC NATURE PRINTING, PART 1 OF 6

Learn how to make lovely prints from natural objects using a simple, direct technique in which a pigment-covered object is pressed onto paper or another receptive surface, revealing a delicately textured, life-size image of itself.

The basic, direct printing method requires a clear work space in a well-lit area where you can keep all materials close by. You will need the following materials:

Water-based block printing inks (such as Graphic Chemical brand)
Water-soluble vehicle (such as Graphic Chemical brand)
Soft rubber brayers in assorted sizes
Palette (sheet of glass) and palette knives or ink spreaders
Tweezers
Paper for practice printing

Printmaking papers
Water and mild liquid soap
Paper towels
A variety of pressed leaves and plants

Prepare for inking by setting up a clear work area and assembling all of your materials within easy reach.

135

BASIC NATURE PRINTING, PART 2 OF 6

Inking

With a practice sheet of paper ready, begin the inking process.

1. To ink palette, squeeze a 1/4-inch (6 mm) blob of ink near the top edge. Place the tip of the palette knife in the middle of the ink and draw it straight down the palette, making a thin smear about 3 to 4 inches (7.6 to 10 cm) long.
2. Dip the corner of a clean spreader into the can of vehicle and mix a few drops into the ink smear with the same downward-drawing motion for several seconds. Lay the spreader at the top of the palette.
3. Select a sturdy, flat leaf. Roll an appropriately sized brayer back and forth along the ink smear, allowing the ink to just coat the brayer. Slightly widen and lengthen the ink by rolling the brayer back and forth, thinning out the ink and evenly distributing it on the brayer. The ink should be tacky and shiny; if it's dry and dull, add another drop of vehicle. You want a very thin layer of ink— when the ink is an even, translucent film on the palette, you're ready to ink the leaf.
4. Lay the leaf underside-up on a clean area of the glass and roll the brayer gently over it from stem to tip. Roll the brayer over the ink to get an even layer of ink on it, and reink the leaf again, and maybe even a third time. The leaf should now be sufficiently coated.

BASIC NATURE PRINTING, PART 3 OF 6

Printing

5. Carefully lift the inked leaf by its stem with tweezers, position it over the paper, and place it inked-side down. Do not move the leaf once it's on the paper.

6. Cover the leaf with a piece of newsprint or paper towel. If you prefer to see the leaf while you print it, cover it with a freezer bag. Keep on hand some cover sheets that are a little larger than your plant.

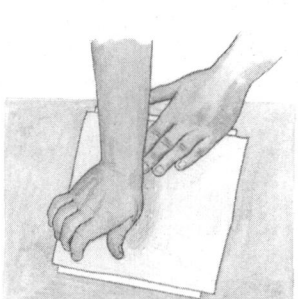

7. Press with your hands. For a small leaf, press with the heel of your hand. For a large leaf, press your left thumb firmly at the center of the leaf to anchor it, then use the thumb, fingers, or heel of your other hand to press all around the leaf, radiating from the center outward to the edges. Press the body of the leaf first, the stem last.

8. Slowly remove the paper covering. Wipe the ink off the tweezers, then grasp the stem of the leaf and lift it straight up and off the print. Lay the leaf on the glass for reinking.

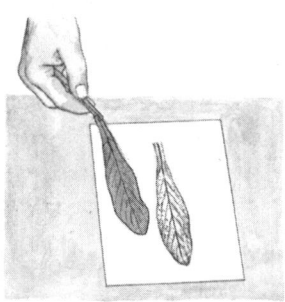

9. Lay prints in a row to air-dry for 1 to 4 weeks before storing, mounting, or framing.

137

BASIC NATURE PRINTING, PART 4 OF 6

Ink Application Tips

- Try inking leaves and plants on both sides, then using a folded sheet of paper to create a double print.
- Make an indirect print as a result of your direct print. The negative image left on the brayer after inking a leaf can be rolled onto a printing surface, thus creating an indirect print. Another way to capture this image is to roll a large, clean brayer over an already-inked object and then roll the brayer on a printing surface. This method works best with the very sensitive composition brayers and polyurethane brayers, although soft rubber brayers also work.

Clean Up

1. Soak brayers in a sink of soapy water for 1 to 2 minutes, then wipe ink off with a sponge, rinse, and dry.
2. Scrape excess ink from glass palette. Spray palette with water, let stand a minute, and wipe clean.
3. Leftover ink can be covered with a loose-fitting lid or plastic wrap and stored for future use.

138

BASIC NATURE PRINTING, PART 5 OF 6

When you first begin printmaking from nature, you'll want to try printing with just one color at a time. But after you've had some practice, try experimenting with multiple colors.

- Paint the protruding veins of a leaf with a contrasting color from the leaf body. To do this, ink the underside of the leaf with one color, then gently roll a brayer inked with a different color over only the veins of the leaf before printing.

* Apply a thin wash of one or more watercolor paints to add color and depth to a finished print once the ink has dried.
* Experiment with combining colors by smearing and then rolling 2 or 3 colors side by side on your palette to fit the width of a 3 1/2-inch (8.8 cm) or larger brayer. Roll the brayer back and forth until an even film appears showing each distinct color.

BASIC NATURE PRINTING, PART 6 OF 6

Display Ideas and Tips

* Crop nature prints so that the margin is even all around. Slip prints into sturdy clear-plastic envelopes and tack them onto a wall or wall-mounted cork strip.
* Mount a length of molding to a wall, with lip facing up, and line up firmly backed or matted prints.
* Plate stands or small table easels make appropriate holders for matted prints and for nature-printed herbals or journals.
* Store unprotected prints in Mylar or acid-free paper envelopes in a cool, dark, airy place.
* Acrylic box frames are inexpensive and come in a large variety of sizes. It is very easy to insert and remove prints, so they can be changed frequently. Make a wall arrangement with several box frames to be changed seasonally or just to accommodate your latest nature prints.
* Nature prints on soft Asian papers, such as *sumi,* can be fastened on very inexpensive wooden embroidery hoops for interesting wall art or a pleasing gift. Use fabric markers for lettering or a border (regular markers bleed on soft paper).

BUBBLE PRINTING

The bubble pattern is found frequently in nature: in rushing water, honeycombs, seedpods, and the tiny world of cell structure.

What You Will Need
Mild liquid soap
Several colors of water-soluble bottled pen ink
Wide-top containers or jars
Drinking straws
Printing paper or plain-colored gift wrap

1. Set out a container for each ink color. Put 1 inch (2.5 cm) of liquid soap in each. Add 1 tablespoon (15 ml) of ink and 1 straw to each container, and mix.
2. Blow through the straw until bubbles come up over the top of the container.
3. Remove the straw and lay a sheet of paper on top of the bubbles. On contact, the pattern will appear on the paper. Repeat the process with the other ink colors on the same sheet of paper to make a multicolored design.
4. Thin paper will buckle as it dries; to flatten, apply a warm iron to the dried print. These designs make delightful pictures just as they are, or you can add nature prints of leaves and other objects.

Adapted from *Nature Printing with Herbs, Fruits & Flowers* by Laura Donnelly Bethmann

MAKE A PRESSED-HERB WINDOW ORNAMENT

As herbs bloom, save the tiny blossoms and a few leaves. Press and dry them to use in this wonderfully elegant and delicate ornament. Make a few and tie them to the ends of window-shade pulls so they hang suspended in the light.

What You Will Need

Small pressed and dried cuttings from herb plants (such as thyme, sage, lavender, marjoram, rue, hyssop, the individual florets of chives and bee balm, and the smaller leaves of bay and costmary)
2 microscope slides
Transparent glue
Sewing needle or pin
1/8-inch-wide (3 mm) satin or grosgrain ribbon

1. Arrange the cuttings on a microscope slide. Secure carefully with tiny drops of glue applied with the point of a needle or pin. Let dry.
2. Cover the arrangement with the other microscope slide. Secure at the corners with additional glue droplets. Press until dry.
3. Make a 1-inch (2.5 cm) loop of the ribbon and glue it to the center of the top edge. When the loop is dry, make a border with the rest of the ribbon, covering the raw edges of the glass. Beginning at the top center, glue the ribbon in place all the way around, ending at the top center and leaving 4 to 5 inches (10 to 12.7 cm) of ribbon at each end. Let dry.
4. Tie the ends of the ribbon in a bow around the hanging loop. Trim the ends to an attractive length.

Adapted from *Herbal Treasures by Phyllis V. Shaudys*

SPICY LEMON-VERBENA POTPOURRI

The very name *lemon verbena* conjures up pleasant memories for many people. It has a sweet, warm, comforting scent—not as sharp as lemon, not as sweet as orange. It makes a pretty green-and-yellow potpourri.

1/2 teaspoon (2.5 ml) best lemon-verbena oil
1/2 cup (118 ml) cellulose fiber
2 cups (473 ml) lemon-verbena leaves
1 cup (237 ml) calendula petals
1/2 cup (118 ml) crushed Ceylon cinnamon
2 tablespoons (30 ml) cracked cloves
1 tablespoon (15 ml) benzoin granules

Combine the oil and cellulose and allow to blend for 24 hours. Add all other ingredients, shake well, and age. If at the end of 3 weeks the fragrance is not quite strong enough, add more combined oil and cellulose fiber.

MIXED-BAG POTPOURRI

1 quart (946 ml) dried herbs and flowers
1/2 cup (118 ml) patchouli
1/4 cup (59 ml) sandalwood chips
1/4 cup (59 ml) vetiver roots
1 teaspoon (5 ml) each frankincense, myrrh, ground cloves, and ground cinnamon
1 tonka bean, finely chopped
1/4 cup (59 ml) ground allspice
10 drops rose oil
1 cup (237 ml) ground orrisroot

Gently mix together the ingredients of your potpourri. Store in a tightly closed container for 3 to 4 weeks until scents are well blended.

USES FOR POTPOURRI

- Sweet bags are a fine way of keeping fragrance in the living room. Make these from any square of fabric. Put half a cup of potpourri in each square, tie shut, and tuck the finished balls behind chair or couch cushions.
- Citrus-spice is especially effective against stale smoke odors.
- Cloves have long been the remedy for the mustiness in trunks, storage areas, and basement rooms.
- Lavender bags are one sure way of freshening clothes closets. Combine cedar, a moth repellent, with lavender for a sweeter aroma. Hang these over the closet rod for lasting aromas among the clothes. Replace after one season.

Gardening

TIPS FOR A HEALTHY CHIVE HARVEST

Chives can be harvested from the moment they begin to grow in spring through the early frosts of autumn. Chives delight gardeners by being among the first shoots of green to appear in the herb garden. Still, do let the plant grow to at least 6 inches (15 cm) in height before you begin tentatively pruning for your kitchen. This will ensure that growth will continue throughout the season.

Always cut each leaf or flower stalk off at the lowest point you can reach. Whatever is left of a stalk will turn brown and hard after you cut it, and leaves will become brown at the ends. Neither of these features makes an attractive addition to your garden.

When harvesting chives, use a sharp knife to trim stalks and leaves close to the base of the plant.

CARING FOR SUMMER BULBS

Disbudding

Some summer bulbs, primarily dahlias, benefit from disbudding. As flower buds develop, pinch out the side buds and allow only the center bud to develop. It will become much larger than if it had been left in a spray of flowers.

To produce more compact, stockier plants with more flowering stems, pinch out the growing tip during the first 4 to 6 weeks of growth, encouraging side shoots.

Staking Tall Bulbs

Some taller-growing summer bulbs, such as gladiolus and tall dahlias, will probably need to be staked. Stakes should be set into the ground at planting time so bulbs will not be injured later on. Stems can be secured to a stake with a twist tie; be careful not to injure the stem. Large plants or clumps of smaller plants can be staked with a hoop or cage.

PLANTING BARE-ROOT ROSES IN 5 EASY STEPS

1. Prepare the site. Dig each hole 15 to 18 inches (38 to 46 cm) wide and deep. Mix a quart of peat moss, compost, or other organic material with the soil removed from the hole. Form a blunt pyramid of some of this mixture in the hole.
2. Remove any broken or injured roots or canes and canes less than pencil thick. Position rose on soil pyramid so the bud union is just above ground level after the soil settles (in mild climates) or about 1 to 2 inches (2.5 to 5 cm) below the surface (in areas with below-freezing winters). Spread roots in a natural manner.
3. Work soil mixture around the roots to eliminate air pockets. Firm soil around roots and add more soil until hole is three-quarters full.
4. Fill hole with water and let it soak in, then refill with water. After water drains again, check bud union to make sure it's at the proper level—if not, add more soil. Fill hole and tamp slightly. Trim canes to 8 inches (20 cm), making cuts at a 45-degree angle about 1/4 inch (6 mm) above outward-facing buds.

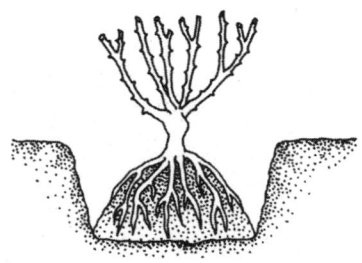

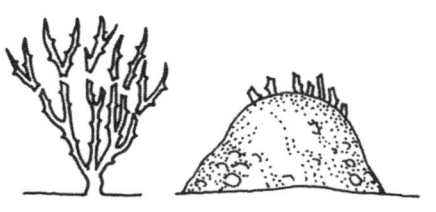

5. Mound soil around and over the plant to 6 inches deep. When buds sprout, gradually and gently remove soil mound (over 2 weeks or so), checking every 2 to 3 days. Loosen name tag so it does not inhibit growth. When vigorous growth starts, apply plant food according to manufacturer's directions.

148

TEN STEPS TO BEAUTIFUL ROSES, PART 1 OF 2

No doubt, roses are one of the best gardening buys around. To ensure a return on that investment, here are ten easy steps to successfully growing beautiful roses.

Step 1: Choose Well
Visit local public rose gardens to see which plants do well in your climate. Talk with neighbors or others in your area who grow roses and discuss the ones that have done well for them. Joining the local rose society is also a great way to get tips on which roses will work well for you.

Step 2: Provide a Great Location
Roses should get at least 6 hours of sunlight a day, the best soil possible, and excellent drainage. They should be planted somewhere accessible, away from large trees and eaves and gutters where falling water, snow, and ice could be damaging.

Step 3: Super Soil
Roses grow best in a slightly acid soil with a pH of 6.0 to 6.5. You can help your soils with additives and fertilizer if necessary.

Step 4: Planting Perfectly

It's helpful to plant bare-root roses at the correct time and to follow certain procedures to ensure success. See tip 149 for a chart showing ideal planting times and spacing.

Step 5: Mulching

Mulching reduces the need for weeding and watering by inhibiting weed growth and slowing soil-moisture evaporation.

TEN STEPS TO BEAUTIFUL ROSES, PART 2 OF 2

Step 6: Watering

Soil moisture and excellent drainage are essential. Never let more than the top inch or so of soil dry out during the growing season. Water slowly and deeply in the early morning—the soil should be soaked at least 12 to 18 inches (30 to 46 cm) deep.

Step 7: Feeding

Here is a basic fertilizer program for roses that repeatedly bloom throughout the summer: one feeding in early spring when buds begin to break, one when buds have developed, and one about six weeks before the first fall frost. Use an all-purpose dry granular garden fertilizer like 10-10-10 if plants are mulched or 5-10-10 if they are not. Use a formulation without nitrogen, such as 0-10-10, for the final feeding.

Step 8: Pruning

Make cuts at a 30- to 45-degree angle at a point 1/4 inch (6 mm) above an outward-facing bud eye. Prune in early spring when the buds begin to swell, and remove all dead wood (healthy wood is white in the center) as well as crisscrossing, weak, or damaged canes. Through the growing season, prune only diseased parts or faded flowers, cutting the stem just above the first live leaflet below the flower.

Step 9: Pest Control

Use preventative maintenance. Remove and destroy any diseased foliage and flowers, and treat with the correct pest control as soon as you spot pests.

Step 10: Winter Protection

Prepare the roses just before the first hard freeze in fall or early winter. Where winter temperatures dip below 20°F (-7°C), remove all leaves around and on the plants. Apply a final spraying of fungicide, work in a feeding of 0-10-10 around each plant, water it well, and prune roses to one-half their height and tie their canes together. If winter temperatures drop to 0°F (-18°C), protect the base of each plant with an 8-inch (20 cm) mound of organic material. If temperatures fall below 0°F (-18°C), increase the mound to 12 inches (30 cm); you may add another 8 to 10 inches (20 to 25 cm) of loose mulch on top, or cover the mounds with caps.

STOPPING WEEDS

Tough perennial weeds have a habit of showing up when you're not prepared to deal with them. Keep a few short, broad boards handy and throw them on top of knots of Bermuda grass to slow them down until you have a chance to dig them out. Colonies of quack grass and johnsongrass can be held in check with boards, too, until you have time to give them the careful digging they deserve.

Smooth crabgrass (Digitaria ischaemum)

GETTING RID OF VINE WEEDS

Weeds that grow as vines pose special problems. Their growth habit makes it possible for them to invade the garden virtually unnoticed. Get to know all of the vining weeds that turn up in your garden so you can eliminate them when they're young, before they get a strong hold on your favorite plants.

If you miss a few and discover them after they've tied themselves in knots around your plants (but before they've begun to flower), you don't need to untangle the stems and pull them out unless you really want to do so. Pulling out an extensive vine may mangle its support plant so badly that it's not worth doing. Instead, sever the base of the vine with pruning shears and let it die while still bound around other plants.

PURPLE IN A POT

Tender lavender can be grown in pots. Choose a container that is about 2 to 5 inches (5 to 12.7 cm) larger in diameter than the root ball of the plant. Make sure the pot has good drainage holes, and choose a growing medium that drains well. If roots are soggy for any length of time, a root rot quickly develops and will kill the plant. A soilless mix of peat, vermiculite, and perlite can work well. Many premixed soilless planting mediums can be found at local garden centers.

Container-grown lavenders can be outdoors all summer long. During the summer the plants will need plenty of water and fertilizer. Apply a liquid fertilizer of 20-10-20 about once a month. After bringing them inside in the fall, give the lavenders a lot of sunlight. Stems will weaken if they don't receive enough sun. Artificial light indoors can work well, and you may be rewarded with blooms in midwinter!

153

THE TAMING OF THE SLUG

Knowing something about slugs helps a little in getting rid of them. They cannot survive in areas of high temperature and low humidity. They seek cool, damp places and usually work at night. In the daytime they seek protective covering, which makes them easier to catch and kill.

Lay a few boards or shingles between the rows in your garden. The slugs will collect under them. A sprinkle of salt causes them to shrink up and die.

The mulch that keeps soil moist also provides protection for the slugs. If slugs have become a major problem in your garden, cultivate between the rows, clean up the old debris or mulch, and pile it a distance from the garden or in your composting pile.

Or try the beer trick—plant throwaway bottles in the rows with just the tops sticking out, and put about 2 inches (5 cm) of beer in the bottom of each. Beetles as well as slugs will be attracted and fall in. Simply replace the bottles a couple of times during the season.

154

RABBIT-PROOFING YOUR GARDEN

Only about 7 percent of all rabbits live to be a year old, but you may feel that the entire surviving population is in your garden.

Rabbits frighten easily—a toy snake or even an old piece of hose left in the garden will fool them, at least temporarily. A dog tied near the garden will keep them away, and an outdoor cat, if a good hunter, can eliminate them altogether. Another approach is to bury empty soda cans and bottles along the border with about 4 inches (10 cm) of the tops poking above the soil. The sound of the wind whistling through the openings scares rabbits away (or at least hurts their ears).You can also fill bottles or jars with water and place them around the garden. The rabbits will be frightened by the reflections of lights or of themselves.

If none of these approaches appeals to you, enclose the garden with a 48-inch-tall (120 cm) poultry fence buried 10 inches (25 cm) in the ground. This keeps rabbits at bay and blocks burrowing animals as well.

155

DISCOURAGE THE DEER

The Cooperative Extension Service of Orange County, New York, recommends hanging bags of human hair in trees to discourage browsing by deer. The hair can be collected from barber shops or beauty parlors and stuffed into old nylon stockings or plastic mesh produce bags, such as onion bags. A bag about the size of a softball should be hung in the tree to be protected. If the problem is severe, try hanging a bag in every tree.

156

STAKING TOMATOES

Set stakes when you set out your transplant, and keep in mind that your tomato plant will get quite tall by fall. Stakes should be 6 to 8 feet (1.8 to 2.4 m) tall and no thinner than 1 by 2 inches (2.5 by 5 cm). Drive them deeply into the ground; your tomato plant will get heavy as it grows and bears fruit.

As your tomato plant grows, tie it to the stake using coarse twine or fabric. Knot the tie around the stake, then around the plant.

When the plant becomes as tall as its stake, pinch off the growing point at the top. Remove any new flowers that form; this will direct the plant's energy into the fruit it has already set.

157

ARE GREEN TOMATOES ANY GOOD?

Green tomatoes are well worth harvesting. Those in the light green stage will ripen, providing good eating long after the vines have been killed by frost. Harvest them before that frost and try one of several methods to save them. One method is to pull up the entire plant, roots and all, and hang it upside down in a place where frost will not reach it. Another method is to pick the light green tomatoes, wrap them individually in newspaper, then keep them in temperatures of 55°F to 65°F (13°C to 18°C), where they will ripen during the next 6 weeks.

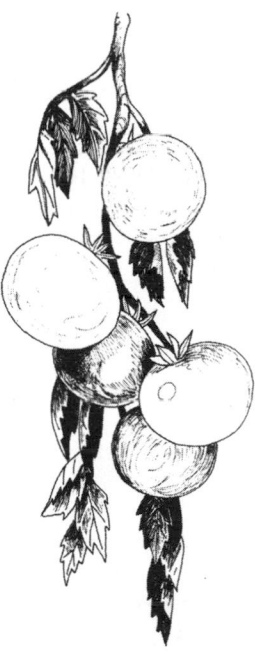

SAVING TOMATO SEEDS

Tomatoes are either hybrid or open pollinated. If they are hybrid, they will not breed true from the seeds. If you have an open-pollinated variety, however, you can save the seeds for planting next year.

1. Look for the healthiest plant that suits your needs, whether it fruited early, bore well, or had the tastiest fruits. Mark the plant or plants by tying a colored flag to the stake, cage, or trellis near the plant.

2. Leave a tomato or two on the plant until they're just past perfect but not rotting. This will guarantee mature seeds. Pick the tomato, cut it in half, and use a spoon to scrape out the seeds and surrounding membrane.

3. To ferment the seeds, place them, still encased in their gooey membrane, in a jar and add about 1/4 cup (59 ml) water. Put the cap on the jar, but don't screw it on tightly. Keep the jar on the kitchen counter. The contents will turn murky and will begin to

smell a bit ripe. Stir daily. The good seeds will sink to the bottom and the infertile ones will float along with the fermented pulp. After 2 or 3 days, pour off the floaters and the liquid. Dump the good seeds into a strainer and wash them well.

4. Spread out the rinsed seeds on several layers of newspaper to dry. After a few days, they should be dry and will not stick to the paper. If the seeds seem to dry slowly, change the newspaper every day. When thoroughly dry, place the seeds in an airtight container and store in a cold, dry place until ready to plant.

Adapted from *Step-by-Step Gardening Techniques Illustrated,* by Nancy Bubel and illustrated by Elayne Sears

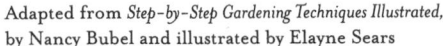

159

STARTING A NEW HEDGE

It is important to get your hedge plants off to a good start. Each one should grow in a bushy form at about the same speed as all its companions. Start with healthy, compact, small plants, if possible.

Begin shearing while the plants are still young, just as they start to grow noticeably. Even if you want the head to grow to 4 feet (120 cm), don't wait until it gets to that height before shaping it.

1. You can dig a hole for each individual plant, but it's easier to get them in a neat row if you plant them in one long trench.

2. If you are planting a straight hedge, use a string stretched taut to mark the line. Unless you're installing a mass planting, never plant a hedge more than one plant wide. For easier shearing, set the plants in a single line (unless you plan to use the plants as a high windbreak or snow trap).

3. Set out the plants 2 feet (0.6 m) apart, measuring from the center of each plant. Plant tall-growing hedges, such as a lilac hedges, several feet apart—the exact distance depends on how quickly you want a tight hedge. Prune the new plants to equal heights.

From *Pruning Made Easy* by Lewis Hill

160

HOW TO PRUNE TREES

The cardinal rule of pruning a tree is *cut cleanly and leave no stubs*. A dead stub will rot and die, and is vulnerable to infections that can spread to the rest of the tree. Either cut close to the main branch or immediately above a bud.

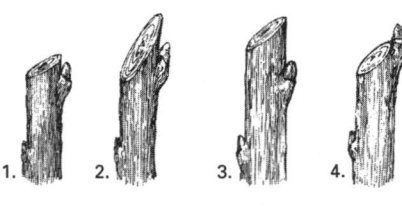

From left to right: the first cut is done correctly; the second cut leaves too much surface; the third cut leaves too long a stub; and the fourth cut was made too close to the bud.

When cutting above a bud, which will stimulate new growth, make the cut just above a bud growing in the desired direction. (A bud on the outside of a branch will grow out; one on the inside will grow in—less desirable.) Make sure the cut is slightly angled and close to the bud. After the cutting, use a knife to trim back any loose bark to the point where it is firmly adhered to the wood, and make sure there are no ragged edges. Coat cuts of more than 1 1/2 inches (3.8 cm) with commercial wound dressing (which contains antiseptic) to speed the tree's healing.

Make your pruning cut just above a bud growing in the direction you want the new growth to take.

161

PRUNING LARGE TREE LIMBS

When sawing off a sizable limb, the main danger is that the limb will split off before you have completed your neat, clean saw cut. A simple cutting method avoids this hazard.

Make a cut about one-third of the way through the branch, 10 to 15 inches (25 to 38 cm) out from the main trunk. Saw from the bottom up (*fig. 1*). Make a second cut farther out on the branch, this time from the top down and cutting all the way through (*fig. 2*). The limb will often break off, but the ragged edge will extend no farther than the first cut you made (*fig. 3*). Then cut the remaining stub flush and parallel to the main trunk (*fig. 4*), and trim away any loose bark with a knife (*fig. 5*).

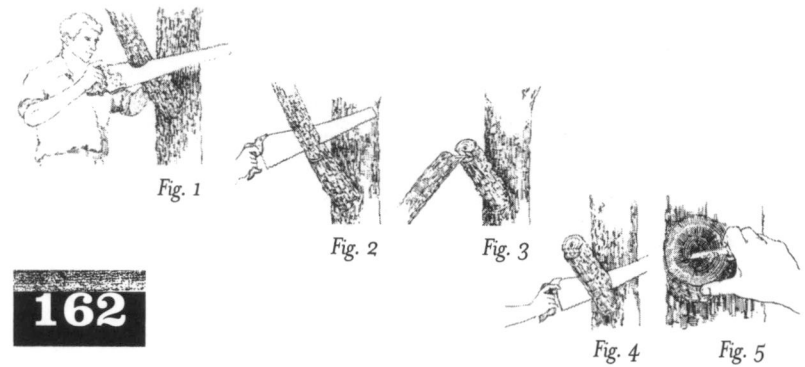

Fig. 1

Fig. 2   Fig. 3

Fig. 4   Fig. 5

162

SWEET CORN TIP

Sweet corn is at its tender, sweet, juicy best for only a few days. That moment of perfection occurs about eighteen to twenty days after the silks have been pollinated. This is the milk stage, when the kernels contain as much moisture as they will ever have. The juice in the kernels is milky, and the usual test of readiness is to puncture a kernel with your fingernail to see if milky juice spurts out. If you are too early, the juice will be watery. Too late (about twenty-eight days beyond pollination), and the kernels will turn doughy.

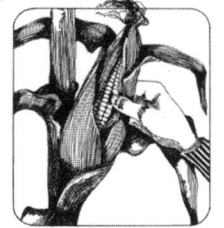

163

THE RIGHT WAY TO PICK STRAWBERRIES

The most natural way to pick strawberries is not the best way. That way is to grasp the berry and pull. This bruises the strawberry and usually leaves the cap on the plant, opening the center of the fruit to spores of decay organisms. Fingers gradually get dirty and sticky using this method, and the dirt gets on the berries.

Instead, grasp the stem close to the cap, twist, and pull, leaving as short a stem as possible attached to the cap to avoid puncturing other strawberries and exposing them to rot. Don't pile them high in the picking container; this will crush and damage them.

Pick strawberries early in the day. They are firmer then and easier to handle than when picked in the heat of the day.

164

HARVESTING FROM A WIDE ROW

Harvesting from a wide row is a simple matter. Just keep picking the largest vegetables, whatever they are. Harvest the biggest carrots, the largest beans, and so on, and leave the smaller ones so they can continue to grow. This way, few vegetables get overripe, seedy, or woody tasting.

When you are harvesting greens such as spinach, chard, and lettuce, don't be too dainty about it. Cut off all the leaves of a plant to within an inch (2.5 cm) of the ground. The plant will grow more leaves.

A plant's main purpose is to grow seed so that it can produce another generation. As long as you prevent it from going to seed, it will continue to try. You will be amazed at the number of times you can cut back a leaf crop in a wide row and have it continue to produce. It's the old story: keep your garden picked, and it will continue to grow more; let it go to seed, and it's finished.

See tips 57 and 58 for information on wide-row planting.

THE MYTH OF WEEDY MANURE

Some gardeners are reluctant to use manure to enrich their soil for fear that it contains many weed seeds. Yet the number of weed seeds in manure depends on what the animals eat and can be very high or close to nothing. As long as the animals that produce the manure you put into your garden do not subsist on weeds, you can use the manure with confidence to improve your soil's structure and fertility. Also keep in mind that it's easier to control weeds than it is to grow healthy flowers and vegetables in weak, infertile soil.

Health and Wellness

166

SAFETY FIRST

It's always a smart idea to have a first-aid kit on hand, especially in any situation (such as camping or traveling abroad) when medical help may be difficult to summon quickly. Also have a reserve of any medication that is needed on a regular basis. If you wear glasses or contact lenses, store a spare pair where you will find it in an emergency.

First-Aid Supply Checklist

Adhesive strips
Adhesive tape
Antibiotic ointment
Antiseptic wipes
Aspirin, ibuprofen, acetaminophen, or other over-the-counter analgesic
Burn ointment
Children's pain reliever
Decongestant tablets
Elastic bandage
Ethyl alcohol, hydrogen peroxide, or other disinfectant
First-aid book
Gauze bandages (2- and 4-inch/5- and 10-cm)
Gauze pads
Hydrocortisone cream
Oral thermometer
Prescription medications
Safety pins
Scissors
Tourniquets

ESSENTIAL OILS AND SUN EXPOSURE

While it's always important to exercise good common sense when going into the sun, be especially careful after you've used essential oils. Some oils, including bergamot and other citrus oils, such as lemon and orange, may increase the skin's sensitivity to the sun. Citrus oils can also increase the skin pigmentation in some people. Lemongrass, a fast-growing grass often used in culinary arts, may also increase sensitivity to the sun and have an irritant effect when used directly on the skin, due to some of the key chemical constituents it contains. If these oils are not properly blended and applied evenly, skin darkening and irritation could result.

If you want to be on the safe side, you can purchase bergamot with the bergaptene (the component of the oil that can lead to increased pigmentation) removed.

BEE-STING CARE

If you get stung by a bee, remove the stinger quickly by scraping it with your fingernail. Don't try to pull it out with your fingers— this will only force more venom into your body.

MAKING POULTICES AND PLASTERS

Poultices and plasters are applied directly to the skin to relieve inflammation, venomous bites, blood poisoning, and the like. They help cleanse the area and draw out infection, toxins, and foreign bodies. They also relieve pain and muscle spasms.

Poultices

A poultice is a warm, moist mass of powdered or crushed fresh herbs. To make a poultice, moisten the herb with hot water, witch hazel, herbal tea, or herbal tincture and apply to the skin. If necessary, reapply after it cools. (In a pinch, you can also make a poultice by chewing the herbs and applying them directly to the skin.)

Plasters

A plaster is just like a poultice except that the herb is placed between two thin pieces of cloth instead of applied directly to the area.

Plasters are wonderful for treating bruises, strains, and sprains.

170

GREEN TEA: ANTIOXIDANTS IN A CUP

For thousands of years, healers and monks have noted the many benefits of tea, particularly green tea, including its ability to offer refreshment, increase alertness, and stave off disease. Yet it is reassuring to know that pharmacologists, chemists, physicians, nutritionists, and others in the field of health science are also recognizing the health-giving properties of tea.

Studies of tea's value to maintaining good health have been reported in medical journals throughout the world. Most notable have been studies conducted by the *Journal of the Japanese Society for Food Science and Technology*, Tufts University, Harvard University, the National Cancer Institute, and U.S. teaching hospitals such as Johns Hopkins. All of these studies concur on one point: green tea is an inexpensive, healthful drink with possible long-range benefits, especially if taken daily throughout one's life.

The studies suggest that green tea may help lower the risk of cancer, inhibit aging, reduce the risk of cardiovascular disease, help lower blood-sugar levels, fight viral infections, and even prevent cavities, bad breath, and gum disease. While drinking green tea will certainly cause no harm, the best reason to drink it is that it does have time-tested benefits, such as antioxidation of fats and possible anticancer properties.

ASIAN FUSION TEA

6 tablespoons (90 ml) Gen-Mai Cha or other loose green tea
3 cups (24 fl oz/709 ml) boiling water
1 1/2 cups (12 fl oz/355 ml) cranberry juice
1/2 cup (4 fl oz/118 ml) pure maple syrup
6 tablespoons (3 fl oz/90 ml) amaretto

1. Brew the tea in the boiling water, covered, for 5 to 7 minutes. Add the cranberry juice and maple syrup and return to low heat to warm.
2. Pour 1 tablespoon of amaretto into each of six teacups, then pour in the cranberry tea. Serve with a smile.

Yield: 6 servings

NATURAL INSECT-BITE OINTMENT

Make an ointment from 1 cup (237 ml) of fresh basil, 1/2 cup (118 ml) of fresh oregano, and 1 cup (237 ml) of fresh rosemary or fresh savory with 2 cups (474 ml) of petroleum jelly. Spread over the bites. (Lesser quantities can be made by halving or quartering the recipe.)

WILTING HERBS

Before using herbs to make an infused oil or a salve, you need to wilt the plant material to allow most of its moisture content to evaporate. (Excess moisture can cause mold or botulism.) Simply lay the fresh herbs out on a screen or on paper towels in a place with plenty of air circulation and away from direct sunlight. After 24 hours, they should be nicely wilted, and most of the moisture they contain should have evaporated.

MAKING INFUSED OILS: THE SUN METHOD

Begin with top-quality extra-virgin olive oil.

Step 1: Fill a clean, dry, wide-mouthed glass jar to the top, loosely packed, with fresh herbs. Cover with the oil and stir with a wooden spoon or chopstick (anything nonmetal) to release any trapped air bubbles. Top off with more oil, seal, and set in a warm, dry spot, such as a sunny windowsill or the top of a water heater, for 2 to 6 weeks.
Step 2: Press the oil through cheesecloth to filter out the spent plant matter. Then let the oil stand so any water will separate. Pour off the water and store the oil in a sealed container in the refrigerator, where it will keep for up to 6 months.

MAKING INFUSED OILS: THE STOVE-TOP METHOD

Begin with top-quality extra-virgin olive oil.

Step 1: For a yield of 2 cups (473 ml), use 2 cups (473 ml) of dried herbs and 4 cups (946 ml) of oil. Place the herbs in a double boiler; cover with the oil. Heat, uncovered, over boiling water for about 3 hours. Don't let the oil bubble or smoke—long, slow cooking produces the best result.

Step 2: Strain the oil by lining a wire strainer with muslin or a coffee filter. Place the herbs in the strainer, and press to remove as much liquid as possible.

Step 3: Bottle the liquid and store in the refrigerator, where it will keep for up to 6 months.

SPRAIN PAIN RELIEF

This is a nice massage oil for soothing strains, sprains, and pains of all kinds. See tips 174 and 175 for instructions for making infused oil.

1/2 cup (4 fl oz/118 ml) arnica-infused oil
1/2 cup (4 fl oz/118 ml) St. John's wort–infused oil
1/2 cup (4 fl oz/118 ml) valerian-root-infused oil
3–5 drops tea tree essential oil
3–5 drops wintergreen essential oil
Contents of a vitamin E capsule

Combine the infused oils of arnica, St. John's wort, and valerian root. Add a few drops of tea tree and wintergreen essential oils and the vitamin E oil. Stir well. Store in the refrigerator, where the oil will keep for up to 6 months. Apply as needed.

VERSATILE YARROW

Yarrow is said to be named for the ancient hero Achilles, who was said to have used the herb to treat his wounded soldiers. Yarrow was indeed a popular wound treatment for the ancient Greeks, and it continued to be popular into the mid-nineteenth century, when it was used by field doctors in the American Civil War.

Native Americans used yarrow to halt bleeding and promote wound healing. It's not known whether European settlers introduced yarrow to the New World or if it is native to North America. Nevertheless, it is quite a useful plant.

To treat a minor cut or scrape that is bleeding, take a clean leaf or two of yarrow, crush it, and apply it to the wound. The hemostatic and antiseptic properties should help to stop the bleeding and promote healing.

Yarrow (Achillea millefolium)

Home

HOW MUCH WATER IS ENOUGH

When considering whether the springs and/or dug wells on a plot of land will provide enough water for your home, consider the following average consumption needs:

Adult or child	*50–100 gallons (42–86 UK gal/190–378 l) per day*
Baby	*100 gallons (86 UK gal/378 l) per day*
Automatic washer	*30–50 gallons (25–42 UK gal/113–190 l) per use*
Shower or tub	*25–60 gallons (21–50 UK gal/95–227 l) per use*
Milking cow	*30–35 gallons (25–29 UK gal/114–132 l) per day*
Dry cow	*10–15 gallons (8–12.5 UK gal/38–57 l) per day*
Horse	*6–12 gallons (5–10 UK gal/23–45 l) per day*
Hog	*2–4 gallons (1.6–2.3 UK gal/7.5–15 l) per day*
Sheep	*2 gallons (1.6 UK gal/7.5 l) per day*
25 chickens	*1–3 gallons (0.8–2.5 UK gal/4–11 l) per day*
Garden (1,000 sq ft/ 92.9 sq m)	*70 gallons (58 UK gal/265 l) per day or 700 (583 UK gal/2,650 l) every 10 days*

Most important, try to be as certain as possible that there is good water, that it is reliable throughout the year, and that whatever system is or will be in place functions well with minimum maintenance.

A FEW WORDS ON WATER

Drinking and bathing in high-quality water is the most natural way to hydrate your body and preserve and promote your good health. Most tap water from public water supplies is loaded with chlorine and often laced with other chemicals as well. Some of these chemicals are intentionally added to protect our health. Fluoride, for example, is a highly controversial additive intended to harden children's teeth and prevent tooth decay. But other chemicals slip through in minute particles as traces of environmental pollution. If your skin is dry or irritated after bathing, and particularly if you notice white residue on your skin, you might want to invest in a water filtration system.

WHO'S THE TRASH THIEF?

If you are mystified as to the identity of the garbage thief that comes in the night, study the clues. A dog will knock over the can, tear open all your neat brown paper bags, and strew the debris over a wide area. An opossum takes what it wants and drags it along the ground while it eats, leaving a trail. A raccoon chooses its menu, washes it carefully, then stays to eat. A crafty raccoon can open a trash container without knocking it over and delicately help himself.

Solution: A teaspoon of ammonia in each trash can and a little sprinkled around the garbage-can area will help to discourage dogs, raccoons, opossums, and skunks. Ammonia is also a good disinfectant.

MAKING YOUR OWN BUILDING MIXES

Ready-Mix Concrete

Concrete is made by mixing cement, sand, gravel, and water. For small jobs, you can purchase ready-mixed concrete. However, if you want to mix your own, simply combine the following ingredients:

1 part cement
2 parts sand
3 parts gravel

Ready-Mix Grout Mortar

Grout is a fine-grained cement mortar used to fill the cracks between mosaic pieces. You'll find it at ceramic-tile supply and hardware stores. To provide a more interesting design to your mosaic or tile work, color it using grout dyes available at ceramic supply stores. You can buy dry, ready-mixed mortar or make your own by mixing together the following ingredients:

1 part Portland cement
3 parts sand
2–3 tablespoons cement bonding adhesive per gallon (6.67 pts/3.8 l) of water

HOW TO REPAIR SCREENS

Your problem: It's nearing the end of summer and your screens have seen lots of wear and tear. Bugs are starting to come in through small holes, and these holes are only going to get bigger with time.

What You Need:

Screening or ready-cut screen patches
Shears
A ruler or small block of wood with a straight edge
Fine wire or nylon thread

Save That Screen

1. Trim the hole in the screen to make smooth edges (*fig. 1*).

2. Cut a rectangular patch an inch (2.5 cm) larger than the hole.

3. Remove the three outside wires on all four sides of the patch (*fig. 2*).

4. Bend the ends of the wires to a 90-degree angle. An easy way is to bend them over a block or the edge of a ruler (*fig. 3*).

5. Put the patch over the hole from the outside. Hold it tight against the screen so that the small, bent wire ends go through the screen (*fig. 4*).

6. From the inside, bend down the ends of the wires toward the center of the hole. You may need someone outside to press against the patch while you do this (*fig. 5*).

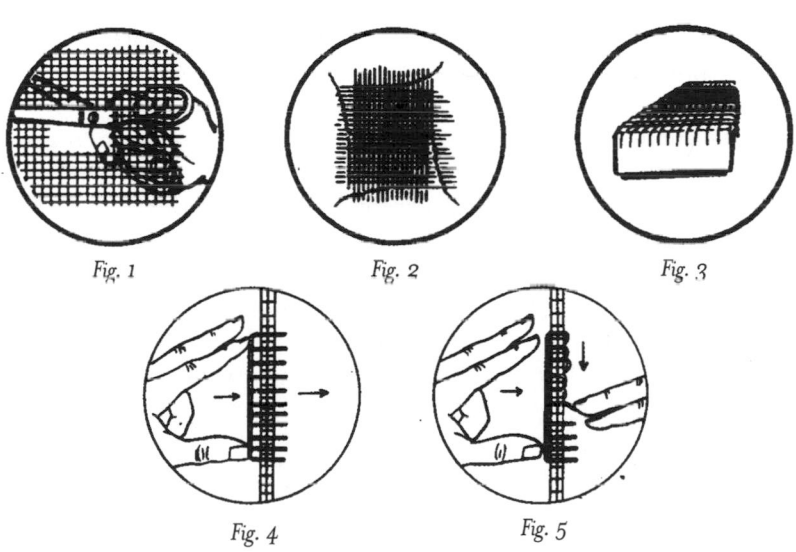

Fig. 1   Fig. 2   Fig. 3

Fig. 4   Fig. 5

QUICK SCREEN FIX

To quickly mend a screen that has a small slit in it, stitch back and forth with a fine wire or a nylon thread (see illustration). Use wire that is a matching color so it blends in.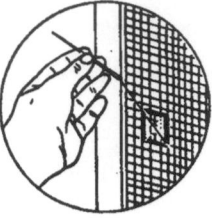

PATCHING LEAKY CRACKS IN BASEMENTS, PART 1 OF 2

If you are certain that water is leaking in at only one or two obvious places and the rest of the foundation is reasonably well water-proofed, it may be very possible to cure the leak with hydraulic cement. This cement can be used even as the leak occurs because it must be applied to a wet surface. The cement works by expanding as it sets, thereby filling and sealing the crack.

To prepare the surface for the cement, use a hammer and masonry chisel to enlarge the crack so that it forms a kind of dovetail shape, narrower at the surface and wider at the rear (see illustration). The purpose of the dovetail shape is that the cement will have the firm support of the masonry to hold it in place.

Use a wire brush to remove any chips and loose pieces of masonry. Following the directions on the cement package, mix only as much as you need immediately, because it sets very quickly. The area to be patched should be soaked thoroughly with water before you apply the cement. This prevents rapid hydration and improper setting. Then fill the crack and hold until it stiffens.

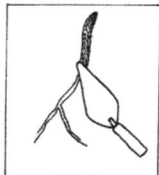

Patching a wall crack with hydraulic cement

PATCHING LEAKY CRACKS IN BASEMENTS, PART 2 OF 2

Hydraulic cement can also be used along the joint of the floor and wall. Make sure the surface is free of all dirt and dust. Chip away any loose mortar and make a dovetail-shaped opening along the joint (see illustration). A vacuum cleaner does a good job of removing dust particles. After wetting the area, mix only as much cement as you need. Use a pointed trowel to force the cement into the opening and smooth the surface.

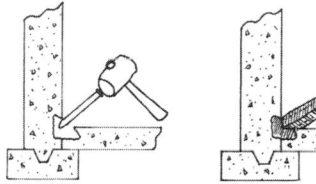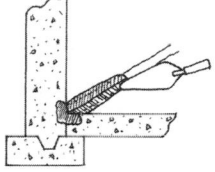

Patching a joint crack with hydraulic cement

POOR DRAINAGE: WHAT CAUSES IT?

For problems caused by poor drainage around the foundation of a house, there are some steps that should be taken before attempting any repairs.

Many basement flooding problems caused by poor drainage have been corrected by the proper installation and repair of roof gutters and proper positioning of the downspouts. Where do the downspouts drain the water? They should carry the water either to a storm sewer or a dry well. If there is neither, there should be splash guards at the bottom of the downspouts to carry the water at least 8 to 10 feet (2.4 to 3 m) away. Check the gutters and clean them of any leaves or debris. During a rainstorm, go outside and check for leaks or breaks. Repair any damage to the gutters caused by ice and snow.

Check the grade of land away from the house. There should be a gradual sloping away so that the surface water will run off before being absorbed into the soil. Lay a board perpendicular to the foundation and place a 4-foot level on the board—the bubble should be off center toward the house. If it isn't, you will probably need to have the land regraded.

Last but not least, check the soil by digging a hole down to the base of the footing—if the soil is loose and loamy, it is a better drainer than if it is packed and has a heavy clay texture.

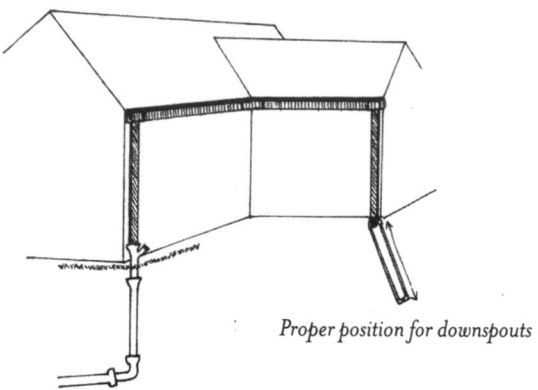

Proper position for downspouts

FIX STICKING OR DRAGGING DOORS

1. Tighten screws in the hinges. If screws are not holding, replace them, one at a time, with longer screws. Or insert a matchstick in the hole and put the old screw back in (*fig. 1*).

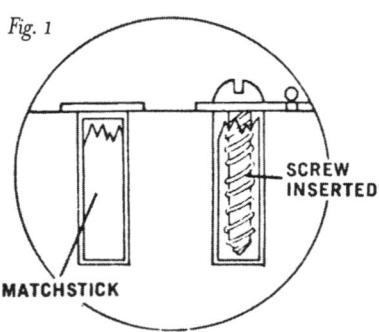

Fig. 1

SCREW INSERTED

MATCHSTICK

2. Look for a shiny spot on the door where it sticks. Open and close the door slowly to find the spot. Sand down the shiny spot (*fig. 2*). Do not sand too much, or the door will not fit as tight as it should.

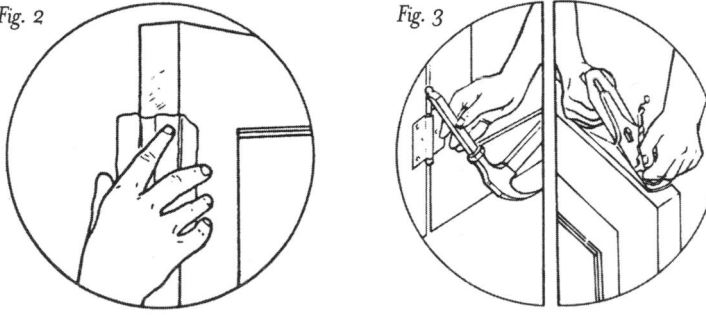

Fig. 2   Fig. 3

3. If the door or frame is badly out of shape, you may have to remove the door and plane down the part that drags (*fig. 3*).

Note: Sand edges of the door before painting to prevent paint buildup. This can cause a door to stick.

Autumn

AUTUMNAL EQUINOXES, 2008–2020

Times given are Eastern Daylight Saving Time (EDT)

2008	Monday	Sept 22	11:44 a.m.
2009	Tuesday	Sept 22	5:18 p.m.
2010	Wednesday	Sept 22	11:09 p.m.
2011	Friday	Sept 23	5:04 a.m.
2012	Saturday	Sept 22	10:49 a.m.
2013	Sunday	Sept 22	4:44 p.m.
2014	Monday	Sept 22	10:29 p.m.
2015	Wednesday	Sept 23	4:20 a.m.
2016	Thursday	Sept 22	10:21 a.m.
2017	Friday	Sept 22	4:02 p.m.
2018	Saturday	Sept 22	9:54 p.m.
2019	Monday	Sept 23	3:50 a.m.
2020	Tuesday	Sept 22	9:30 a.m.

AUTUMN HOLIDAYS

(United States and Canada)

COLUMBUS DAY · *second Monday in October*
THANKSGIVING DAY (CANADA) · *second Monday in October*
HALLOWEEN · *October 31*
DAYLIGHT SAVING TIME ENDS · *first Sunday in November*
ELECTION DAY (U.S.) · *Tuesday after the first Monday in November*
VETERANS DAY/REMEMBRANCE DAY · *November 11*
THANKSGIVING DAY (U.S.) · *fourth Thursday in November*

Animals

BIRD IDENTIFICATION 101

When bird watching, closely observe and take note of all the physical characteristics you notice, and then look for a matching picture in your guidebook. Ask yourself these questions:

- Does the bird show any splotches of color?
- What kind of beak does it have? What kind of tail?
- Any discernible pattern such as stripes or rings?
- Any markings around the eye, head, back, or breast?
- When the bird is in flight, do you notice any particular characteristic, like gliding, dipping, or undulation?
- Do any flashes of white or some other color appear on the wings or tail when the bird moves? Where did you see the color?
- What about its shape—is the bird chunky or slender?
- Does it walk, hop, perch quietly, or flit about?
- Does it say anything?
- What about size? Give yourself some mental image to compare the bird to. Was it the size of a sparrow, a robin, or a crow?

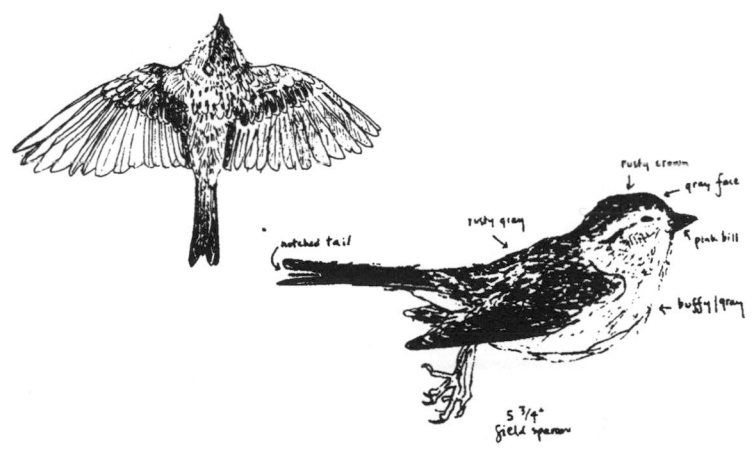

189

KNOW YOUR BIRD WORDS

Altricial: Bird that is born naked and helpless (for instance, songbirds).
Precocial: Bird that is born with down feathers and the ability to walk (for instance, ducks).
Hatchling: A baby bird that is completely dependent on its parents for warmth and food; nestlings are too young to leave the nest. This term is usually used to describe altricial birds.
Chick: A young precocial bird.
Fledgling: To fledge means to "grow feathers"; fledglings have matured enough to leave the nest but may not yet be able to fly, or may be able to do so only for short distances. They are still cared for by their parents, gradually becoming self-sufficient. This term is usually used to describe altricial birds.
Raptor: Bird of prey.
Pin feathers: The first feathers to emerge on altricial birds.
Talons: The powerful claws of a bird of prey.

190

SAVE THE STALKS

If you live in a colder region, leave any flower stalks standing after the first fall frost so birds can feast on the seeds all winter, and wait until spring to cut back the plants.

191

DIVIDING A BEE COLONY

There are several methods of dividing a colony of bees. Probably the simplest is to remove four to six combs of brood, with the adhering bees and old queen, to an empty hive. Fill the remaining space of both hives with empty combs or frames with brood foundation. Move the new divisions, with the queen, to a new location. This may be near the old location, but preferably with the entrance turned at a right angle to the parent hive. The parent hive should be given a  ripe (capped) queen cell or a new, young queen within 2 hours and no later than 24 hours after making the division. Dividing should be done during the middle part of the day, when many of the bees are away from the hive.

192

SWARM CONTROL

If you're a beekeeper, the last thing you want is swarming—more than half of your bees moving out of your hive to a different location they've selected. Swarms can be prevented, however, because bees will give you fair warning of their plans. They'll build a number of queen cells, which provide the hive with a queen when the reigning queen leaves with the swarm.

If your bees start building queen cells, you can cut out or destroy the cells every 8 to 10 days. They may be destroyed by sticking the point of your hive tool into them in such a manner that the larvae are killed. You must be very thorough in destroying queen cells—if only one is missed, the colony is likely to swarm. Before destroying any queen cells, you should check them closely to make certain they are not supersedure cells. If you were to destroy all such cells, your colony might be left queenless. If the cells are supersedure cells, leave one so that the new queen can emerge, and destroy the remainder. Also destroy the old queen, if you can find her.

If destroying queen cells doesn't stop the bees' desire to swarm, you may want to divide the colony and increase their numbers. It would be better to do that than to risk losing the swarm if it should come out on a day when no one is at home.

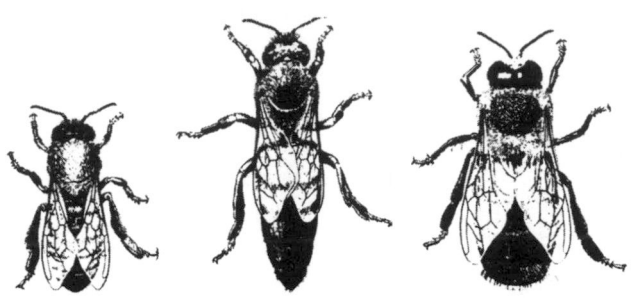

Worker, queen, and drone bees

THE RUN-IN SHED

A run-in shed is a three-sided shelter that allows horses to come and go as they please, taking advantage of the shed's shade in the heat of the day and the sun's warmth during cold winters. The three sides offer shelter from the wind, no matter which direction it's blowing; the sloping roof protects against rain, sleet, and snow.

DIFFERENT USES FOR DIFFERENT HORSE BLANKETS

Type	Use
Cotton or cotton/polyester sheet	*Keeps off dust or flies, provides warmth during cool weather*
Wool cooler (usually 85–100% wool)	*Cools a hot or sweaty horse*
Acrylic Baker blanket	*Provides moderate warmth in a stall*
Cotton duck with blanket lining	*Provides moderate warmth in a stall*
Nylon with fiberfill insulation and nylon lining	*Provides a high degree of warmth in a stall*
Nylon with foam insulation and fleece lining	*Provides a high degree of warmth in a stall*
Nylon Gore-Tex waterproof laminate	*Protects from wind and water, provides warmth outside*
Canvas turnout rug, often with blanket lining	*Protects from wind and water, provides warmth outside*

195

THE IDEAL CHICKEN FENCE

Whether your chickens have only a small yard or are free to roam the range, you'll need a stout fence to keep them from showing up where they aren't wanted and to protect them from predators. The fence should be at least 4 feet (120 cm) high so predators won't climb over and chickens won't fly out. It may need to be higher if you raise flyers such as Leghorns, Hamburgs, Old English, or many of the bantams.

The ideal chicken fence is made from tightly strung, small-mesh woven wire. Yard-and-garden fencing, which has 1-inch (2.5 cm) spaces at the bottom that graduate to wider spaces toward the top (thus using less wire to keep the cost down) makes a good secure fence for the coop. The smaller openings at the bottom keep small chickens from slipping out and small predators from slipping in.

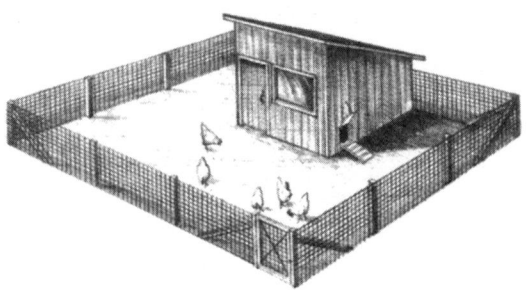

196

SOLVING COMMON DOG BEHAVIOR PROBLEMS: JUMPING UP ON PEOPLE

Dogs jump up on people to get attention. Puppies should be taught from a very young age not to jump. The key in preventing and stopping jumping is not to give the puppy or dog any type of positive attention when she does jump. Don't pet her or talk to her in any way that she might misunderstand as approval.

Allowing a dog to jump up on people will eventually cause you trouble. The dog might be muddy and get someone's clothes dirty. The person may have his arms full of groceries, including eggs and breakable bottles. The person may be elderly or handicapped. In any case, it's not a good behavior to allow.

Solution: If your puppy is young enough, use a stern voice to say "Off!" as you take her paws off you and place them on the ground. Then praise the dog. If you see that the puppy is coming over and has that "I'm going to jump on you" look, give her a firm

"Off" before she jumps and you'll be one step ahead. As she sits down, praise her. For a large dog, you can take a small step forward as she approaches and lift one knee to block her from full-body contact, at the same time giving her a stern "Off." The minute she sits down, praise her.

For a dog that is resistant to the solutions above, I suggest that she be taught the "Sit" command. As the dog approaches, give the "Sit" command and praise as she sits (see tip 197).

TEACHING A DOG OR PUP TO SIT

The sit can be easily taught with a treat and a little physical help. Your puppy should be in a relatively calm mood when you teach her the sit. With her standing in front of you and facing to your right, show her the treat, say "Sit," and move the treat to her nose and slightly over her head, at the same time lightly pushing down on her rump. If the dog sits, immediately give her the treat and praise. Keep the praise calm so that you can repeat the exercise several times. Within a few tries, the dog will sit without the push on her rump. Then you can tell her "Sit" and not offer the treat until she does. This usually takes only one lesson to learn. If possible, try to have several practice sessions in one day.

When you teach your puppy to sit, hold a treat above her nose and use light pressure on her rump. Don't forget to praise her when she does it right!

WHOLESOME HONEY DOG TREATS

If your dog likes things a bit sweet, she'll love these healthy treats.

2 cups (10 oz/300 g) rice flour
2 cups (10 oz/300 g) unbleached white flour
2 cups (12 oz/340 g) whole wheat flour
2 cups (7 oz/200 g) quick-cooking oats
1/2 cup (2 oz/57 g) wheat germ
1 3/4 cups (14 fl oz/414 ml) water
3/4 cup (6 fl oz/177 ml) low-fat milk
1/2 cup (6 oz/170 g) pure honey

Preheat the oven to 350°F (180°C). In a large bowl, combine all ingredients; mix well.

On a floured surface, knead the dough until it is firm.

Roll the dough to 1/4-inch (6 mm) thickness. Cut with the cookie cutter of your choice. Transfer the cookies to a baking sheet.

Bake for 30 to 45 minutes, or until the cookies are dry and firm to the touch. Turn off the heat; let the cookies stand in the oven until hard, 1 to 2 hours.

TREATING OTITIS NATURALLY

To treat your pet's otitis, otherwise known as ear cankers, simply combine 1/2 teaspoon (2.5 ml) lemon juice and 1 1/2 teaspoons (7.5 ml) warm water. Drop into the affected ear.

200

TIPS TO SAVE YOU FROM CAT SCRATCHES

- Never pull your hand away from your cat quickly during an attack. She will interpret this as play and chase it, and you will reinforce her behavior.
- Don't play rough with your kitten. When her claws get sharper and her jaws get stronger, it won't be so cute!
- Don't bother your testy cat while she eats, bathes, or sleeps.
- Pay attention to her tail while you are petting her. If it begins to move from side to side in quick, sharp movements, this is a sign she's ready for you to stop.
- Don't ever react to an attack by hitting your cat. She will feed into your aggressive attitude and will assume that this is your personality. Remember, there is no such thing as an alpha cat in the feline mind.

201

HINTS FOR BREAKING A CAT'S BITING OR SCRATCHING HABIT

Immediately react to any unwanted bite or scratch by letting out an exaggerated yelp or "No!" Do not respond with physical aggression. This will only reinforce the nipping, biting, or scratching behavior of your cat. As soon as she has understood that she hurt you, speak in a calm, soothing voice. If she continues to act aggressively or play rough, yell out another "Ouch!" and stop playing.

Cooking

DRY YOUR OWN MUSHROOMS

To dry mushrooms, wipe them clean, string them together using a needle and thread, and hang them in an airy location. Or place clean mushrooms on several thicknesses of newspaper, turn them several times as the day progresses, and change the newspaper as moisture is absorbed. Place the mushrooms in a dry, airy spot (in direct sun if you wish, but don't forget to bring them in at night).

In one or two days the mushrooms will be almost brittle. After the drying process, the mushrooms must be heated in a 175°F (80°C) oven for 30 minutes to destroy insect eggs.

To condition the mushrooms, place them in a large, open container such as a large enameled canner pot. (Don't use a pot that is aluminum or porous, because it might affect the flavor or consistency of the mushrooms.) Put the pot in a warm but dry and airy place. For the next 10 days or 2 weeks, stir the mushrooms once or twice a day. Don't add newly dried mushrooms to the batch in the pot, as you want it all to finish drying at the same time.

Once the mushrooms are conditioned, store them in a cool, dry place for up to 6 months.

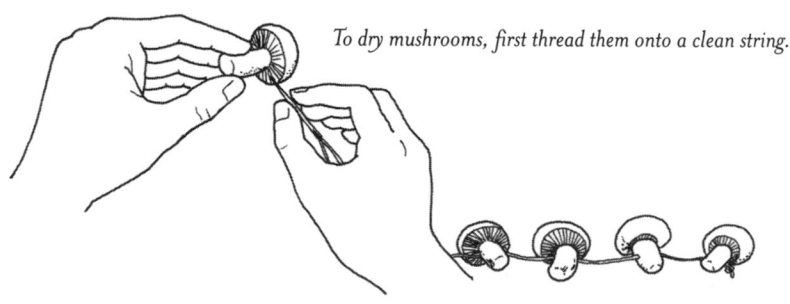

To dry mushrooms, first thread them onto a clean string.

SPLIT PEA SOUP

This is a wonderful early fall dish.

1 pound (454 g, about 2 1/4 cups) green or yellow split peas
6 cups (48 fl oz/1.4 l) chicken or vegetable stock
2 tablespoons (2 oz/28 g) butter
1 teaspoon (5 ml) salt
1 whole clove
1 medium onion, chopped
1 celery rib with leaves, chopped
1 small clove garlic, minced   .
1 carrot, chopped
1 small potato, unpeeled and diced
1 cup (5.25 oz/151 g) cooked chicken or turkey, diced (optional)

Wash and sort the split peas. Put them in a 6-quart (6 l) kettle with all the other ingredients except the chicken or turkey. Bring to a boil. Lower the heat, cover, and simmer, stirring occasionally to keep the peas from sticking to the bottom of the pan, for 2 to 3 hours. The peas and vegetables should be very soft and begin to fall apart. The thicker part of the soup will tend to sink to the bottom of the pan and should be stirred up before serving, or you can puree the soup before serving. Stir in the chicken or turkey, just about 5 minutes before serving. Parmesan cheese makes a good garnish.

Yield: 6–8 servings
Time: 2–3 hours (if peas are soaked first; preparation time after soaking is 30–40 minutes)

COOKING OLDER VEGETABLES

For optimum nutritive value, color, and eating quality, harvest or hold vegetables the least possible time before preparing or cooking. As vegetables mature, their sugar turns to starch, which is why older peas and corn are less sweet. You can add a pinch of sugar when cooking older vegetables, but *never* add baking soda. This was done in past generations to keep a bright green color, but properly cooked vegetables retain their lively green color anyway. Baking soda in cooking water destroys many nutrients—especially the B vitamins.

SWEET-ONION SALSA

Sweet-onion salsa is especially nice on steak or grilled fish. Try making it with Vidalia, Walla Walla, or Maui onions.

1 large sweet onion, minced
Cold water
1 tablespoon (15 ml) balsamic vinegar
1/2 teaspoon (2.5 ml) sugar
3 tablespoons (45 ml) green onions, thinly sliced
3 tablespoons (45 ml) fresh flat-leaf parsley, minced
2 teaspoons (10 ml) jalapeños, minced

Cover the minced sweet onion with cold water. Let sit for 30 minutes, then drain in a strainer and pat dry with paper towels.

Combine the sweet onion with all of the other ingredients in a fairly small bowl and refrigerate, covered, for at least an hour, stirring from time to time.

Yield: About 1 1/2 cups (355 ml)

NEED JUST A BIT?

If you are preparing a recipe that calls for a small amount of vegetables and you want to avoid waste, it is easy to get just the amount you need from a supermarket salad bar. Suppose you want 1/2 cup (2 oz/57 g) of sliced mushrooms, a few strips of green pepper, or 1/4 cup (6 oz/170 g) of black olives for garnish. Buy just what you need, and none will go to waste.

PEANUT BRITTLE

Butter to grease a cookie sheet
1 1/3 cups (10.67 oz/300 g) sugar
One 6 1/2 ounce (149.5 g) can cocktail peanuts

Butter a cookie sheet very thoroughly.

Cook the sugar in a frying pan over low heat until it has melted and turned a light brown. Stir in the peanuts, then pour onto the baking sheet.

Immediately start stretching the candy by pressing it out with the back of two spoons. Don't touch it with your hands, as it will be very hot. Keep this up, working quickly, until the brittle is no more than 1 peanut deep.

When the candy is completely cool, break it into pieces. Store in an airtight container.

CANDY-MAKING TEMPERATURES

When reading recipes for candy making, you'll probably notice that some temperature-related terms keep coming up. Here are the basic temperature stages of candy making:

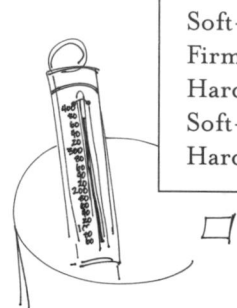

Soft-ball stage	234°F–240°F (112°C–115°C)
Firm-ball stage	244°F–250°F (117°C–121°C)
Hard-ball stage	265°F–270°F (129°C–132°C)
Soft-crack stage	275°F–280°F (135°C–137°C)
Hard-crack stage	285°F–300°F (140°C–149°C)

candy thermometer

APPLE OR CRAB-APPLE JELLY (WITHOUT PECTIN)

4 pounds (1.8 kg) apples
4 cups (32 fl oz/946 ml) water
3 cups (24 oz/675 g) sugar

Use hard, tart fruit. Wash apples, discarding stems and blossom ends. Cut apples into small chunks. Place in a kettle. Add water. Bring to a boil and simmer 25 minutes. Place fruit and juice in a suspended cheesecloth jelly bag. Let juice drip overnight. In the morning, measure 4 cups (946 ml) of juice into a kettle, add sugar, heat, and stir until sugar dissolves. Bring to a boil and cook rapidly until jelly test is met. Skim off foam. Pour into hot glasses and seal.

Yield: Four to five 8-ounce (226 g) glasses

BATHING TIME FOR CANNING

Many traditional canning recipes may indicate that after being sealed, jars filled with jelly should be immersed in a boiling water bath for 5 minutes. This is no longer the accepted standard. New canning standards from the USDA recommend that the boiling water bath should be extended to 10 minutes.

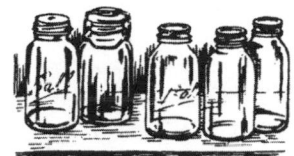

PUMPKIN SOUP

You can use corn chips to decorate this soup. Or serve it in a pumpkin tureen.

1 small pumpkin, about 3 pounds (1.4 kg), or 3 cups (19.25 oz/546 g) cooked pulp
2 tablespoons (1 oz/28 g) butter
1/2 cup (3–3.5 oz/85–99 g) onion, finely chopped
4 cups (32 fl oz/946 ml) chicken or vegetable stock
1/4 teaspoon (1.3 ml) ginger
1/4 teaspoon (1.3 ml) nutmeg
Corn chips
Black olives (optional)

To make pumpkin puree, preheat oven to 375°F (190°C). Wash pumpkin, cut in half, remove seeds and fibers. Place halves, cut-side down, on oven rack. Bake about 40 minutes or until flesh is fork tender. Cool slightly. Scrape flesh from shell and puree in blender. (You can also use home-canned or frozen pumpkin.)

In a soup pot, melt butter and sauté onion until transparent. Add stock, spices, and pumpkin.

Bring to a boil, reduce heat, and simmer for about 10 minutes. Serve with crushed corn chips on top. Or make a ring with the corn chips and use olive slices to make a jack-o'-lantern face on this rich, heavy soup.

Yield: Approx. 6 cups
Time: About 1 hour

CONVERTING RECIPE MEASUREMENTS TO METRIC

Use the following chart for converting U.S. measurements to metric. Since these conversions are not exact, it's important to convert the measurements for all of the ingredients to maintain the same proportions as the original recipe.

To convert to	From	Multiply by
milliliters	teaspoons	4.93
milliliters	tablespoons	14.97
milliliters	fluid ounces	29.57
milliliters	cups	236.59
liters	cups	0.236
grams	ounces	28.35

APRICOT-ALMOND BREAD

Apricots and almonds are a time- and taste-tested combination. Cardamom and nutmeg complete the flavor magic.

1/2 cup (4 oz/113 g) sugar
2 tablespoons (1 oz/28 g) butter or margarine

1 egg
1 cup (8 fl oz/237 ml) buttermilk
1/2 cup (1 oz/28 g) bran
1/2 cup (2 oz/57 g) wheat germ
1 cup (4 oz/113 g) almonds, coarsely chopped
1 cup (6 oz/170 g) dried apricots, coarsely chopped
1 cup (5 oz/150 g) unbleached flour
1 cup (6 oz/170 g) whole wheat flour
1/2 teaspoon (2.5 ml) nutmeg
1/2 teaspoon (2.5 ml) cardamom
1 tablespoon (15 ml) baking powder
1/2 teaspoon (2.5 ml) baking soda
1/2 teaspoon (2.5 ml) salt

In a large bowl, cream the butter and sugar until fluffy. Add the eggs and buttermilk and mix well. In another bowl combine the remaining ingredients. Add them to the creamed mixture and mix just enough to combine thoroughly. Spoon the batter into greased pans and bake at 350°F (180°C) until a tester comes out clean. Cool in the pans for 10 minutes and then remove to a rack to cool completely.

MORE QUICK TIPS FOR QUICK BREADS

Listed below are a few tips to make your quick breads even quicker—and more fail-proof.

- Allow thick bread batters that do *not* contain baking powder to rest in the pan for 10 minutes before baking. A lighter loaf will result.
- Fill pans no more than two-thirds full.
- Place filled pans in the center of the oven.
- No need to preheat the oven. Save energy instead.
- Use whole wheat *pastry* flour instead of regular milled whole wheat flour for a lighter loaf. It's processed from soft wheat, which contains less gluten. (Gluten makes quick breads tough.)
- Add nuts and dried fruits to the dry ingredients to coat them with flour so they don't sink to the bottom of the loaf.

- Mix dry ingredients together in a large bowl. Combine them with a wire whisk to distribute the leavening agents evenly and to add air to the mixture.
- Mix wet ingredients together in another bowl (use the same wire whisk), and with a spoon, stir them quickly into the dry ingredients.
- Do not combine wet and dry ingredients until you are ready to bake, or some of the leavening action will be lost.
- Test the loaf about 10 minutes before you think it will be done. As soon as the tester comes out clean when inserted in the center of the loaf, and the bread begins to pull away slightly from the sides of the pan, the bread is done.
- When loaves are done, cool them in the pans for 10 minutes; then remove to a wire rack. If they cool completely in the pans, condensation will make them soggy.

For more on quick breads, see tips 118 and 119.

215

BUTCHERING AND CURING PORK

Pork is not aged like beef but should be thoroughly chilled before cutting or curing. Let it hang for 24 hours where the temperature is between 32°F and 35°F (0°C to -1°C).

When the carcass is chilled to the bone, cut the skin, holding the two sides together, and lay each half on the cutting table to cut as the illustrations show.

Cutting the Meat

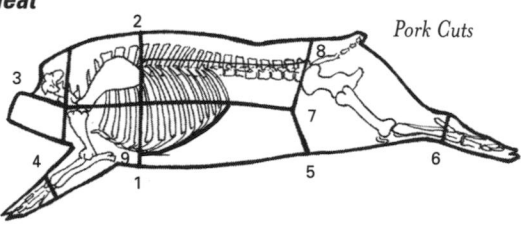

Pork Cuts

Cut 1: Cut between the fourth and fifth ribs.
 Use a saw to cut through the backbone.
Cut 2: Cut off the jowl. Trim to a square.

Cut 3: Separate the butt from the shoulder.

       Trim the shoulder to look like a small ham.

Cut 4: Saw off the front foot.

Cut 5: Cut off the ham at the joint. Trim to round off the corners.

Cut 6: Cut off the hind foot.

Cut 7: Using a saw, cut the center piece in half lengthwise.

Cut 8: Trim the fat back from the loin.

Cut 9: Cut the spareribs from the top of the back.

Curing the Meat

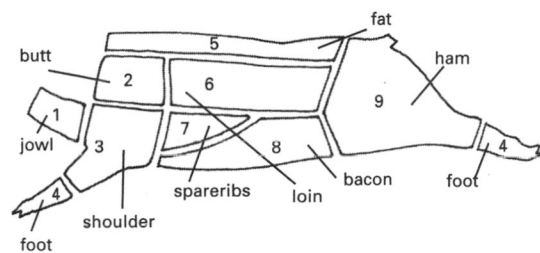

1. Cure the jowl as a bacon square.
2. The Boston butt is cured or ground for sausage.
3. The shoulder can be cured as a picnic ham or roasted fresh.
4. Simmer or pickle the feet.
5. The fatback can be cured or used in lard or sausage.
6. Cut between the ribs for loin chops or a roast. Pull out the meaty strip of tenderloin and cut the remainder into short ribs.
7. Spareribs can be baked or simmered.
8. Bacon is cured.
9. Ham is cured.

216

HOMEMADE LARD

After butchering a pig, you can make pure, white lard from the back and side fat. It should be rendered over very low heat in a large, heavy kettle. Cut up or grind the fat to speed the process, and stir it frequently to keep the pieces from sticking. As the lard cooks out, the cracklings will float to the top. As they do, skim them off and drain them. They are delicious in corn bread.

When all the pieces have floated to the top, turn off the heat and let the liquid cool for 30 minutes. Ladle the lard into small coffee cans or plastic containers without disturbing the settlings on the bottom. Strain what is left through a piece of muslin and package separately. Store lard in the refrigerator. For long-term storage, keep it in the freezer.

Bonus Tip
If you've recently butchered a hog, sheep, or calf, you can use the intestinal fat from the hog and all the fat from the sheep and calf to make soap and candles.

DIFFERENT GAME FOR DIFFERENT TASTES

Small Game
Rabbit meat is fine grained and mild flavored.

Squirrel meat is similar to rabbit except it has a stronger flavor. Most rabbit recipes can be used for squirrel.

Opossum is a rich food, and it is not for everyone. But to those who like it, there is nothing better than roast 'possum.

A very clean animal, the muskrat feeds only on plants and roots, which gives the meat a sweet flavor.

Because of its strong flavor, woodchuck should be parboiled in salt water for 20 minutes before baking or using.

Big Game
Although usually thought of as deer meat, venison is the meat from any antlered game animal, including deer, caribou, elk, and moose.

The meat from young animals is tender, with a mild flavor. The texture is similar to veal or beef, but without the marbled fat of beef, it tends to be dry.

The meat from old animals and mature bucks during the mating season may be tough or strong tasting.

Bear meat is dark and well flavored.

The texture and flavor of wild boar is much like that of pork, except there is little fat.

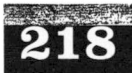

218

MINIMIZING STRONG WILD GAME FLAVORS

Many people like the flavor of game—once they've acquired a taste for it. It is like ripe olives or Limburger cheese; few people like it the first time. If you have not yet acquired the taste, there are ways you can minimize the strong flavor of wild game.

- **Soak it.** Cover the meat with water in which 3 tablespoons (45 ml) of salt or 3 tablespoons (45 ml) of vinegar have been mixed. Soak the meat for no more than 30 minutes; soaking too long can make the meat soft and watery.
- **Disguise it.** Baste a roast with marinade or gravies rich with garlic or spices. Serve steaks and roasts with flavorful sauces and gravies.
- **Stuff it.** Fill the cavity of whole animals with sliced onions or orange halves. Discard the stuffing after baking.
- **Combine it.** Make stew or ground meat with half game and half beef or pork. Cook a venison stew or pot roast with potatoes and carrots.
- **Parboil it.** Simmer the meat in water before frying or baking. Discard the cooking water.
- **Hunt early in the season.** The meat of large game animals becomes much stronger in taste with the approach of the mating season.

219

PREPARING A GAME BIRD

Preparing a game bird is similar to preparing domestic fowl (see tips 309 and 310). Just follow these simple steps:

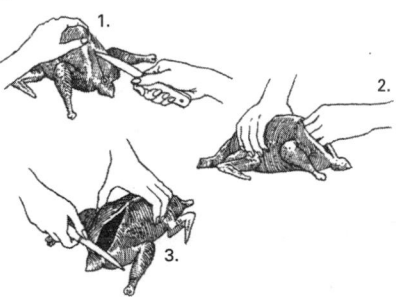

1. Slit skin from vent to breastbone.
2. Reach into body cavity and remove entrails.
3. Cut off tail.

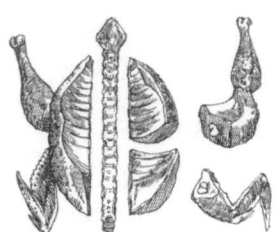

Cut larger game birds into breast pieces, wings, legs, and thighs. The bony back pieces usually are discarded or simmered in water to make soup stock or gravy.

PREPARING SMALL GAME

Skin the small game as the illustration indicates. When the skin has been removed, cut the abdomen just through the muscle and remove the entrails, being careful not to burst the bile sac. Save the heart and liver and discard the rest. Wash the carcass under running water, wrap in a damp towel, and refrigerate—I day for young animals and up to 4 days for older animals.

Small game may be fried, braised, baked whole, or cut in several pieces. Tougher cuts and meat from older animals should be cooked as you would older chickens.

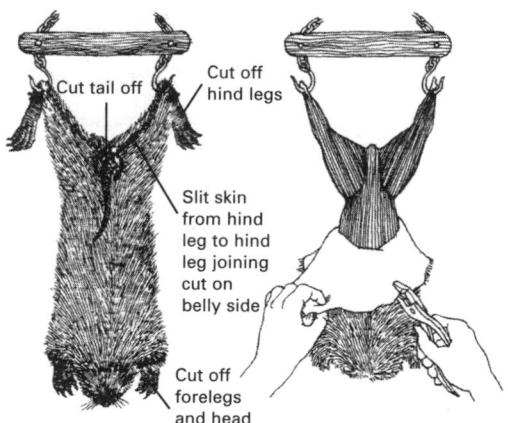

(1) Cut off the head, tail, and forelegs. (2) Cut just through the skin around the hock of each leg. (3) Hang the animal by the hind legs (or fasten it to a table). (4) Slit the skin from hind leg to hind leg and foreleg to foreleg through the neck opening. (5) From the top, fold the skin over and peel it off, wrong-side out, as you would a tight sweater.

SQUIRREL SKILLET PIE

This is a wonderful dish for squirrel meat, which is similar to rabbit except it has a stronger flavor.

1 squirrel, cleaned and cut up
1/2 teaspoon (2.5 ml) salt
Water to barely cover
1/2 cup celery (2 oz/56 g), chopped
1/4 cup (2 oz/56 g) butter or margarine
1/4 cup (1.5 oz/40 g) onion, minced
1/4 cup (1.25 oz/38 g) sweet red or green pepper, chopped
1/4 cup (1.5 oz/40 g) flour
Salt and pepper
2 packages canned, ready-to-bake biscuits

Cover squirrel pieces with salted water. Add chopped celery, cover, and simmer until the meat is tender. Remove the meat, but save the cooking liquid. When the meat has cooled, pull it from the bones in fairly large pieces. Set aside.

In a large iron skillet, melt butter or margarine over low heat. Add onion and peppers and cook about 5 minutes, until onion is transparent but not browned. Blend in flour and cook until mixture bubbles, stirring constantly. Pour in 2 cups (16 fl oz/473 ml) cooking liquid. Cook until thick and smooth, stirring constantly. Season to taste with salt and pepper. Add meat and reheat to boiling. Turn off heat. Top with canned biscuits and bake at 350°F (180°C) for 10 to 15 minutes, until biscuits are browned.

BOSTON BAKED BEANS

Here's a standard baked bean recipe in the New England tradition. You'll note the absence of tomato or catsup. That's because the colonists did not eat tomatoes and, in fact, thought they were poisonous until after 1800.

2 cups (1.25 lbs/567 g) small white beans
6 cups (3 pints/1.4 l) water
1/2 teaspoon (2.5 ml) salt
3/4 cup (2 oz/57 g) salt pork cubes
1/4 cup (1.5 oz/44 mg) brown sugar
1/4 cup (3 oz/88 mg) molasses
1/2 teaspoon (2.5 ml) dry mustard

Soak the beans overnight or use the quick-soak method [see below]. Put the beans in a kettle with 6 cups of the soaking water or fresh water. Add the salt. Bring to a boil, lower the heat, cover the pan, and simmer the beans until tender, about 2 hours.

Mix the beans and all the cooking water in a baking dish with the salt pork, sugar, molasses, and dry mustard. Cover the casserole and bake the beans at 225°F (107°C) for 6 to 8 hours or longer. Check occasionally to see if you need to add more water. You may raise the heat and shorten the baking time, but the long, slow cooking produces tastier beans.

Time: 8 to 10 hours (after beans are soaked)
Yield: 8 to 10 servings

The Quick-Soak Method

The quick-soak is good when you haven't planned ahead to soak beans overnight. Put the beans in a large pot, cover them with water, bring to a boil, and cook for 2 minutes with a lid on the pan. Then remove the pan from the heat and let the beans stand, covered, for 1 to 2 hours. This is equivalent to as much as 15 hours of plain soaking.

THANKSGIVING LEFTOVER MASH

1–2 tablespoons (0.5–0.75 fl oz/15–30 ml) extra-virgin olive oil
1 pound (454 g) cooked, unpeeled minipotatoes, quartered
1 pound (454 g) cooked turkey, diced
1 cup (5–6 oz/142–170 g) dried cranberries
3 shallots, finely chopped
2 tablespoons (30 ml) fresh marjoram, chopped (or 2 teaspoons/10 ml dried, crumbled)
1/2 cup (4–4.5 oz/113–128 g) sour cream
1/4 cup (2 fl oz/59 ml) half-and-half
1/2 teaspoon (2.5 ml) salt
Freshly ground black pepper

Heat a large cast-iron skillet on medium-high, then heat enough olive oil to amply coat the bottom of the pan. Add potatoes and turkey and toss with sturdy tongs. Add cranberries, shallots, and marjoram; toss again. Reduce heat to medium and cover.

Mix sour cream and half-and-half in a small bowl until smooth. Add salt and several coarse grinds of pepper, and stir. Add sour-cream mixture to potatoes and turkey and mix well.

Cover skillet and let sit for 5 minutes, then stir well. Cook, covered, for another 10 minutes or so over medium heat, stirring occasionally. Uncover and raise heat to medium-high. Watch that mixture does not stick to pan too much or get too dry. If it does, drop a tablespoon or two of olive oil into a clear spot in pan, let heat, and toss mixture into hot oil.

Cook, uncovered, at medium-high until crisp and browned, stirring frequently to prevent burning. Add salt and pepper to taste. Serve hot.

Crafts

224

APPLE-PRINT GIFT WRAP

This is a great project for kids as well as adults. Make apple-printed gift wrap by stamping on plain-colored paper.

What You Will Need
3 large apples
Knife
6 colors of finger or tempera paints
6 paper plates or pie tins
Newspaper
Plain construction or gift-wrap paper
Smock

1. Cut each apple in half crosswise.
2. Cut a design on the flat surface of an apple half. The flat, raised areas will print.
3. Pour a different color of paint onto each paper plate. Spread out the newspapers over your worktable and place a piece of construction paper on top.
4. Carefully dip the flat surface (the design) into the paint, and then press it on the paper.
5. By the time you've finished cleaning up your workspace, your gift wrap should be dry and ready to use!

Note: The paints may make the apples slippery and hard to hold on to. Try using corn-cob holders to get a better grip.

APPLE-CONE TREE

These are delightful and aromatic gifts. If your dried apple slices have not been treated with a sealer, keep the tree away from areas of high humidity.

What You Will Need

1 large pinecone (6–8 inches/15.2–20 cm tall)
Dried apple slices (approx. 1 1/2 cups/9 oz/255 g)
Glue gun and glue sticks
Small sprays of baby's breath
3 or more 6-inch (15.2 cm) lengths of 1/8-inch (3 mm) ribbon

1. Level the bottom of the pinecone by rocking it back and forth on a flat surface to break off uneven petals from the bottom.
2. Cut a large, dried apple slice in half and fold to form a cone shape. Glue the ends together and let dry. This will form the base of the tree. Apply hot glue to the tip of the cone-shaped apple slice and place the pinecone over the tip. Let dry.
3. Starting at the top of the pinecone and using the smallest apple slices first, insert the apple slices between the cone petals, skin-side out, to test for fit before gluing. To glue, run a small bead of hot glue along the edge of each apple slice and insert the slice between the cone petals.
4. Glue small sprays of baby's breath scattered around the cone. Tie 6-inch (15.2 cm) lengths of ribbon into small bows and glue them onto the edges of the cone petals. You can also tie ribbon onto small pieces of cinnamon sticks, and glue the sticks onto the cone.

Adapted from *Herbal Treasures*
byPhyllis V. Shandys

BRAIDING ONIONS

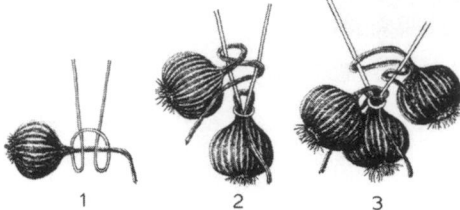

1. *Loop string around onion top.*
2. *Braid in second onion as shown.*
3. *Repeat with third onion and others.*

1   2   3

MAKE YOUR OWN
LAVENDER-SCENTED CANDLES

Scented candles are expensive to buy but not that difficult to make. Lavender makes a delightful scented candle that's sure to ease your nerves while it cleanses the air.

2 pounds (908 g) paraffin wax
2 colored crayons or a colorant for wax (optional)
2 cups (473 ml) lavender blossoms, or 4 cups (946 ml) fresh flowers
Candle molds (old cans work well)
Petroleum jelly
Candle wicking
A pencil

Break up the wax and crayons into small pieces and melt in a bowl over a saucepan of hot water. Keep heat very low and watch carefully; paraffin is extremely flammable. Stir in color, if using.

Remove from heat and then add the lavender. Coat the molds with petroleum jelly, and drop a length of wick into each mold so that it touches the bottom. Wind the other end around a pencil resting across the mold's rim to keep the wick centered as you pour in the hot wax.

When the wax cools to a gel, pour it into the molds. Allow the candles to set overnight.

For more on making candles at home, see tips 316 through 325.

DECORATIVE CANDLE WRAPPING

Candles make wonderful gifts, whether or not you make them yourself. They are a great addition to gift baskets because they add color and texture and because they're useful.

Tissue Paper

For a single candle, simply roll tissue paper securely around it and tape it or tie it with ribbon. To wrap pairs or multiple candles, roll the paper completely around the first candle, then insert the second one so that it does not touch the first and continue rolling. This way, the candles are separated from one another by a layer of paper and serve as stiffeners for each other.

Fabric and Ribbon

For gift giving, it's a great idea to wrap the bottom half of a candle in fabric or interesting paper tied with a bow. This allows the top half of the candle to be exposed so people can see, feel, and smell it. If necessary, add a piece of cardboard for extra stiffness before wrapping. This method works best for undecorated candles, since the fabric wrap might cover or clash with the design of the candle.

CHOOSING QUILT FABRICS

Picking out fabric is easily one of the best parts of quilting—maybe the most difficult as well. Where do you start? Think about your project. Will it go in a particular room? Is it a gift for a baby? A wedding? This can help determine which colors and patterns to use.

A few other suggestions: First, go to the fabric store with plenty of time, and go alone or with a patient friend. Second, look around at all the fabric; don't just grab the first three bolts and run. There may be a particular fabric you just *have* to use; this can be a good starting point for adding coordinating fabrics, picking and choosing as you try different combinations. Third, try to use a light, a medium, and a dark fabric in your quilt, and to vary the size of the prints. By varying the scale of the prints and the values of the colors, you add depth and spark to your quilt. A "viney" all-over print, oversize prints, and stripes will also add variety and interest. Don't try to match every color!

One hundred percent cotton fabrics are recommended as they are easier to handle than the thinner polyester blends.

Once you have decided on your fabrics, the next question is how much to buy. In general you'll be better off buying more than you need to make allowances for mistakes, to compensate for shrinkage, and in case you change the pattern.

TYING A QUILT

When you finish a quilt top and have the backing prepared, you can proceed to tie the quilt. Spread the backing, right-side down, onto a large, clean, flat surface. Pin or tape the backing straight and taut. Place the batting onto the backing and pat it smooth. Layer the top, right-side up, onto the batting. Pin through all three layers, starting in the center and working out to the edges. Place pins approximately 6 inches (15.2 cm) apart.

Using crochet-cotton thread or a washable yarn and a long thin needle, stitch and tie double knots throughout the quilt, making sure you go through all three layers. The ties should be no more than 5 to 6 inches (12.7 to 15.2 cm) apart in any direction. Any more than that and the batting may bunch and shift after the quilt has been washed. Tie according to your block design—in the corners of each block, the middle, and along each edge—anywhere the ties do not obstruct the design of the block.

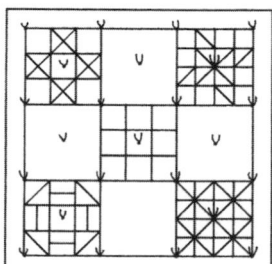

Remove all pins and release the quilt from the floor or table. Now the quilt is ready for binding.

CARING FOR YOUR QUILTS

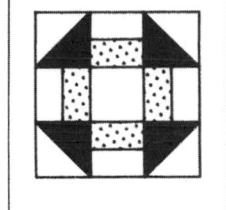

Most quilts made today can be washed. Use a mild soap or one especially made for quilts. Wash in warm or cold water on a delicate cycle or hand wash in the bathtub.

Dry in a large dryer on a delicate setting. Placing a couple of dry towels in the dryer with the quilt may help absorb the tumbling of the quilt. Or lay the quilt flat on a sheet to dry. Hanging a wet quilt on a clothesline causes too much strain on the batting and the stitches and may damage the quilt.

Dry cleaning is not recommended as some fabrics may react to the solvents by running or discoloring.

Pieces that are not soiled but are merely dusty, such as wall quilts, may be freshened by putting them in a dryer with a couple of damp washcloths or hand towels on an air-only cycle. This removes the dust without having to wash and soak the piece.

Never store your quilts in a plastic bag. The fibers need to breathe. Condensation may build up and stain a quilt sealed in plastic. A zippered pillowcase is a safer alternative, as are special acid-free boxes and tissue paper usually available by mail order.

Be careful of the amount of light your quilts receive. Give your wall hangings a rest after 3 to 6 months of display. Any light, not just direct sunlight, can cause fading.

NEW ENGLAND BAYBERRY POTPOURRI

Most of us know the warm, balsamic aroma of bayberry candles, since every gift shop seems to sell them. With imagination, you can make a potpourri with almost the same wonderful fragrance that this shrub provides along the coast.

1/2 cup (118 ml) cellulose fiber
1/2 teaspoon (2.5 ml) bayberry oil
1 cup (237 ml) uva-ursi leaves
1/2 cup (118 ml) oakmoss
1/2 cup (118 ml) juniper berries

Mix the cellulose and oil and allow to set for 24 hours. Then add the other ingredients. Shake and age for 3 weeks. You may want to adjust the scent with more leaves or more oil. Package in a large clamshell for a delightful seaside touch.

WORKING WITH GRAPEVINES TO MAKE WREATHS

When creating your own decorative grapevine wreath, keep in mind the following tips:

- Grapevine creations are meant to be uneven and irregular—even lopsided. Stress the vine's natural state and beauty.
- Pick fresh, live vine. It is quite flexible and can be bent, shaped, and twisted easily.
- Begin with the thicker end of the vine and work toward the thinner end.
- Incorporate natural bends, angles, and forks for shaping and reinforcement.
- To remove bark easily, gently bend the vine back and forth so the bark cracks and separates.

- Young vine is often long and thin—great for small wreaths and rings—but it snaps more easily than older vine.
- Readjust your wrapping to avoid placing knobs on a curve or bend.
- Be patient with the vine to learn what it can and cannot do. This will help avoid breaks.
- If your vine does break, simply tuck the broken end into the wreath and begin in that area with another piece of vine.
- Determine which side of the wreath is the front; bend the tendrils on the backside toward the center or to the sides. Cut off any tendrils that will prevent the wreath from laying flat against a wall.

MAKE A FALL BITTERSWEET WREATH

To make a fall bittersweet wreath, use a grapevine wreath as the base. Lay the bittersweet in a circle on top of the grapevine like a crown. Lace a single long piece of grapevine in and out over the bittersweet, so the bittersweet is lashed to the wreath. This way the bittersweet won't move around, disturbing the beautiful berries. When the season is over or the berries have faded, the bittersweet can easily be taken off by undoing the thin grapevine.

MAKE A TEARDROP WREATH

A teardrop shape will set your wreath apart from the ordinary. You can decorate it point-up or point-down. It is also a perfect use for a vine with a wide fork or natural angle.

1. Select a good-size, medium-weight vine that has either a sharp angle or wide fork. Trim off any unwanted branches.

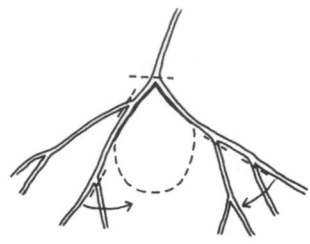

2. Beginning with one length of vine, form a teardrop (following the natural curve of the vine) and make a simple overhand knot. As you wrap and add additional vines, the natural angle will keep the point sharp. An additional angled piece or two may be added to reinforce the point. You may use single vines, heavy vines, or branched vines; wrap it tightly or loosely; crisscross or follow one direction—just as long as you include natural right angles to make the point sharp.

236

QUICKIE SPICE WREATH

These adorable aromatic wreaths can be created in miniature to use as favors or made large to serve as decorations. For a variation, apply the project steps below to a Styrofoam ball and present it as a topiary decoration.

What You Will Need

Styrofoam ring or cardboard
Brown florist tape or textured fabric
Hanger
Glue
Assortment of dried materials from herb garden or spice cupboard
Ribbon (optional)

1. Wrap a Styrofoam ring of desired size (purchased at any craft shop) or a ring cut from cardboard with brown florist tape or textured fabric.
2. Attach a small hanger at the back.
3. Cover the wreath generously with glue. Embed bay leaves; small nuts, pinecones, or acorns; bits of cinnamon bark; vanilla beans; whole cloves, star anise, aniseed, dill, cumin, caraway, poppy seeds—anything dried from your herb garden or spice cupboard. For color, glue on cardamom, dried orange peel, petals, rose hips, candied ginger, pistachios, whatever is available. Look around you, especially on the spice shelf in your favorite store, with an eye toward color, size, shape, and texture as well as fragrance.
4. Allow your wreath to dry thoroughly.
5. Fasten on a bow if you wish.

Adapted from *Herbs for Weddings & Other Celebrations* by Bertha P. Reppert

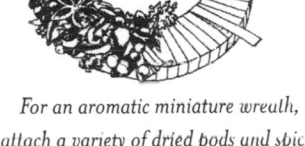

For an aromatic miniature wreath, attach a variety of dried pods and spices to a small wreath form.

MINIATURE TUSSIE MUSSIES

Miniature tussie mussies make elegant hangings or ornaments and are a perfect way to use pieces of herbs and flowers that have broken off from wreaths.

What You Will Need
Styrofoam
8-inch (20 cm) lengths of fine wire
Short lengths of cord
Very small sprigs and pieces of flowers, herbs, and spices
Glue
Narrow width of lace
Sturdy white paper
Florist tape
Short length of 1/4-inch-wide (6 mm) ribbon

1. Cut a piece of Styrofoam about the size of a nickel. Double a length of wire and push the folded point through the center of the Styrofoam to make a handle. Leave about an inch of the loose ends protruding from the bottom (*fig. 1*). Thread the cord under the wire loop on top of the Styrofoam, and tie it off to make a loop handle.

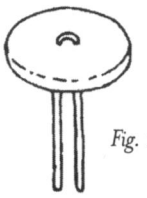

Fig. 1

2. Push the stems of the herbs into the Styrofoam. If you have one, use a single, tiny rosebud in the center. Use glue to affix any herbs, spices, or flowers that don't have a sturdy stem. Use single rosebuds or florets of statice, tansy, or another flower to make a tiny bouquet on the Styrofoam, filling in the spaces with tiny whole cloves, tiny sprigs of baby's breath, leaves of boxwood, or other tiny blossoms. Allow to dry.

3. Wrap the lace around the base of the tussie mussie; cut to fit and glue around the edge. Cover the bottom with a fitted circle of white paper, first snipping off any stem ends that may protrude.

4. Wrap together the two loose ends of the wire with florist tape. Then finish off with a tiny bow of ribbon in a matching or complementary color (*fig. 2*).

Adapted from *Herbal Treasures* by Phyllis V Shandys

Fig. 2

CORN-HUSK DOLLS

In colonial times children made corn-husk dolls after the harvest in the fall. This is a fun project for kids around Thanksgiving (and is an especially good use of all the leftover husks from corn casserole).

What You Will Need

Dried corn husks and corn silks
Water
Yarn or string
Scissors
Fine-point color markers
White glue and brush

1. Prepare the husks by soaking them in warm water until they bend without cracking. Slit some into narrow strips to use for tying. (You can also use yarn or string for tying.)
2. To form the head, lay several husks on top of one another. Fold in half. Tie under the fold to make the head. The part below the head will make up the body.
3. Slip some folded husks between the body husks, below the tie. Let them stick out on both sides to form arms. Tie at the place the wrists should be, and cut off the extra length of husk at the end of each hand.
4. Tie the body husks again under the arms to make a waist. For a girl doll, arrange the lower part of the husks into a skirt. For a boy doll, separate the husks into two parts and tie at the ankles.
5. Glue corn silk to the head for hair. Add facial features with colored markers.
6. Use extra husks, corn silk, twigs, and buttons to make a broom, rake, pocketbook, hat, or other accessories.

Gardening

GREEN MANURE CROPS

A green manure crop is usually a small-grain crop that is tilled under before it matures. The decaying tops and roots provide organic matter and some nutrients to help build up the soil. This process increases soil aeration, water-holding capacity, and stimulates microbial activity in the soil.

Some of these grains grow best in summer and will not tolerate a frost. Others will survive the winter and are useful in preventing soil erosion during this time. Some commonly used green manure crops are listed below, along with their time and rate of seeding.

Crop	Seeding Time	Time to Turn Under
Winter rye	Early fall	Very early spring
Buckwheat	Early summer	Early fall
Ryegrass	Early fall	Early spring
Millet	Early summer	Early fall
Soybean	Early summer	Early fall

KEEPING YOUR GARDEN GREEN

Vegetable gardens can be a pleasure to view in the summer and an eyesore in the fall. You can change that by growing green manures.

Gardeners in the north can have a green garden right up to the first snow by planting

a crop such as annual ryegrass. A heavy, rich growth will appear in only a few weeks.

Southern gardeners have a much bigger variety from which to choose. Crimson clover and blue lupine are two good selections. Vetch, field peas, annual sweet clover, and bur clover are others. In both the north and south, a wide band of kale can be grown to provide a contrast and to offer good eating for many months.

The following crops are adapted to all areas of the United States:

Barley
Kale
Oats
Rye
Ryegrass, annual
Vetch, hairy
Wheat

HOW TO PLANT GREEN MANURES

1. Prepare Soil

Turn under crop residues and weeds, and let them decompose. Rototill soil to a fine texture. Add fertilizer and lime if they are needed.

2. Sow Seed

Broadcast seeds by hand. Check the seed packaging or ask at your garden center to determine how much seed you will need.

3. Cover Seed

Rake it in, or go over the area with a rear-mounted rotary tiller set at a very shallow depth. Roll it, or simply walk on the seedbed.

4. Water If Dry

If the weather is hot and dry, water the plot so the seeds are moist until they put down roots.

LUCKY CLOVER

To improve your soil, plant clover—it absorbs nitrogen from the air and thus enriches the soil. Clover is one of the best green manures, with species for many purposes.

Red Clover: A perennial if not cut before it sets seed, it will usually die the year it is planted. It prefers well-drained soil that is not too acid, and it won't tolerate as much heat and dryness as alfalfa. Its strong taproot has many branches. Red clover will produce a large mass of green material, plus nitrogen.

Alsike Clover: This foraging crop will grow in poorly drained areas and in soil too acid or alkaline for red clover. Its root system is less extensive, but it's a strong nitrogen producer.

White Clover: A low, creeping perennial often found on lawns, this good green manure tolerates excessive moisture, demands heavy feeding, and produces rich organic matter.

Crimson Clover: Popular where winters are mild, it is planted in the fall. It grows rapidly in spring and decomposes rapidly when turned under, so it is excellent for land that supports warm-season crops.

243

LEAF MOLD

In a hurry-up world, the making of leaf mold is largely forgotten. Because leaves have little nitrogen, they decompose slowly and do not heat up as they would if high-nitrogen material were added to them.

The 2-year process of decomposition can be hastened by running the leaves through a shredder before piling them. Fence in the pile with wire netting to keep the leaves from spreading back across your lawn. Stamp the pile down. Expect to see it half its original size when the leaves have turned to leaf mold and are ready for use. After a year, turn the pile, cutting and mixing it as much as possible. In this stage the leaf mold can be used as a mulch and will be welcomed by the earthworms in your garden.

244

PREP HANGING PERENNIALS FOR WINTER

To prepare and carry a hanging perennial basket through the winter, follow these easy steps:

- **Keep abreast of evening temperatures**. If even a hint of frost threatens, bring baskets in for the night. Baskets can be kept happily blooming for weeks into the fall if protected from the cold. Most hanging basket plants are not cold hardy, though, and will not survive a freezing night forgotten on the porch.

- **Keep an eye on basket plants as fall advances.** Stop feeding and cut back on watering. This will encourage the physical hardening the plant must undergo to survive the winter. Once they begin to enter dormancy, bring them in.
- **Place the plant in a dimly lit, cool but not freezing spot (45°F–50°F) for the winter.** Be sure it's a spot in which the plants won't be totally forgotten. They will still need water every 3 or 4 weeks. The garage is fine if you are in an area that doesn't dip much below 40°F in the winter. A corner of the basement, a root cellar, beneath stairwells—anyplace that stays cool, but does not freeze, will do.
- **Check plants periodically.** Don't be discouraged if they drop leaves. As long as they don't freeze or dry out, they'll make it.

PLANTING TIPS FOR SPRING-FLOWERING BULBS

- Until you plant your bulbs, be sure to store them in a dark, dry, and cool but not freezing area so they will not grow, rot, or shrivel up. A good place to store them is in a covered box inside the garage; do not keep them in the house as the heat will cause them to start growing.
- You can plant spring-flowering bulbs anytime in the fall until the soil freezes; if you can't plant them all at once, start with the smaller, earlier-flowering bulbs. Begin with crocus, squills, glory-of-the-snow, winter aconite, and other tiny bulbs and tulips and daffodils.
- Bulbs in general prefer sun to light shade. If you are planting under a large tree, the bulbs seem to be in heavy shade. But since most bulbs bloom before trees leaf out, this shade is not a problem. However, many hours of shade cast from the side of the house will be a problem, and the planting site should be moved.

A SELECTION OF SPRING-FLOWERING BULBS

Flower	Height	Blooming Time
Snowdrop	4–6"	Early spring
Crocus	3–5"	Early spring
Anemone blanda (wildflower)	5"	Early spring
Grape hyacinth (Muscari)	6–10"	Early spring
Early tulips	10–13"	Early spring
Hyacinth	12"	Early spring
Daffodil	12"	Midspring
Darwin hybrid tulips	28"	Midspring
Crown imperial (Fritillaria imperialis)	30–48"	Midspring
Late tulips	36"	Late spring
Dutch iris	24"	Late spring
Allium giganteum	48"	Late spring

WINTER CARE FOR SUMMER BULBS

All summer bulbs need to be lifted from the ground and stored over the winter, as they cannot withstand freezing temperatures. Tuberous begonias are best dug up before the first fall frost. Others should remain in the ground until the foliage is blackened by frost. Be careful when digging not to cut or damage the roots, corms, tubers, or bulbs.

After digging up the bulbs, wash off as much soil as possible with a gentle spray of water and dry them in a sunny spot for several days. Store bulbs in a dark, dry area at 40°F to 50°F (4°C to 10°C). A good method of storage is in dry sphagnum peat moss in a plastic bag. Check the bulbs often to make sure they are in good condition. If they have started to grow, they need a cooler spot. If they have started to rot, allow the packing material to dry out somewhat.

For advice on dividing summer bulbs, see tip 67.

GROWING IRISH POTATOES IN THE FALL

Irish potatoes can be planted as a fall crop in any section of the country where there is a 90-day period relatively free of extreme heat just prior to the first killing frost, and thus, fall growing is popular in many southern areas. The Irish potato, being a cool-weather crop, needs a fairly cool period to mature, but it can withstand short periods of heat rather well. And since a severe frost will kill the plant, it must be given time to mature before the first fall killing frost.

A gardener should determine the first average killing-frost date in his or her area, then count back about 90 days to establish the sowing date.

Don't Reuse Beds

If you are in a long-growing-season area and thus could grow consecutive Irish potato crops, avoid using the same bed that was used for the spring crop. Introduction of another potato crop shortly after harvesting one will give the fungi a chance to progress, possibly out of control.

For information on planting Irish potatoes in spring, see tip 53.

GARLIC: THE GOOD GARDEN NEIGHBOR

Garlic is not attacked by many insects. It can, in fact, be considered a deterrent to infestations that might affect other crops, which makes it popular as a companion planting with other garden favorites, including tomatoes, fruit trees, and roses.

WHEN TO PLANT GARLIC

The usual advice given would-be garlic growers is to plant in fall. However, the ideal planting time varies with your preference as well as where you live.

Northern gardeners will be well advised to plant in fall (for instance, in late September) before the first frost, then, after 3 or 4 days of watering, apply a mulch to help protect the garlic through the cold winter. Good mulches include shredded leaves or grasses (but not quack grass), peat moss, cocoa shells, and seaweed.

Gardeners in such semitemperate growing zones as Ohio feel it's best to plant their garlic in early spring—March or, at the latest, April.

Those in the Deep South have more latitude. Floridians will probably do best if they plant, just as in the North, in fall, looking forward to the cooler days of winter.

HOW TO PLANT GARLIC

Professional garlic growers refer to "garlic seed." What they mean is the cloves of garlic themselves. Thus when you plant cloves of garlic from a grocery store, you are planting "seed."

Garlic seed of very high quality can be bought from mail-order sources. If, though, you use store-bought garlic for your seed, use only the large cloves from the outside of good-size heads. If you want to use "seed" from home-grown garlic, store it in whole heads until your next planting season. Separated cloves dry out too fast.

If you are planting in fall in a cold climate, put the cloves 2 to 4 inches (5 to 10 cm)deep. Otherwise, plant them about 1 inch (2.5 cm) deep. In either case, the cloves should be placed pointed-end up, they should be set at 3- to 5-inch (7.6 to 12.7 cm) intervals, with at least 18 inches (45.75 cm) between rows.

You will find that garlic sprouts very quickly—sometimes in as little as 3 days. However, it has a long way to go before each clove becomes a new head.

It's very important to water your newly planted cloves thoroughly for their first 3 days in the ground. After this, you can settle down to a routine similar to that you would use for any other root vegetable—watering only every few days.

TEST SOIL IN THE FALL

Do your soil test in the fall. Extension service offices are often swamped with requests in the spring, causing delays of up to a month. By having the soil test results on hand early, you'll be able to purchase the necessary fertilizers during the winter. And you'll be gardening in the first good spring weather, rather than fighting the crowds at the local garden supply store.

STARTING ONIONS FROM SEEDS

To give the onions the longest possible growing season, seeds should be sown outdoors in fall where winters aren't too severe (Zone 7 and warmer). In Zone 7, sow onion seeds (intermediate-day or short-day varieties) from late August to mid-September; in warmer parts of Zone 8 and Zone 9, sow in October (short-day varieties). In colder zones where the growing season is long enough (100 to 120 days; the actual length of time needed depends on the variety), you can sow seeds outside in early spring. Plant seeds a month before the final spring frost, when the soil has warmed to at least 45°F (about 7°C). In areas with shorter seasons, start seeds indoors (see tip 349).

A POSTFROST VEGETABLE HARVEST

Want to have freshly picked garden vegetables even after the frost sets in? The following root crops can be stored in your garden and harvested postfrost:

- **Radishes.** Winter radishes are excellent winter keepers. Although they can be stored in moist sand in a root cellar, they're best left in the garden under a heavy straw mulch and harvested when needed.
- **Parsnips.** The colder temperature changes starches in the roots into sugar. Store roots right in the ground where they grow, digging them up as you need them throughout the winter, knowing they'll be sweet and delicious. Mulch the parsnips with up to 12 inches of straw to keep the soil soft enough to dig. Even if there's snow on the ground, you can have fresh, tasty parsnips.

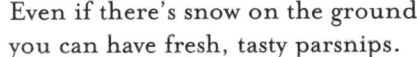
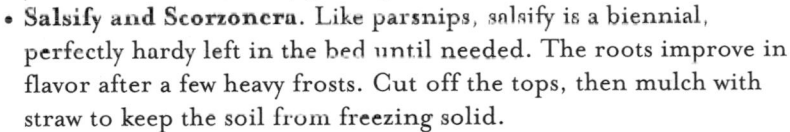

Parsnips
(Pastinaca sativa)

- **Salsify and Scorzonera.** Like parsnips, salsify is a biennial, perfectly hardy left in the bed until needed. The roots improve in flavor after a few heavy frosts. Cut off the tops, then mulch with straw to keep the soil from freezing solid.
- **Celeriac.** Like most fall root crops, celeriac should remain in the ground until after a few frosts. The cold weather converts starch in the roots into sugar. If your soil doesn't freeze hard, it's easier to keep celeriac right in the garden, under an 8- to 12-inch mulch of straw, to use as needed.
- **Rutabagas.** Harvest rutabagas after a few frosts, but before the ground freezes.

MORE COLD-WEATHER HARVEST VEGETABLES

This cold-storage method works well with certain crops: simply leave them in the ground until they are needed. For some, the protection of a blanket of hay or straw or leaves is advised, for others even this is not needed.

- Kale is a hardy vegetable and can be harvested and used in place of spinach well past Christmas in even the coldest parts of the country. Just let it grow.
- Jerusalem artichokes are poor "keepers," but keep well if left undisturbed in the ground. Dig them up when you want them. If the digging promises to be hard in colder areas, put down a layer of hay or leaves, and the digging will be easier. You'll miss a few of the 'chokes as you harvest them, and those will provide you your next season's crop.
- Cabbage can be left in the garden until well after the first frosts, though Halloween or severe freezes may finish the cabbages. Brussels sprouts will produce long after the first frosts, too.

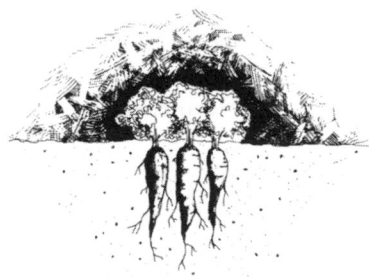

PLAN AHEAD FOR IN-GARDEN VEGETABLE STORAGE

Plan on this storage when you are planting your garden. Some crops should be planted in mid-summer so they mature in the late fall.

Try to keep all of the "storage" crops in one area of your garden. It makes for easier work in the fall, when you should be cleaning out your garden, rototilling it, and planning a cover or green manure crop. If all of those storage crops are in one area, cleaning will be much easier. And so will harvesting in the dead of winter, when finding the vegetables can be a task.

HARVESTING AND STORING CARROTS

The largest carrots will have the darkest, greenest tops, but don't leave the roots in the ground too long or they'll be tough. Most carrots are at their prime when they're about an inch in diameter at their crowns.

When harvesting, drench the bed with water first, making the carrots easier to pull. When you find a carrot large enough, grasp the greens at the crown and gently tug with a twisting motion. If the greens snap off, carefully lift the roots with a spading fork. Use damaged roots first and store unblemished roots for later use.

There are three ways to store fresh carrots: leave them in the ground under a heavy mulch, store them in a root cellar or underground barrel, or keep them in the crisper bin of the refrigerator. The thick-cored varieties store the best. If you want to preserve them longer, you can freeze or can them with little difficulty.

258

HARVESTING SQUASH

A ripe squash is easily detected; if your thumbnail cannot penetrate the skin, it is mature. But check the color first. If you test an immature squash and you do penetrate the skin, that squash will not store as long. There is no hurry to harvest winter squash and pumpkins; they cannot overripen on the vine. Just pick the mature fruit sometime before the first frost.

Autumn Gardening

259

STORING SQUASH

Winter squash and pumpkins must be cured before they can be put into storage. This will dry and harden their skins. Ideally, they should be left to cure in a warm, well-ventilated place for about 10 days. Look for a spot, perhaps on a sunny porch or by a woodstove, where the temperature ranges between 75°F and 85°F.

Ideal storage conditions for these vegetables is in a cool, dry place, approximately 50°F, 50 to 70 percent humidity, with moderate air circulation. A basement or attic with a fan might be just the thing. They should be set securely on shelves, not touching one another.

Outside storage might run the risk of freezing your vegetables, and storing them inside the home where temperatures run above 55°F will cause them to get stringy. Even under the best conditions pumpkins and winter squash will not stay perfect forever. Eventually the starch content will turn to sugar and the water content will increase. For this reason some people freeze, dry, can, or pickle some pumpkin or squash for use during the late winter months.

Bonus Tip: Acorn Squash

Don't cure the acorns. They may lose moisture, turn orange, or become stringy.

Health and Wellness

MAKING A SALVE

Salves are used for a variety of skin problems, as well as to provide protection against the elements.

Step 1: Gather 2 to 3 ounces (56 to 84 g) of dried or freshly wilted herbs and 1 pint (473 ml) of olive oil. Then use one of the following methods: On the stove top, combine the herbs and oil in the top of a double boiler. Heat over boiling water for at least 40 minutes, then remove from heat. Alternatively, put the herbs in a jar and cover with oil, making sure there are 2 to 3 inches (5 to 8 cm) of oil over the herbs. Run a knife around the edge of the jar to release any trapped air bubbles. Set the jar on a sunny windowsill for 2 to 6 weeks.

Step 2: Press the mixture through cheesecloth to separate the oil from the spent plant matter.

Step 3: To give the salve the proper consistency, use 1/4 cup (59 ml) grated beeswax for each cup of infused oil. Combine in the top of a double boiler. Heat until the beeswax is completely melted and the ingredients are thoroughly combined.

Step 4: Test the consistency by taking a spoonful of the mixture and putting it in the refrigerator for a minute or two. If it becomes too hard, add more oil. If it doesn't harden, add a bit more beeswax.

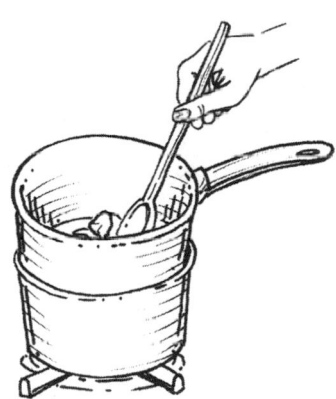

Heat the beeswax in a double boiler, stirring constantly so it doesn't burn.

Step 5: Divide the mixture among several glass containers. Allow the mixture to cool, then seal the jars tightly. Store in the refrigerator for up to 2 years.

CATNIP: NOT JUST FOR CATS

Commonly thought of as a treat for cats and frequently found stuffed in cat toys, this useful herb can also promote rest, improve digestion, calm and soothe upset stomachs, and relieve the symptoms of colds, flu, and fevers. It even contains antiseptic properties with which minor skin lesions can be treated. The volatile oils contained in catnip can absorb intestinal gas, so it is an age-old remedy for childhood colic. Taken before meals, it can be used to stimulate the appetite. The fresh leaves contain vitamins A, B, and C.

Catnip (Nepeta cataria)

TURNIP-AND-HONEY SYRUP
TO SOOTHE THE THROAT

This old turnip-and-honey remedy is excellent for calming a scratchy throat.

1 medium-size winter turnip (also called a rutabaga)
Honey

Wash and peel the turnip. Slice it straight across the bottom to make it level so that it can sit up without falling over. Then cut the turnip into four equal wedges.

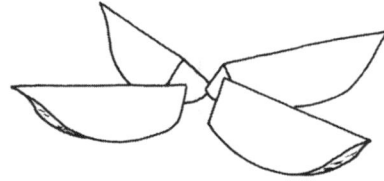

Spread the cut sides of each wedge with a liberal amount of honey and then put them back together again, re-forming your turnip. Set in a bowl to catch the liquid.

Cover the bowl and allow to sit for 24 hours, or until you see that you have collected a good amount of liquid in the bowl. Store the liquid in your refrigerator, and drink to soothe a scratchy throat.

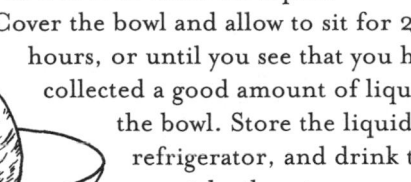

263

THROAT-SOOTHING PASTILLES

These pastilles (pronounced *pas-TEE*) are easily made at home.

1 1/2 cups (12 fl oz/355 ml) water
1 teaspoon (5 ml) dried horehound leaves
1/8 teaspoon (0.6 ml) dried thyme
A pinch of dried mallow flower
  (if mallow is unavailable, you can use hollyhock or musk mallow)
2 teaspoons (10 ml) dried mint leaves
2 1/4 cups (18 oz/506 g) sugar
1/2 teaspoon (2.5 ml) cream of tartar

In a saucepan, bring the water to a boil and then remove from heat. Mix in the horehound, thyme, mallow flower, and mint. Allow to steep for 1 hour. Strain into a separate pot. Add the sugar and cream of tartar to the strained liquid and stir over medium heat until the sugar is dissolved. Then cook without stirring until the mixture reaches the hard-crack stage (300°F/150°C). Pour into a greased pan. When the mixture has cooled a bit, score it into pieces. When completely hardened, break it into smaller pieces.

For a lemon flavor, mix 1 teaspoon (5 ml) of dried horehound, a pinch of mallow, 2 tablespoons (30 ml) of fresh lemon balm, 1/2 teaspoon (2.5 ml) of lemon thyme, 2 teaspoons (10 ml) of dried mint, and a few drops of lemon oil. Proceed as directed above.

HINTS OF MINT

Often taken after dinner, mint tea is said to promote digestion. The menthol in peppermint has been found to relieve indigestion, flatulence, and nausea. It may also help relieve menstrual cramps.

Mint Varieties

By far the most popular and easy-to-grow tea herb, mint comes in a variety of flavors, from citrus to peppermint. Many people do not realize how many mint varieties there are.

Apple mint (*Mentha suaveolens*)
Chocolate mint (*M. x piperita* "Chocolate")
Curly mint (*M. aquatica* var. *crispa*)
Ginger mint (*M. spicata* "Ginger")
Grapefruit mint (*M. suaveolens x piperita*)
Orange mint (*M. x piperita* var. *citrata*)
Peppermint (*M. suaveolens* "Variegata")
Spearmint (*M. spicata*)

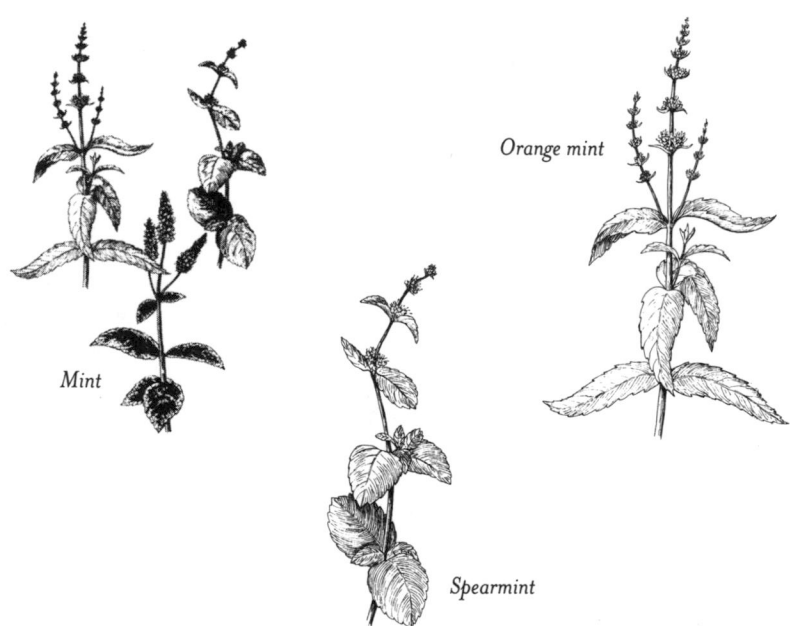

Orange mint

Mint

Spearmint

HERBAL HAIR AND MASSAGE OIL

This is a terrific conditioning oil for all hair and scalp types. It makes a wonderful body massage oil as well.

1 tablespoon (0.5 oz/14 g/15 ml) dried chamomile flowers
1 tablespoon (0.5 oz/14 g/15 ml) dried rosemary
1 tablespoon (0.5 oz/14 g/15 ml) dried horsetail
1 cup (8 fl oz/227 ml) almond or sesame oil

Combine the ingredients in an airtight container. Let stand for several days (or even weeks, if time allows), stirring or gently shaking the mixture frequently.

Strain the oil and discard the spent herbs. Store the oil in dark glass bottles in a cool, dark place. The oil will keep for 3 to 4 weeks.

Use the oil as a treatment for your hair, or to massage the body or scalp.

Yield: Approx. 1 cup (227 ml)

WHY USE NATURAL OILS IN MASSAGE BLENDS?

Synthetic oils, petroleum products, and mineral oils create a barrier on the skin. This may seem helpful, but they do not allow the skin to breathe. Vegetable oils are closer to natural human oils and are better for people. Unfortunately, most commercial cosmetics contain mineral or synthetic oils. And if you go for a massage, a budget-conscious masseuse may also be using these products. Ask for a natural vegetable oil. And certainly do not skimp at home, either.

RELAXING FOOT MASSAGE OIL

Are your feet tired and aching? Treat them to some relief. After washing and stretching your feet, use this fabulous aromatherapy herbal oil to further enhance your relaxed mood and soften any rough skin.

2 teaspoons (10 ml) soybean, jojoba, extra-virgin olive, or almond oil
2–6 drops (depending on strength desired) lavender, German chamomile, orange, or clary sage essential oil

Mix all ingredients thoroughly in a small bowl.

Massage into feet. Apply pressure as needed to alleviate fatigue and tension. Put on socks afterward. You may be ready to climb into bed at this point.

Yield: I treatment

STEP-BY-STEP FULL-BODY MASSAGE, PART 1 OF 2

What You Will Need
Space heater (if necessary)
Relaxing music
Massage lotion, oil, or cream
Bowl
Pillow
Top and bottom sheets
Blanket or two

1. Make sure the room is comfortably warm; use a space heater if necessary. Put on some relaxing music.
2. Wash your hands thoroughly and make sure nails are short.
3. Pour a couple glugs of oil into the bowl to start.
4. Oil your hands and rub them together to warm the oil.

5. Start with your "client" lying face-up with his head on a pillow and his body under a sheet (and a blanket, if needed). Apply the oil to the throat using gentle side-to-side strokes.
6. Gently swipe across the chin, above the lips, and then across the forehead.
7. Using your fingertips, gently massage in upward strokes, starting at the jaw outside the mouth, coming up along the side of the nose, then across the bridge of the nose.
8. Make several spiraling, circular motions spanning the entire forehead; end up above and outside the eyes.
9. Press the cheekbones using slight pressure from the outside to the inside. Use a spiral, circular stroke on the cheeks.

STEP-BY-STEP FULL-BODY MASSAGE, PART 2 OF 2

10. Press along the sides of the neck, working outward to the shoulders.
11. Massage the crown of the head using the fingertips. Press gently, working down and around to the back of the skull.

Step 11

12. Uncover one arm, leaving the rest of the body draped. Gently holding the wrist, shake the arm from side to side. With both hands around the arm, gently squeeze. Work back and forth, starting at the shoulder and working down to the hand.

Step 12

13. Do the same on the other arm and then each leg.
14. Have the "client" turn over, and work on the back. Starting at the base of the spine, gently push on the spine, working up to the top of the shoulders. Rub the shoulders and top of the back all over.

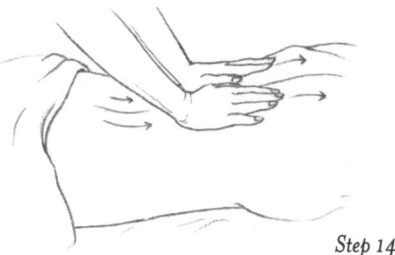

Step 14

270

BASIC MASSAGE STROKES FOR REVITALIZATION

Effleurage

This is a gliding stroke over the surface of the skin, usually done with oil or cream. Massage normally starts with light effleurage to gently connect with the person, soothing her nervous system. Gradually, deeper strokes may be applied to increase circulation.

Petrissage

This kneading movement lifts, presses, and rolls muscle tissue away from the bone to increase circulation of blood and lymph and to detoxify the muscles.

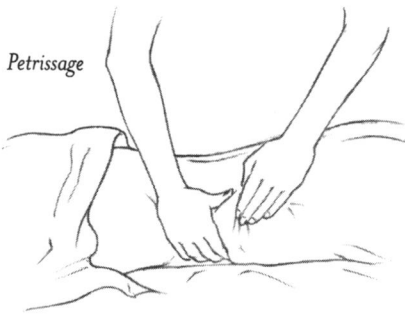

Petrissage

Compression

Compression is direct pressure to the body and affects muscular, nervous, and energy systems. This is done with the thumbs, the whole hand, and even the elbows.

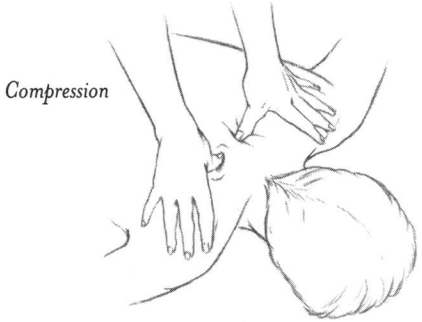

Compression

Rocking

Rocking is a smooth, rhythmic motion that soothes the nervous system. Gently shaking the limbs or rocking parts of the torso encourages the person to let go of tension.

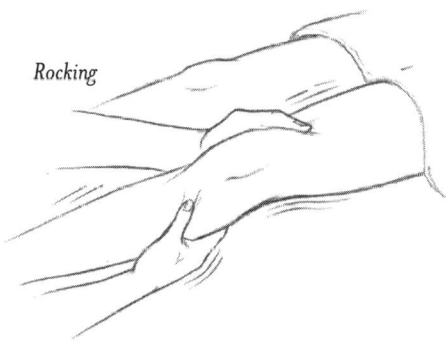

Rocking

Home

EMERGENCY FOOD IDEA LIST

In the event there's a power failure in your area, it's a good idea to keep extra long-storage food on hand. Here are some suggested items for your emergency pantry:

Main Dishes in a Can	Fruit and Vegetables	Beverages
Baked beans	Canned fruit	Bottled water
Beef stew	Dried fruit	Canned and bottled
Chicken and	Canned vegetables	fruit juices
noodles	of all kinds	Canned and bottled
Chili		vegetable juices
Corned Beef		Canned milk
Hash		Coffee and tea
Pork and beans		Nonrefrigerated
Sardines		milk
Soups		Powdered milk
(not condensed)		Soda and seltzer
Spaghetti/macaroni		
dinners		
Tuna or salmon		

BRIGHT IDEA

Power failures due to snowstorms, sleet, hurricanes, and other natural disasters are often preceded by a warning. In such cases, heat stews, soups, beans, spaghetti, and other one-pot meals and pour them into insulated thermos bottles, where they will keep warm for up to 12 hours.

It's also a good idea to store as much water as possible. Fill your washing machine, sinks, bathtub, and any clean containers. Buckets, dishpans, empty soda bottles, barrels, large pots, plastic storage bins, and even sturdy plastic bags can be used to hold water for a few days.

If the outage is weather related, you may have access to unlimited water supplies (snow in the North and rain in the South). Use this water for sanitation, or purify for drinking (see tip 273).

PURIFYING WATER

Here are two simple ways:

- Boil the water for 5 minutes. For every 1,000 feet (304 m) above sea level, boil 1 additional minute.
- Add 1 halazone tablet to each quart of water. Let it stand for half an hour. If the water is murky, double the number of tablets and the amount of time you let it stand. Halazone tablets are available at camping stores and pharmacies.

CRUISING FOR TIMBER

Start 10 to 20 feet (3 to 6 m) from your property line or the edge of the woods. Mark a *crop tree,* a straight, tall tree that you want to save and use for lumber someday. A crop tree should be free of signs of internal disease: swollen stems, seams or breaks in the bark, open wounds, or poorly healed branch stubs. After marking your first tree, pace off 20 feet (6 m) parallel to the property line or the edge of the stand. Mark the closest crop tree or one that might become a crop tree. If there are no trees within 5 to 7 feet (1.5 to 2 m) around you, take another couple of steps and try again.

Keep this up until you reach the end of the stand or the edge of the plot you want to work with. Turn at a right angle and pace off another 20 feet (6 m). Pick a crop tree, mark it, then turn again and go back, parallel to the first line. Continue this process, marking all the crop trees in your lot.

275

IDENTIFY YOUR TIMBER TREES

The best wood for burning is hardwood, and although you'll do most of your firewood cutting in the late fall and early winter, it is a good idea to take inventory in the spring and summer. During these times you can identify trees by their seeds and leaves. Here is a sampling of some good timber trees' leaves.

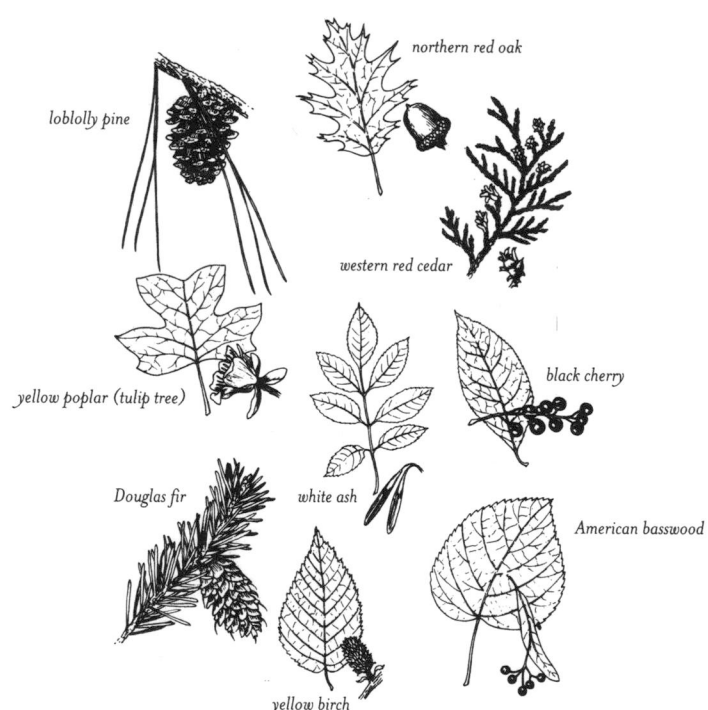

northern red oak

loblolly pine

western red cedar

yellow poplar (tulip tree)

black cherry

Douglas fir

white ash

American basswood

yellow birch

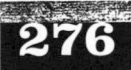

FELLING A TREE

Always cut trees in the late fall; with the leaves off, you can easily determine which way a tree is leaning. Before you begin, take a pair of lopping shears or a handsaw and clear away brush around the tree. Plan the landing zone—you should fell your tree in the general direction of its crown lean and the angle of its trunk. But you can "aim" the tree so that it does not get hung up in another tree or smash young saplings. Finally, plan your escape route and walk along it to avoid any surprises when you clear out.

Notch cut: This is the first cut, made on the side of the tree toward which it will fall. First, make a cut parallel to the ground more than a quarter and less than a third of the way into the trunk. Cut down into this cut to make a 45-degree notch.

Fall cut: This cut should be parallel to the bottom of the notch cut and about 3 inches above it. It creates a hinge that controls the fall of the tree. By making one side of the hinge fatter than the other, you will be "holding a corner"—the tree will fall in the direction of the deepest cut. Go easy at the start of the fall cut, but keep your saw running at full speed. When you reach the middle of the cut, apply a little more pressure and cut as fast as the saw comfortably allows.

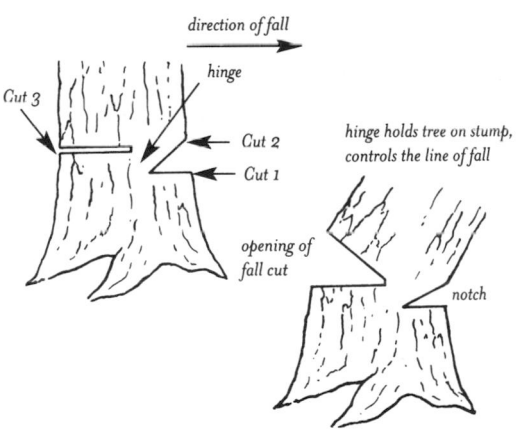

direction of fall

hinge

Cut 3

Cut 2

Cut 1

hinge holds tree on stump, controls the line of fall

opening of fall cut

notch

DRYING FIREWOOD

If you can manage it, dry your wood in the woods, close to where it was cut. Dry wood is much lighter than green wood, so it is easier to transport. Wood should be dried to 20 percent moisture before it is suitable for burning. This takes six months to a year. Dry wood feels dry to the touch when the bark is peeled off, and its ends contain deep cracks. Check your wood carefully before you burn it; wood that is still green causes creosote to build up in your chimney, which can cause disastrous chimney fires.

Wood dries faster with a "solar drier," which is simply a sheet of heavy-duty clear plastic secured over your pile. Leave the end that faces the prevailing wind open for plenty of air circulation (see figure). Set logs lengthwise along the bottom of the pile for a base. Logs dry most effectively when stacked log-cabin style, with each level set at a right angle to the one below it. If you do not cover your wood, stack it with the bark facing up. If you do cover it, the split sides should be faceup.

A standard cord covered with plastic

HOW TO REPAIR A CRACK AROUND A BATHTUB OR SHOWER, PART 1 OF 2

If there's a crack between the bathtub and wall, it should be filled to keep out water, which can damage the walls and house frame. The crack can also catch dirt and look unsightly.

What You Need

There are two types of waterproof filler: waterproof grout and plastic sealer. Grout comes in powder form. It must be mixed with water. You can mix it in small amounts at a time. Plastic sealer comes in a tube. It looks like toothpaste. It is easier to use than grout, but costs more. Read instructions on the package before you begin your project.

Prepare the Surface

Remove the old crack filler from the crack (*fig. 1*). Wash the surface to remove the soap, grease, and dirt. Dry the surface well before you make repairs.

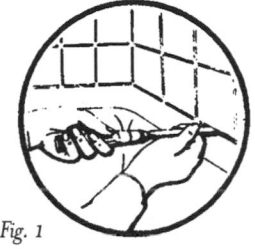

Fig. 1

HOW TO REPAIR A CRACK AROUND A BATHTUB OR SHOWER, PART 2 OF 2

Repair the Crack Using Grout

Put a small amount of grout in a bowl. Slowly add water and mix until you have a thick paste (*fig. 2*). Put this mixture in the crack with a putty knife (*fig. 3*). Press in to fill the crack (*fig. 4*). Smooth the surface (*fig. 5*).

Wipe excess grout from the wall and tub before it gets dry and hard. Let the grout dry well before anyone uses the tub.

Discard any leftover grout mixture (do *not* pour it down the drain) and wash your bowl and knife right away.

Fig. 2

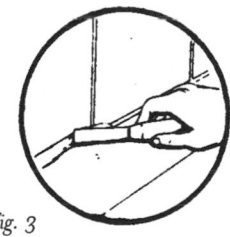

Fig. 3

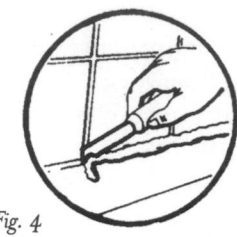
Fig. 4

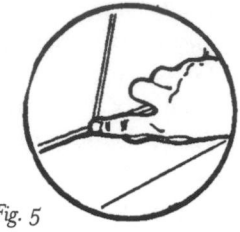
Fig. 5

Repair the Crack Using Plastic Sealer

Squeeze the plastic sealer from the tube in a ribbon along the crack (*fig. 6*). Use a putty knife or spatula to press it down and fill the crack. Smooth the surface. Work fast! Plastic sealer dries in a very few minutes. Keep the cap on the tube when you're not using it.

Fig. 6

280

CLEANING HARDWOOD FLOORS

Day-to-Day

A few precautions will keep your hardwood floors looking like new. Frequent sweeping or vacuuming will remove dust, crumbs, and grit that can get ground into the finish with every step.

Weekly

Start with a good vacuuming, then a bucket of cool water and a mop. Most everyday dirt will come up with a simple damp mop followed by a drying cloth (old cloth diapers work best). Hot water should be avoided as it will make the top layer of finish just tacky enough to set the dirt.

If a stronger solution is needed, use a very small amount of a mild detergent, such as Ivory liquid dish soap or Murphy Oil Soap, in cool water. Always dry hardwood floors with a soft cloth after mopping.

For very dirty floors, gradually strengthen the cleaning solution, avoiding cleaners with ammonia. The rough side of a kitchen or bath sponge, used gently, will remove tough scuff marks and set-in dirt. If you are uncertain about the effect a cleaner will have on the finish on your floor, test it in an inconspicuous place first.

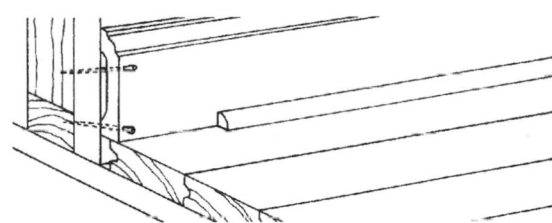

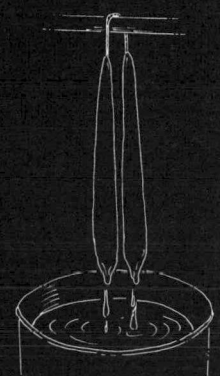

Winter

WINTER SOLSTICES, 2008–2020

Times given are Eastern Standard Time (EST)

Year	Day	Date	Time
2008	Sunday	Dec 21	7:04 a.m.
2009	Monday	Dec 21	12:47 p.m.
2010	Tuesday	Dec 21	6:38 p.m.
2011	Thursday	Dec 22	12:30 a.m.
2012	Friday	Dec 21	6:11 a.m.
2013	Saturday	Dec 21	12:11 p.m.
2014	Sunday	Dec 21	6:03 p.m.
2015	Monday	Dec 21	11:48 p.m.
2016	Wednesday	Dec 21	5:44 a.m.
2017	Thursday	Dec 21	11:28 a.m.
2018	Friday	Dec 21	5:22 p.m.
2019	Saturday	Dec 21	11:19 p.m.
2020	Monday	Dec 21	5:02 a.m.

WINTER HOLIDAYS

(United States and Canada)

CHRISTMAS · *December 25*
BOXING DAY* · *first weekday after Christmas*
NEW YEAR'S DAY · *January 1*
MARTIN LUTHER KING DAY · *third Monday in January*
INAUGURATION DAY · *January 20 (2009, 2013, 2017)*
GROUNDHOG DAY · *February 2*
LINCOLN'S BIRTHDAY · *February 12*
VALENTINE'S DAY · *February 14*
WASHINGTON'S BIRTHDAY · *February 22*
PRESIDENTS' DAY · *third Monday in February*

*CANADIAN FEDERAL HOLIDAY

Animals

FEEDING OUR FEATHERED FRIENDS

Freezing temperatures, chill winds, snow cover, and lack of natural food make winter the most obvious time to keep bird feeders full. Nights are long and temperatures plummet. A study of chickadees found that they could put on as much as 7.5 percent of their body weight during the day, only to burn it off by the following morning. Birds will be most active in their search for food first thing in the morning and again just before nightfall. Make sure feeders, water, and grit are accessible at these high-demand times.

Freezing weather places a tremendous energy demand on a wild bird's system. Because of this, high-fat/high-protein/high-energy foods are more important in the winter than any other time of year. They are referred to as "heating foods." Nuts are one example, and suet—the hard, white beef fat found behind the kidneys—is a favorite winter offering. It is gratefully accepted by at least eighty different species of North American birds.

Winter Feeder Tip
Winter feeders need a sunny, sheltered location that will allow the birds to keep warm and the seeds to stay dry. Remember in winter to remove snow from feeder platforms.

SWEETENING SUET FOR BIRD FEED

Suet, which contains protein and fat, is a high-energy food. All insect eaters (especially woodpeckers) like suet.

Suet is available at the meat counter in the supermarket, or you can use your own fat trimmings from steak or roast beef. In winter, use as-is; in the heat of summer, suet melts and must be rendered to increase its hardness and to prevent it from turning rancid.

You can "sweeten" the suet by adding other ingredients such as millet, oatmeal, peanut butter, cornmeal, seeds, nuts, raisins, and cooked rice. Birds love the added tidbits but aren't fussy about what they are. Some particularly good combinations:

Combination 1
1 cup (8.5 fl oz/237 ml) melted suet or fat
1/2 cup (3.5 oz/100 g) rolled oats
1/2 cup (3.5 oz/100 g) raisins or peanuts
1/2 cup (2.75 oz/78 g) cornmeal
1/2 cup (24 oz/680 g) seeds

Combination 2
1 cup (8.5 fl oz/237 ml) melted suet or fat
1/2 cup (4 oz/113 g) chunky peanut butter
1 cup (4 oz/113 g) sunflower seeds or mixed grains

To make a simple suet feeder, place a ball of hardened suet mixture in a loosely knitted twine or yarn sack.

CHRISTMAS-TREE BIRD FEEDER

Transform a living tree in your yard, or, after you finish with your Christmas tree, stake it outside and decorate it for birds to use as a feeding station.

Decorate your tree with:

- Pinecones stuffed with peanut butter
- Strings of cranberry, popcorn, and dried fruit
- Small mesh bags of suet

- Nosegays of wheat or other grains
- Half-rings of oranges filled with birdseed
- Small ears of corn
- Small dried heads of sunflowers

Also especially appropriate at Christmastime are decorative strands of whole peanuts, popcorn, caramel corn, dried or fresh berries, and pieces of fruit. Wrap around trees, hang from a window to the feeder, or weave into holiday wreaths, and watch the birds cheerfully dismantle them.

CHICKENS: COLD-WEATHER WARNINGS

In winter, rapidly disappearing feed may signal that your chickens are too cold. Eliminate indoor drafts and increase the carbohydrates in the scratch mix. However, it may also mean your chickens have worms—take a dropping sample to your vet for testing—or that other animals, like rodents or opossums, are dipping into the trough.

BUYING USED HORSE TACK

When looking to buy tack, do not eliminate the possibility of buying used items. Sometimes, by looking on the bulletin board of your tack store or by searching the columns of your local horse news or online postings, you can find a used item that will save you a great deal of money. If you are not experienced enough to detect a fatigued saddle tree or a "white elephant" bridle, take a knowledge-able person along with you. Whether you buy new or used tack or equipment, give it an initial safety check and cleaning before putting it into service. Then inspect it regularly for signs of stress and wear, replace worn portions, and have the item repaired as needed.

CARING FOR LEATHER HORSE TACK

After investing time and money in finding good tack, it's important to protect your investment by caring for the leather. Leather's greatest enemies are water, heat, dirt, and the salt from sweat. Fine leather articles should be stored at room temperature and out of direct sun and light. Humidity should be moderate, and the room should be well ventilated and as dirt-free as possible.

If a dehumidifier is impractical, discourage mold and mildew by wiping leather articles periodically with a mild acid solution, such as white vinegar and water or a 1 to 1 ratio of rubbing alcohol and water. If mildew persists, wash with thick suds of germicidal or fungicidal soap and then expose the leather to air and sunlight.

For routine leather care, follow these three steps: clean it, feed it, seal it. To clean leather, warm water and Turkish toweling may be all you need. If the saddle is tooled, you may want to try a naturally made oil-based soap, such as Murphy, as well. Once the leather is cleansed, rinsed, wiped, and partially dry, nourish the flesh side with oil (pure neat's-foot oil is best) or grease (beware overfeeding, however, which makes leather flabby and greasy). Once the leather is dry, seal in the oil with soft soap or hard wax, which will also make daily removal of sweat and mud much easier.

Leather articles should be covered with fabric when not in use. Take care of your leather tack items, and they will last a long time. (And they'll take care of you—when you least expect it but most assuredly will appreciate it!)

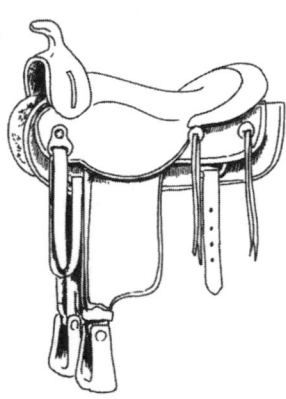

PAPER-TRAINING A PUPPY

Paper-training is a convenient method for apartment dwellers and for those with little access to an outside area. The puppy is confined to a small, noncarpeted area in which the whole floor is covered with newspaper. Since the whole area is covered, the puppy will have no choice but to relieve himself on the paper.

After several days, begin removing some of the paper. The puppy has become used to the idea that he should relieve himself on the newspaper, and he won't eliminate on the area of the floor that's bare.

Eventually, you might use a large litter pan or plastic blanket box with a paper liner in the bottom. Without a litter pan, the dog may think any paper object on the floor is a fair target. Once the puppy is dependably eliminating in the litter pan, you can gradually give him more access to the house.

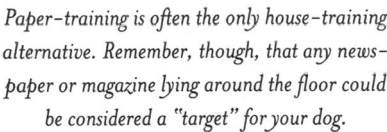

Paper-training is often the only house-training alternative. Remember, though, that any newspaper or magazine lying around the floor could be considered a "target" for your dog.

TEACH YOUR DOG TO STAY

This is a very important obedience command to teach your dog. If you ever see your dog entering a dangerous situation, such as crossing a busy road, you'll be happy you taught him this.

With the dog in a sitting position, tell him "Stay," give a slight backward pressure to the leash, and put your flat hand, palm forward, between you and his face. Then pivot in front of the dog so you are facing him. Praise your dog if he doesn't move, then pivot back to his side. Repeat this several times, eventually lengthening

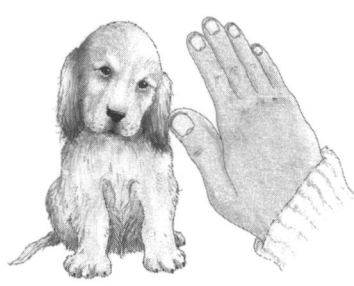

the time and distance you are away. When the dog has mastered this in the sit position, you should teach him to stay in the down position using the same method.

Stay: When you tell your dog to stay, your hand should look like a solid barrier in front of his face.

289

"CATCH OF THE DAY" DOG TREATS

3 cups unbleached wheat flour
1/2 cup (8 oz) cornmeal
1/2 cup wheat germ (8 oz)
1 cup (8 oz) water
1/2 cup (4 oz) vegetable oil
1 can (6 oz/170 g) tuna in water, drained, rinsed, and drained again
1 clove garlic, chopped

1. Preheat the oven to 350°F (180°C). In a large bowl, combine all ingredients.
2. On a lightly floured surface, knead the dough until it is firm.
3. Roll the dough to a 1/2-inch thickness. Use a fish-shaped cookie cutter (or whatever shape you prefer) to form the cookies. Transfer the cookies to a baking sheet.
4. Bake for 30 minutes. Turn off the heat; let the cookies stand in the oven until hard, 1 to 2 hours.

IS FELIX FANCY FREE?

Body language is an important clue to determining your cat's mood. If you are unsure about how your cat feels around you or other people, look for these signs:

- A cat sprawled out on her back, showing her belly, feels relaxed, content, and safe.
- A cat with his ears flattened against his head is frightened and angry.
- A cat scurrying madly with her head and body held low has been frightened.
- If your cat lets you play with his paws, he is relaxed and trusts you.
- A cat kneading your lap is expressing affection for you and sometimes also requesting an extended fur rub.
- A cat holding his tail upright with its tip leaning toward his head is curious and playful. If he's walking to you in this tail-high posture, he's coming to say hello.

A cat with tail held high is curious, confident, and ready for action.

ULTRASIMPLE HOMEMADE CAT BED

When topped off with fleece and set in a warm, sunny location, this bed will quickly become a cat magnet. Best of all, it's easy to launder—just remove the fleece blanket and throw it in the washing machine. If you suffer the misfortune of a flea infestation, you can wash the bed as well.

What You Will Need

An old pillowcase
Old towels, rags, or T-shirts
A needle and thread
A small fleece blanket (a baby blanket works well)

Stuff an old pillowcase with layers of rags, worn-out towels, and old T-shirts. Use enough filling to make the bed at least an inch thick and just wide enough to fit inside a standard cat condo.

Sew up the open end of the pillowcase, again adjusting for size, and add a few stitches around the edge to secure the stuffing, so that it won't bunch up when it's washed.

Arrange the cat bed in the area you've selected. Drape the fleece blanket over the bed and tuck in the corners to secure it.

KEEPING CATS OFF CLOTHING

Cats love to sit on our favorite sweater or other clothing, and it's always something that contrasts with their fur color. To help your cat feel closer to you without ruining your clothing, sleep in an old sweater or soft shirt that you don't mind giving up to your furry pal, then use it to line the cat bed. This quick alternative is comforting to your cat when you're not at home, and it just might save your favorite cashmere sweater!

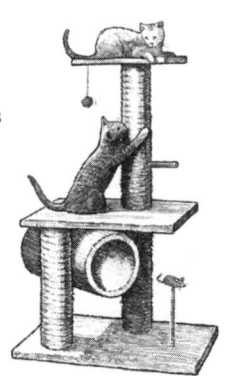

Cooking

TYPES OF WINTER SQUASH

Acorn. An acorn-shaped squash with a dark green rind and golden-yellow, sweet-flavored flesh. These squash are especially good for baking and stuffing. One squash will usually serve two people.
Banana. A very large squash with a long, cylindrical body and small seed cavity. Usually weighs around 10 to 35 pounds.
Butterbush. The bush-type butternut squash with reddish-orange flesh and an average weight of 1 1/2 pounds is nice for baking and stuffing.
Buttercup. Averaging 3 to 4 pounds, this drum-shaped squash has a tough, green rind. It cooks extra dry, but its sweet-potato flavor is good steamed or baked.
Butternut. Bottle-shaped or straight, this squash has a pinkish-tan hide and averages 2 to 4 pounds in weight. Its sweet, nutty flavor and fine texture make it good for pies.
Curshaw. Crookneck or pear-shaped with a light buff or green-striped rind. Good for baking and boiling for mashing. Good for pies and canning.
Delicious. Round, yellow or dark green, heart-shaped squash with orange flesh. Higher in vitamin content than most winter squash.
Hubbard. Comes in green, gold, or blue varieties. Excellent boiled for mashed squash dishes.

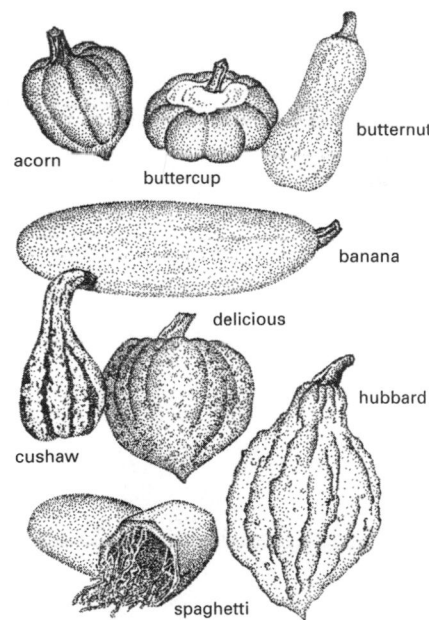

acorn

buttercup

butternut

banana

delicious

hubbard

cushaw

spaghetti

Spaghetti. Not really a winter squash, but it will keep well nonetheless. You can cook this novelty squash in boiling water and then substitute it for any recipe calling for spaghetti. This squash can be cooked and chilled for use in salads, too. Spaghetti squash is oval, with a cream-colored or tan rind and yellow spaghetti-like texture inside.

SQUASH OR PUMPKIN CAKE

4 eggs
1 1/2 cups (12 fl oz/355 g) oil
1 cup (12 oz/350 g) honey
1/2 cup (4 oz/100 g) sugar
2 cups (10.5 oz/300 g) grated raw squash or pumpkin
2 cups (12 oz/340 g) whole wheat pastry flour or white flour
2 teaspoons (10 ml) baking powder
1 1/2 teaspoons (7 ml) baking soda
1 teaspoon (5 ml) salt
2 teaspoons (10 ml) cinnamon
One 8-ounce (227 g) can pineapple, well drained
1/2 cup (2.5 oz/75 g) nuts

Place eggs, oil, honey, and sugar in a blender, in that order, and blend until smooth. Add the squash, a little at a time. Pour into a large mixing bowl, add all dry ingredients, and stir well. Fold in nuts and pineapple. Pour into greased 9 x 13–inch (23 cm x 33 cm) pan. Bake at 350°F (180°C) for 35 to 40 minutes until done.

Yield: 1 large cake
Time: Approx. 1 hour

Frost with your favorite recipe for coconut icing or spread on a mixture of 1/2 cup (4 oz/114 g) cream cheese, 1/4 cup (2 oz/28 g) butter, and 1/2 cup (6 oz/175 g) honey.

SWEET-POTATO PANCAKES

These are a delicious twist on traditional potato pancakes, and they include all the healthful goodness that tofu—a secret ingredient—provides. Serve them with poached eggs for brunch.

1 cup (8 oz/227 g) cooked sweet potato, mashed
4 ounces (113 g) tofu
2/3 cup (1.3 oz/38 g) fresh breadcrumbs
1 tablespoon (15 ml) onion, minced
A few dashes curry powder
1/4 teaspoon (1.3 ml) salt
2 tablespoons (10.25 oz/284 g) unbleached flour, spread on a saucer
2 tablespoons (1 fl oz/30 ml) oil

Using a fork, mix all the ingredients, except the flour and oil, in a small bowl. Mash the tofu as you mix and blend. Form the mix into 4 thin patties. Dip each side of each patty in the flour. Heat the oil in a heavy skillet, and fry the pancakes over medium-low heat for about 10 minutes on each side. The pancakes should be golden brown and crusty on the outside, soft and rich on the inside.

Yield: 4 pancakes
Time: 25 minutes

TIPS FOR COOKING WITH YOGURT

In Baked Desserts, Breads, and Pancakes. Yogurt makes these foods light and moist. If your yogurt is thick or solid, and you want to substitute yogurt for the liquid called for in the recipe, use 1 1/4 cups of yogurt for each cup of liquid. But if there is whey (a watery liquid) separated out on top of the yogurt, your yogurt is liquid enough. Just stir the yogurt well, and measure it cup for cup for the liquid in the original recipe. When using yogurt in baking, add 1/2 teaspoon of baking soda per cup of yogurt to counteract the acid content. (See tip 297.)

In Marinades. Yogurt is a great tenderizer, and it particularly enhances chicken, lamb, and pork. (See tip 298.)

As a Low-Calorie Substitute in Sauces and Dressings. Yogurt can be substituted for mayonnaise, sour cream, and cream cheese when some of the whey is drained off. (See tip 299.)

PUTTING YOGURT TO USE: MUFFINS

This batter will keep several days under refrigeration.

2 eggs
1/3 cup (2.5–3 fl oz; 80 ml) vegetable oil
1/2 cup (4 fl oz/120 ml) honey or maple syrup
1 1/2 cups (12 oz/340 g) plain yogurt
1 cup (4.25 oz/120 g) whole wheat flour
1 1/2 cups (7 oz/200 g) unbleached flour
2 teaspoons (10 ml) baking powder
1 teaspoon (5 ml) baking soda
1/2 cup (2.5 oz/75 g) chopped nuts or 1 cup (5 oz/145 g) blueberries

Preheat oven to 400°F (200°C). Grease the muffin trays.

In a small bowl, beat together the eggs, vegetable oil, and honey. Stir in the yogurt.

In a large bowl, stir together the flours, baking powder, and baking soda. Make a well in the center of the flour, and add the liquids. Stir together until the dry ingredients are moist (a lumpy mixture makes tender muffins). Gently stir in the chopped nuts or berries. (If you plan to refrigerate the mixture overnight, add the berries just before baking.) Fill each muffin cup approximately 2/3 full.

Bake 20 to 25 minutes or until a skewer inserted in the center comes out clean. Remove from the muffin tray immediately and cool on a wire rack, or serve hot.

Yield: 18 muffins
Time: 30–35 minutes

PUTTING YOGURT TO USE:
HOT GRAVY FOR ROASTS

1 cup (8 oz/227 g) yogurt
1/2 cup (4 fl oz/120 ml) vegetable or meat broth
2 tablespoons (0.5 oz/15 g) unbleached flour
Salt, pepper, herbs to taste

Combine the yogurt, broth, and flour. Refrigerate until needed.
Remove excess fat from the roasting pan. Stir the yogurt mixture into the remaining pan juices. Cook over medium heat, stirring constantly, until the gravy is thick and smooth. Thin with more broth or water, if desired. Season with salt, pepper, and herbs to taste.

Yield: Approx. 2 cups (16 oz/454 g)
Time: 10–15 minutes

DRAINING WHEY FROM YOGURT

To drain yogurt, line a strainer or colander with 2 to 3 layers of cheesecloth, or a linen tea towel rinsed in cold water and wrung out. Place the lined strainer over a pan or bowl. Pour the yogurt into the strainer. Refrigerate while the yogurt is draining.

Substitute For	Drain	Yields
Mayonnaise	10–15 minutes	2 cups (16 oz/455 g) yield 1 1/2 cups (12 oz/340 g)
Sour Cream	30 minutes	2 cups (16 oz/455 g) yield 1 cup (8 oz/226 g)
Cream Cheese	6–8 hours	3 cups (24 oz/908 g) yield 1 cup (8 oz/226 g)

Bonus Tip: Lighten Up Cheesecakes

If a cheesecake recipe calls for three 8-ounce packages of cream cheese, drain 9 to 10 cups of yogurt for 6 to 8 hours to get 3 packed cups. The yogurt will act just like cream cheese—for fewer calories.

300

TURNIPS AND RUTABAGAS
(Brassica rapa and Brassica napus)

The turnip was one of the first vegetables cultivated by man. A member of the mustard family, it was at one time as popular as the potato. In the past century, however, the vegetable has fallen out of favor with gardeners, despite new varieties that mature quickly and taste superb.

Although a different species, rutabaga is usually grouped with turnips. The rutabaga is really a weedy offshoot of the cabbage, producing a larger root than the turnip. Popular in Russia, Scandinavia, the British Isles, France, and Canada, rutabagas are often called Swedes or yellow turnips. In the United States, rutabagas are grown even less often than turnips, although they store better and have a sweeter, yellow flesh.

VITAMIN SOUP

Our favorite vitamin-rich soup is great during the winter months. If you put your Crock-Pot on low, you can simmer this soup almost all day. Try different combinations of herbs until you find your favorite flavors.

1 cup (7 oz/200 g) dried beans, any variety
1/3 cup (2 oz/50 g) dried peas
2 cups (9 oz/255 g) carrots, diced
2 cups (14.25 oz/404 g) potatoes, peeled and diced
1 cup (5.25 oz/149 g) rutabaga, diced
1 medium-size onion, chopped
2 teaspoons (10 ml) dried summer savory
1/2 teaspoon (2.5 ml) dried thyme
1/2 cup (120 ml) fresh or frozen parsley, chopped
2 cups (2 oz/50 g) cooked chicken (optional)
1 cup (4 oz/113 g) zucchini or pumpkin, grated (optional)

Soak the dried beans and peas in cold water for 8 hours (or overnight).

Fill the Crock-Pot one-third full with water. Add the carrots, potatoes, rutabaga, onion, beans, and peas. (If you decided to include them, add the cooked chicken and pumpkin or zucchini as well.) Let simmer for 3 hours or until the vegetables are almost tender.

Add the summer savory, thyme, and parsley. Let simmer for another 1 to 2 minutes or until vegetables are completely tender. Serve hot.

THE PERFECT ROAST DUCK DINNER

The secret to roasting a duck is to thaw it slowly in the refrigerator the day before you want to serve it. Remove the bird from the fridge the next morning and let it warm to room temperature as you simmer the giblets. Dry it well inside and out several times, so that by roasting time the skin is as dry as possible. Pierce the fatty parts so the fat will render out during cooking.

Cook the bird at 425°F (220°C) for 15 minutes, then at 325°F (170°C) for 20 to 35 minutes, depending on its size and age. After the skin starts to turn a golden brown, baste frequently with freshly squeezed orange juice and rendered fat.

You can serve the duck halved or quartered, with rice and salad. But so long as you get the bird dry and render out most of the fat in cooking, that crispy skin and dark, flavorful meat with be a culinary delight, no matter how you cut it.

MAKING ROLLS

Any basic white or whole wheat dough recipe can be used to make rolls. If you haven't made rolls before, a good type to start with is the cloverleaf. Just make small balls of dough and stick 3 of them in each hole of a greased standard-size muffin tin. (Aim for dough balls the size of large marbles.) Cover loosely and allow to rise until double in size. Bake in a preheated 350°F (180°C) oven for about 20 minutes or until light brown.

Don't try this with batter bread doughs or rye dough, since they'll be too soft and sticky; however, those doughs, as well as basic ones, can be made into miniature loaves if you have the right little bread pans.

COOKING WITH CRANBERRIES

Cranberries are among the simplest fruits to judge and keep. A bright red berry is a fresh berry, packed with flavor. Beware of any berries with wrinkly skins or squishy bodies. The fresher the berry, the more time you'll have to think up new ways to eat it! Size does not affect the quality of the berry.

Whole cranberries usually keep for several weeks in the refrigerator; in the freezer, they last at least 9 months. Whole frozen cranberries can be substituted for fresh in many recipes, and older frozen berries may be used in recipes that require you to cook the berries. Do be aware, however, of the differences among store-bought varieties of frozen cranberries—some are presweetened and cut, and this variety will not work well in many recipes.

Sweetened dehydrated cranberries and canned jellies and sauces are readily available in supermarkets. Cranberry juices are found in a plethora of forms, including unsweetened concentrates, ready-to-mix concentrates, juice blends, organic blends, and more.

CRANBERRY BUTTER

1 cup (2 sticks/4 oz/110 g) butter or margarine, softened
2 tablespoons (1 oz/25 g) confectioners' sugar
1/3 cup (3.5 oz/100 g) cranberries, mashed

Mix all ingredients in a blender or food processor and blend until smooth. May be kept, refrigerated, for up to 2 weeks.

Yield: 1 1/4 cups

THE IMPORTANCE OF GLUTEN

Gluten plays an important role in bread baking. It is a substance created when the protein in wheat flour is combined with a liquid. The amount of protein in the flour governs the amount of gluten. You can purchase boxes of wheat gluten to add to recipes—especially whole-grain recipes—to help them rise better. Gluten works by forming an elastic network (think kitchen sponge here) that traps the carbon dioxide being released by the yeast, which is what makes bread rise.

TUSCAN COUNTRY BREAD

If fresh sage is available, the mild flavor is distinctive and delicious. If you use dried leaves, 2 tablespoons (30 ml) are enough.

1 cup (5 oz/150 g) unbleached flour
1/2 cup (2.5 oz/75 g) whole wheat flour
1/2 cup (2.75 oz/80 g) cornmeal
1/4 cup (59 ml) chopped fresh sage leaves
1/2 tablespoon (7 ml) baking powder
1/2 teaspoon (2.5 ml) salt
1/4 teaspoon (1.3 ml) ground black pepper (or to taste)
1/4 cup (2 fl oz/59 ml) olive oil
1 egg
1/2 cup (4 fl oz/118 ml) milk
1/4 cup (2 fl oz/59 ml) dry white wine

In a large bowl combine the flours, cornmeal, sage, baking powder, salt, and pepper. In another bowl combine the olive oil, egg, milk, and wine. Stir the wet ingredients into the dry ingredients and mix until just blended. Spoon the batter into greased pans and bake at 350°F (180°C) until a tester comes out clean. Cool in the pans for 10 minutes and then remove to a rack to cool completely.

"REAL" HOT COCOA

Homemade cocoa is *much* better than the packaged supermarket kind. Give it a try!

2 tablespoons (30 ml) unsweetened cocoa
2 tablespoons (1.5 oz/42.5 g) honey
2 cups (16 fl oz/473 ml) warm milk
1/4 teaspoon (1.3 ml) vanilla
2 tablespoons (30 ml) powdered milk (optional)

Blend the cocoa and honey in a cup. Slowly add a small amount of warm milk to make a syrup. Pour the syrup into the remaining milk and add the vanilla. (If you want richer cocoa, put it into a blender and blend in the powdered milk.) Heat the cocoa until hot but not boiling, and serve.

Yield: 2 servings

HOW TO BUTCHER A TURKEY OR OTHER POULTRY, PART 1 OF 2

This is a simple method for killing a turkey or other poultry. Take a 1-gallon (4 l) plastic bottle. Cut off the bottom of the bottle and trim about 2 inches (more if the bird is large) from the top and handle. Hang the bottle upside down by a rope or small hook from a tree or the side of a building. If your bird is large, you can buy a large killing cone from your farm supply store for the same purpose, or hang the bird by its feet.

Pick up the bird by the feet and hold it a minute. This head-down position will put the bird to sleep. Insert the unconscious bird upside down into the large end of the hanging bottle or cone, and pull the head through the narrow end (*fig. 1*).

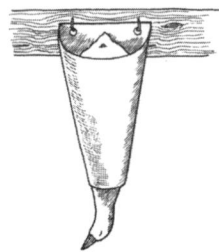

Fig. 1: A goose suspended in a killing cone

Open the bird's beak and, with a sharp knife or ice pick, pierce the back of the roof of the mouth into the brain (*fig. 2*). Immediately pull the head down and cut it off at the neck. Let the carcass bleed out. Meanwhile, fill a pot or tub (large enough to fit the bird) with hot water (140°F/60°C).

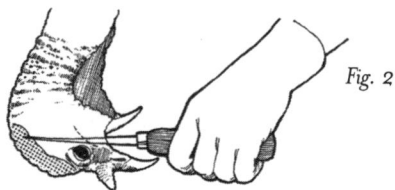

Fig. 2

HOW TO BUTCHER A TURKEY OR OTHER POULTRY, PART 2 OF 2

As soon as the bleeding stops, scald the bird by dipping it up and down for 1 minute in the hot water.

Lay the bird on a table. Pluck out the wing and tail feathers, then the rest of the feathers. On older birds, singe off any hairs over an open flame. Cut off the feet and wash the carcass thoroughly in running water.

Lay the bird on its back and cut off the tail, including the oil sac just above it. Carefully cut around the vent and cut a slit just through the skin from the vent to the breastbone. Reach in and remove the entrails.

Carefully remove the bile sac from the liver, and clean and peel the gizzard. Cut off the neck and pull out the crop and windpipe from the neck opening. Reach in and remove the heart and lungs from the breast cavity. Wash and refrigerate the neck, liver, heart, and gizzard. Discard the rest.

Wash the carcass, inside and out, in cold water. Cover and refrigerate 48 hours and tenderize the meat. After 48 hours the turkey can be prepared for cooking.

ROAST WILD GOOSE

This is an unusual and flavorful twist on traditional Christmas goose.

2 cups (8 oz/227 g) breadcrumbs
1/4 cup (1/2 stick/2 oz/55 g) butter or margarine, melted
1/4 cup (3 oz/85 g) orange, peeled and chopped
1/4 teaspoon (1.3 ml) orange rind, grated
3/4 cup (3 oz/84 g) celery, diced
1 cup (5–6 oz/142–170 g) cooked pitted prunes, chopped
1/2 teaspoon (2.5 ml) salt
1 wild goose, cleaned and aged
Salt and pepper to taste

Sauté breadcrumbs in melted butter or margarine. Add chopped orange, orange rind, celery, prunes, and salt. Stuff goose cavity lightly and place bird in a roasting pan. Sprinkle with salt and pepper. Bake at 300°F (150°C) for 1 1/2 hours, basting frequently with pan drippings.

Yield: 6 servings

THE VERY BEST STUFFING

1 1/2 cups (8–9 oz/227–255 g) dried cranberries
1 cup (8 fl oz/237 ml) white rum
5 cups (12 oz/340 g) fresh corn bread (about 1 1/2 loaves), coarsely crumbled
2 cups (4–6 oz/113–170 g) pecans, chopped
4 stalks celery, chopped
2 Cortland apples, chopped
1 Vidalia onion, chopped
2 teaspoons (10 ml) dried marjoram
2 teaspoons (10 ml) freshly ground nutmeg
2 teaspoons (10 ml) dried sage
2 teaspoons (10 ml) dried thyme
1/2–1 cup (4–8 fl oz/118–237 ml) chicken or turkey broth

Soak dried cranberries in rum for at least 3 hours.

In very large mixing bowl, combine all ingredients except broth. About 1 1/2 hours before turkey is done, add 1/2 cup (4 fl oz/118 ml) broth to stuffing and mix well. If stuffing is too dry, add more broth until slightly moist but not mushy. Spread stuffing in a baking/lasagna pan, cover tightly with foil, and place in oven.

When turkey has 15 minutes more to cook, remove it and stuffing from oven and scoop some stuffing into turkey. (Be careful of steam when removing foil from stuffing.) Put turkey back in oven to finish, and spread remaining stuffing evenly over bottom of baking pan. Return pan to oven, uncovered, until turkey is done, or longer if a crisp topping is preferred (be careful not to burn).

Serve cooked-inside stuffing and crispy stuffing separately to suit different tastes.

PERFECT POPCORN BALLS FOR EATING OR TREE TRIMMING

You will need a candy thermometer for this recipe.

8 cups (34 oz/960 g) popped popcorn (1/3 cup before popping)
1/2 cup (6 oz/170 g) light molasses
1/2 cup (6 oz/170 g) honey
1 1/2 sticks (6 oz/165 g) butter
Pinch of salt (optional)
Needle and heavy-duty thread (optional)

Make the popcorn and put it in a large bowl. Cook molasses with the honey until the thermometer reads 270°F (130°C) for hard-crack stage. Stir in the butter and salt.

Slowly add the mixture to the popcorn, stirring with a wooden spoon until all the popcorn is coated. Butter your hands lightly and shape the popcorn into balls. Set the balls on wax paper and let them harden. To store them, wrap each one in wax paper.

If you'd like to use the popcorn balls as ornaments, string a length of thread, knotted at the end, through the center of each ball. Pull through enough thread so that when you tie a long loop at the end of each, there will be room to hang the balls from the boughs of a tree.

Yield: 16 balls

GINGERBREAD MEN

1/2 cup (4 oz/225 g) softened butter
6 tablespoons (4.5 oz/128 g) honey
1/4 cup (3 oz/85 g) blackstrap molasses
2 cups (10 oz/300 g) unbleached flour

1 1/2 teaspoons (7.5 ml) baking soda
1 1/2 teaspoons (7.5 ml) cinnamon
1 1/2 teaspoons (7.5 ml) ground ginger

Combine the butter, honey, and molasses. Add the dry ingredients and stir until a dough is formed. The dough will be soft and buttery. Divide the dough in half and knead each ball gently. Roll each ball to a thickness of 1/4 inch (6 mm) on a lightly floured board. Cut out each man with a cookie cutter. Place on a greased cookie sheet. Bake in a 375°F (190°C) oven for 5 to 7 minutes. Watch carefully since they burn easily. Decorate with your favorite icing or Almost Buttercream Frosting (below).

Yield: 12 men

Almost Buttercream Frosting
1/2 cup (4 oz/225 g) white shortening
1 teaspoon (5 ml) clear vanilla
1/4 teaspoon (1.3 ml) almond or coconut extract
3 1/2 cups (15.75 oz/447 g) powdered confectioners' sugar
3–4 tablespoons (1.5–2 fl oz/43–57 ml) milk or hot water
Food coloring (optional)

Beat shortening and flavoring for about one minute, then slowly add half of the sugar, mixing in well. Add half of the milk or water and mix well. Gradually beat in the rest of the sugar and just enough milk or water to reach the desired consistency, whether for piping or spreading. Stir in food coloring if desired.

BANANA EGGNOG

1 cup (8 oz/226 g) plain or vanilla yogurt
1 banana, cut up
2 tablespoons (1.5 oz/44 g) honey
2 teaspoons (10 ml) vanilla extract
1 egg

Place all the ingredients in a blender and process for 20 seconds, or until smooth.

Yield: 2 servings
Time: 2 minutes

Crafts

DIPPING CANDLES, PART 1 OF 4

Learn how to dip your own beautiful, long-lasting candles. Remember to take notes so that you can repeat your successes or make adjustments for your next batch.

Materials

Wick (medium-size, 1/0 square braid, or 30-, 36-, or 42-ply flat braid)
At least 6 pounds (2.7 kg) wax in one of the following formulas:

Formula A: 100 percent beeswax
Formula B: Paraffin with 5 to 30 percent stearic acid (10 to 15 percent works well)
Formula C: 6 parts paraffin, 3 parts stearic acid, 1 part beeswax
Formula D: Paraffin and beeswax mixed in any proportion
Formula E: 60 percent paraffin, 35 percent stearic acid, 5 percent beeswax
Color, as desired
Scent, as desired
Double boiler or concealed-element heater
Dipping can, at least 2 inches (5 cm) taller than desired length of candle
1 small piece cardboard
Small metal weights such as washers and nuts
Water bucket tall enough to submerge entire candle
Hook to hang candles on

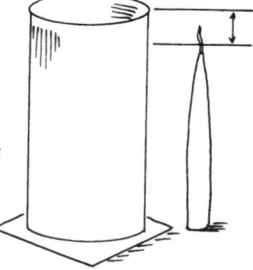

Make sure your dipping can is at least 2 inches (5 cm) taller than the candles you're making.

DIPPING CANDLES, PART 2 OF 4

1. Measure a length of wick equal to twice the length of the desired candles plus 4 inches (10 cm).
2. Tie one small weight on each end of the wick.
3. Cut a 2-inch (5 cm) square of cardboard for a candle frame. Cut a 1/2-inch-deep (12 mm) slash on opposite sides of the cardboard. Find the center point of the wick and align it with the center of the cardboard (1 inch [2.5 cm] from the edge). Push the two lengths of wick into the slashes. Equal lengths of wick should hang on either side of the cardboard square, with a 1-inch (2.5 cm) piece across the top of it.
4. Heat the wax in a double boiler. The wax must be 10 degrees above its melting point (155°F/70°C for medium-melting-point paraffin and stearic acid; 165°F/75°C for the beeswax formula). Add color and scent if desired.
5. Fill a dipping can with wax to 1 inch (2.5 cm) from top. Add wax as needed throughout the process to keep it at this level.
6. Dip the wicks down into the wax until only 1 inch (2.5 cm) of the wicks shows below the cardboard. Hold for 30 seconds (to let air bubbles out of the wicks). When you see no more air bubbles, pull up the wicks slowly and steadily.

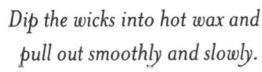

Dip the wicks into hot wax and pull out smoothly and slowly.

DIPPING CANDLES, PART 3 OF 4

7. Hang the wicks by the cardboard on a peg until the wax feels cool. Do not let the wicks bend. Dipping the candles in cold water between each wax dip speeds the cooling process (but be

sure all water droplets have evaporated from the candle before dipping in wax again).

8. When the wax feels cool, redip the wicks. Dip in quickly, up to the same point as before, and pull out slowly and steadily. When the wax is cool again, dip once more. You should see a small wax buildup. If not, allow your dipping wax to cool 5 degrees and repeat these 2 dips. (It's a good idea to rotate the cardboard between dips to avoid bowing the candles or layering the wax unevenly.)

9. Continue the dipping and cooling process (the cooling time will increase as the candle grows) until the tapers are at least 1/4 inch (6 mm) thick at their widest point. The candles will be heavy and stiff enough to weigh themselves down, so you can carefully slice off the bottom of each (removing excess wick and the weights). (To reuse the weights, drop them into hot wax until the wax melts off.)

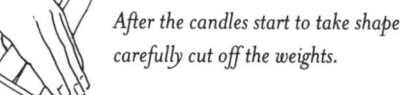

After the candles start to take shape, carefully cut off the weights.

DIPPING CANDLES, PART 4 OF 4

10. Continue dipping until the candles are the desired diameter; 7/8 inch (22 mm) is the most common. Replenish the wax as necessary to maintain a sufficient level for submersion. If the bases are elongated by drips or are uneven as you approach the finished size, trim with a knife and proceed with the last few dips. The dips will round over the bases, giving them a nice shape.

11. Some candlemakers raise the temperature of the wax to 180°F to 200°F (80°C to 95°C) for the last 2 or 3 dips to improve layer adhesion. Some increase the amount of stearic acid for these dips or use wax with a higher melting point. If you have the proper ratio of wax to stearic acid to begin with, this shouldn't be necessary.

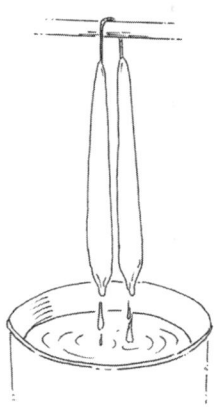

12. If you want a shiny surface on your candles, dip them into cool water immediately after the last dip. Hang the candles on a hook or peg for at least an hour to cool further, then store flat and out of direct sunlight.

Basic tapers are repeatedly dipped in hot wax to build diameter.

320

SHAPING HANDMADE TAPER CANDLES

Dipping candles creates a natural, slim taper, but you can make this shape more pronounced. After you've dipped the wick once, follow these instructions for the next three dips.

1. Visually split the length of the candle into quarters. Dip the candle into the wax leaving only the top quarter exposed. Cool.
2. Immerse the candle for a second dip that reaches only to the halfway point of its length. Cool.
3. Make a third dip that covers only the bottom quarter of the candle. Cool. After the above dips are made, some candlemakers make a taper dip one-third up, and then two-thirds up, to smooth over the first lines. Try this if you find your taper lines are too noticeable.
4. Continue dipping the candle (full length) until it has reached the desired diameter.

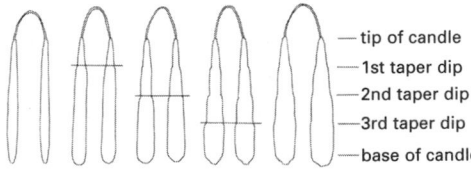

— tip of candle
— 1st taper dip
— 2nd taper dip
— 3rd taper dip
— base of candle

CANDLE-DIPPING FRAME ALTERNATIVES

If you are becoming more experienced at making candles, you might want to try other dipping methods, especially if you plan to dip a large number of tapers.

For dipping two candles at a time, use hollow rods such as drinking straws and metal tubes as frame separators. Knot the wick material and pull the knot inside one of the tubes to make a continuous loop. The separators will be at the bottom and top of each candle.

To dip multiple wicks, hang or knot several wicks over a rod that can be suspended (for example, between two chairs) while the candles cool. If you have a very large dipping tank, you will be able to dip an entire rod's worth of candles at once. If not, you can dip the pairs one at a time, moving the rod in and out of the wax to coat each wick.

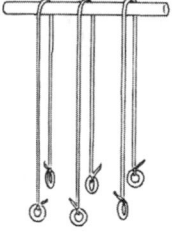

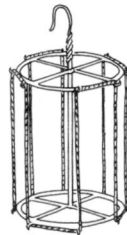

You can buy round, metal dipping frames made to fit into some of the available round dipping cans. These frames have a central part with a hook like a coat hanger. You thread the wicks through four or more protruding rods at the top and bottom. If you are handy with metal, you can make a round frame yourself from old coat hangers or similar-gauge wire.

If you have an oblong dipping tank, you can make a dipping frame from wood or metal. Wind the wick around the frame, spacing the lines properly for the size of the candles you plan to make.

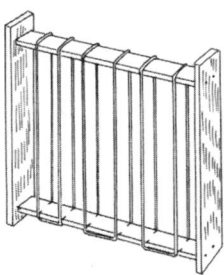

CANDLEMAKING DOS AND DON'TS

Do

- Cover your workspace with newspaper or work on a table that can be scraped clean (wax can be saved and reused).
- Avoid open flames.
- Heat wax in a double boiler (replenish the water often) or a heating vessel with encased elements.
- Keep on hand a fire extinguisher, metal pan lid (to starve a fire of oxygen), baking soda (to smother flames), and a damp cloth.
- Store candles flat in a cool, dark place (wrap scented candles in plastic).

Don't

- Pour wax down the drain—it will solidify and cause a *major* clog. Instead, pour extra wax into cups or tins. After it's cooled, store it in plastic bags for reuse.
- Pour the double-boiler water down the drain. Although it's mostly pure water, it probably contains some wax. You can set it outside or allow it to cool, remove the solid wax from the surface, and then pour it down the drain.
- Use water to extinguish a wax fire. *Never, never, never.* It can cause the wax to splatter and burn you.

WHICH KIND OF WICK IS BEST?

There are three general types of wicks to choose from for candlemaking.

Flat Braid

This is basically what it sounds like—a three-strand braid made of many plies per strand. Flat-braided wick is referred

Flat-braided wick

to by the number of plies in the wick, so the larger the number, the larger the wick. Common sizes are 15 ply (extra small), 18 ply (small), 24 and 30 ply (medium), 42 ply (large), and 60 ply (extra large). This wick is best used for tapers.

Square Braid

These wicks look like round-cornered squares and come in various sizes with various numbering systems. Square-braided wicks are best for beeswax candles. They tend to stand up straighter than a flat braid, burn off in the upper oxidation zone of a flame, and keep a flame centered in its candle.

Cored

Cored wicks, which have a paper, cotton, zinc, or lead core, work best with container candles.

Square-braided wick

As a beginning candlemaker, you will have your best success with wicks by following the instructions in the catalogs or on the packages provided by the supplier.

324

WAX-SPILL CLEANUP

If you ever find yourself with wax spilled on your clothes, don't fret. Try one of the following procedures:

- Wait until the wax cools; if it is sitting on the surface of the fibers, scrape it off.
- Put the clothes in the freezer. Chip off the wax once it's brittle.
- Place the cloth between layers of kraft paper or brown paper bag, and iron the wax out of the cloth and into the paper, changing the paper frequently to prevent the wax from redepositing on the clothes.
- Boil the clothes in water, then wash and dry them. A caution here: when you pull the clothes out of the water, wax can be redeposited in a different place.
- Take the garment to a dry cleaner, letting the cleaner know you

have a wax stain. Dry-cleaning solvent dissolves wax, but it's best for the cleaner to know about the wax for preliminary spot treatment.

CANDLE STORAGE TIPS

- Candles must be stored flat. This is particularly true of long tapers, which tend to bend if airspace is left beneath them.
- Store candles in a place that stays cool and dark year-round. Temperatures above 70°F (21°C) for prolonged periods of time can soften the candles, which can bend or even stick together at these high temperatures. But if they are wrapped and stored properly, your candles should be able to withstand summertime heat.
- Do not refrigerate or freeze candles. This can cause them to crack!
- Candle colors may fade if continuously exposed to light, so be sure to cover the box or close the drawer or cabinet where you store your candles.
- Candle scents dissipate if the candles are not wrapped in an impermeable covering such as plastic.

MAKING SALT-DOUGH JEWELRY

This is a very simple, fun project for kids.

2 cups (12 oz/350 g) whole wheat flour
1 cup (10.5 oz/298 g) salt
3/4 cup (6.25 fl oz/177 ml) water
Nonstick cooking spray
Nylon cording
Pin backs and/or plain barrette pieces
Glue
Watercolors and paintbrush (optional)

Combine the flour, salt, and water in a mixing bowl and mix with your hands until it forms an elastic dough. If it is too dry, add more water; if it is too wet and sticky, add a bit more flour.

Coat a cookie sheet with nonstick cooking spray.

Roll a small piece of dough into a ball. Use a rolling pin to roll it out to 1/4 inch (6 mm) thick. Using cookie cutters, cut out as many shapes as you can. Move the pieces to the cookie sheet with a spatula.

To make beads, roll small pieces of dough into little balls. Place on the cookie sheet and poke a small hole (big enough for the nylon cording) in the center of each with a toothpick.

Place the cookie sheets in a 170°F (80°C) oven for 1 hour. Check the jewelry pieces—they should be hard when tapped. If not, cook longer. When done, let cool for at least 30 minutes.

If desired, paint the jewelry with watercolors and let dry. Or leave the pieces plain.

String beads on nylon cording; glue other pieces onto pin backs and plain barrettes using white glue or a glue gun.

MAKE A HAMMERED PRINT T-SHIRT

This printing technique requires no paint or ink.

What You Will Need
Newspapers
Wax paper
Natural-fiber T-shirt or fabric, prewashed and ironed
Fresh, young leaves
Transparent tape
Hammer with a flat end
Salt or washing soda
Water
Iron

1. Lay a section of newspaper topped with a sheet of wax paper on a hard, flat surface.

2. Spread the T-shirt or fabric on the surface so that the area to be printed on is smooth. Arrange the leaves you want to print. Secure all edges of each leaf to the fabric with tape (*fig. 1*).

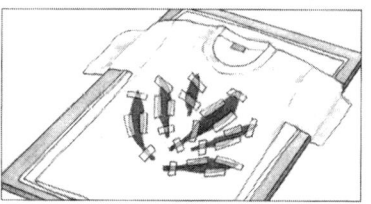

Fig. 1

3. Cover leaves with wax paper. Hammer leaves for several minutes until prints appear (*fig. 2*).

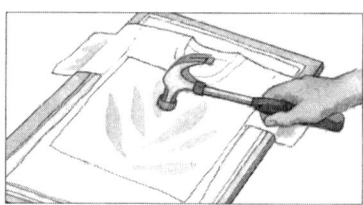

Fig. 2: If the wax-paper cover rips, replace it. Some leaves print better than others, so you may want to experiment first on a piece of scrap fabric.

4. To set colorfastness, soak the T-shirt or fabric in a solution of 1/2 cup (5–5.5 oz/142–156 g) salt to 2 gallons (1.67 UK gal/7.5 l) tepid water, or 2 tablespoons (2 fl oz/30 ml) washing soda dissolved in 2 gallons (1.67 UK gal/7.5 l) tepid water, for 10 minutes. Rinse thoroughly and dry outdoors or in a dryer. Iron.

328

MAINE WOODS AIR POTPOURRI

This is a delightful scent for the holiday season. Add red sumac berries and red rose petals to the potpourri mixture for a festive touch, and package it with a tiny candy cane for a deliciously cute gift.

1 cup (237 ml) fir balsam tips
1/2 cup (118 ml) rose hips
1/2 cup (118 ml) juniper berries
1/2 cup (118 ml) hemlock cones
1/4 cup (59 ml) oakmoss
10 drops fir balsam oil (see note)

Combine the first five ingredients in a jar with the oakmoss on top. Sprinkle with fir balsam oil, stir well, shake, and age at least 3 weeks.

Note: Many fragrance oils are available with Christmasy smells, such as Merry Berry, Christmas Pine, and Elfin Christmas.

GINGERBREAD HOUSE TIPS

Here are some forming and baking tips for creating a fail-proof gingerbread house:

- Be sure the cookie sheets are cool—no warmer than room temperature—for each batch of gingerbread. Hot cookie sheets cause the dough to soften and spread before it can set up.
- Not all parts of a gingerbread house should be cut from the same thickness of dough. Cut the major structural components (main supporting walls) of the thickest dough, 3/16 to 1/4 inch (5 to 6 mm) thick. This makes the finished house more stable. Cut chimneys, trim, and other decorative pieces from dough rolled thinner, but not less than 1/8 inch (3 mm) thick. It is easier to fit together small pieces, such as dormers and chimneys, if they are made of thinner gingerbread.
- Baking time will vary according to the thickness of the dough. Thicker pieces of gingerbread need to bake slightly longer than thinner pieces. Bake different thicknesses of dough on separate cookie sheets.

TEXTURING TIPS FOR GINGERBREAD

When building a gingerbread house (or village!) this holiday season, you can make your work even more realistic by texturing the gingerbread dough.

Before baking, you can create wood grain, boards, bricks, a woven surface, or even a shingled roof. Make planks for a gingerbread barn by scoring the dough with a knife. Gently press into the dough with the knife edge, being careful not to cut all the way through.

Or roll out the dough over a very clean, floured, textured surface, such as a woven placemat. Cut out the pattern pieces and transfer them to foil or a baking sheet by flipping the placemat, dough, and sheet over in one smooth motion. Slowly peel the placemat from the dough pieces.

You can also use icing on baked gingerbread to look like paneling or bricks. Smooth a layer of colored icing (or frosting) on the gingerbread, then pipe icing in the same color or a contrasting color over the frosting to make parallel lines.

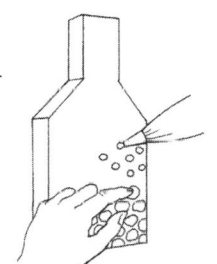

To give chimneys that made-of-stone look, apply a base of frosting and either press candy or nuts into the "mortar" or create stones with icing.

ORANGE POMANDER

Spicy orange pomanders make wonderful holiday gifts and decorations. Hang your pomander in the kitchen, bathroom, or a closet. Its spicy scent will last for years.

What You Will Need
1 perfect orange
1 ounce (23 g) whole cloves
1 tablespoon (15 ml) cinnamon

1 teaspoon (5 ml) nutmeg
1 teaspoon (5 ml) allspice
1/8 teaspoon (0.6 ml) ginger
An 18-inch (46 cm) length of ribbon
Bowl and skewer

1. Push the stem ends of the cloves into the orange—just close enough to touch. Cover the orange completely with cloves.
2. Mix the spices in the bowl. Roll the orange pomander in the spice mixture. Leave the pomander in the bowl in a warm spot for 2 or 3 weeks. Roll it in the spices occasionally to help the orange dry, harden, and shrink.
3. Pierce the pomander lengthwise with the skewer. Thread a double length of ribbon through the top of the pomander. Tie a knot and a bow at the bottom and make a loop for hanging at the top.

332

PAINTED HOLIDAY BREAD

This is a fun, festive project to share with kids. It's an extremely simple and healthy way to let their artistic talent shine through in the kitchen—they just grab paintbrushes and go!

What You Will Need
1/2 cup (4 fl oz/118 ml) milk
4 drops each of red and green food coloring
White bread
2 small bowls
2 brand-new paintbrushes
Toaster

1. Divide the milk between 2 small bowls and mix each with 4 drops of one of the food colorings.
2. Have kids set slices of bread on the counter or work surface and use the paintbrush and milk "paint" to paint a holiday design on the bread. They can make one large design or several small ones.

Only one side of the bread should be painted, and be sure the bread doesn't get too soggy!

3. When the kids have finished their pictures, put the bread in the toaster on a low setting. The heat from the toaster will bake the designs into the bread.

4. The bread can be used just as any other. You can make a whole batch and store it in the fridge, or put it in the freezer so there's always some on hand.

Gardening

PROTECTING ROSES FOR WINTER

Preparation for winter should be done just before the first hard freezing weather in the fall or early winter. First, remove all rose leaves that have fallen to the ground around the plants as well as any foliage still attached to the stems. This reduces the places where diseases can overwinter. Apply a final spraying of fungicide. Work in a feeding of 0-10-10 around each plant, watering in well. Prune roses to one-half their height and tie canes together with twine.

In areas where winter temperatures drop to 0°F (-18°C), the base of each rose must be protected by an 8-inch (20 cm) mound of soil, coarse compost, shredded bark, or other organic material. If using soil, do not pull up soil from the rose bed; instead, bring it in from another part of the garden. This soil will have to be removed the following spring, while the organic material can be spread out as mulch.

Where winter temperatures fall below 0°F (-18°C), the mound is made progressively deeper, up to 12 inches (30.5 cm) in the northern plains. Some gardeners cover this with another 8 to 10 inches (20 to 25.5 cm) of loose mulch, such as pine needles, oak leaves, pine branches, or straw. Where winds are severe, this can be contained in wire or paper cylinders. If temperatures stay below 15°F (-9°C) for extended periods, caps, cones, or baskets over the two layers are recommended.

THE INDOOR GARDENER

No gardeners worth their salt can leave their passion at the patio door. Bring it inside with a few easy-to-grow hanging houseplants. Here are those that will thrive in the low light and humidity of indoor growing conditions:

Achimenes
Asparagus fern
Baby's tears
Begonias (tuberous)
Chenille plant
Christmas cactus
Cissus
Creeping charlic
Creeping fig
Donkey tail
English ivy
Ferns
Kalanchoe (*manginii* and other species)
Pothos
Spider plant
Wandering jew
Wax plant

Check with your local gardening store for information on the care of each of these beautiful, long-lasting plants.

HOMEMADE PLANTING MIXES

Soil-Based Planting Mix

1 part high-quality soil
1 part peat moss
1 part perlite, vermiculite, or clean, sharp builder's sand
1 part compost (optional)

Soilless Planting Mix

1 part #2-grade vermiculite
1 part peat moss

To either mix add 1 tablespoon superphosphate, 2 tablespoons ground limestone, and 4 tablespoons steamed bonemeal per gallon of medium, or substitute a fertilizer mix of your choice.

GROWING HERBS INDOORS

So you want to grow herbs but you do not have the garden space? Or you simply cannot go through another winter without fresh herbs to liven up your meals? Do not despair. Herbs are some of the easiest plants to grow in containers. All they need is adequate light, warm temperatures, fertilizer, and humidity to thrive.

Choose herbs that you often use in cooking, or those that are hard to find in stores. It is preferable to select compact, low-growing herbs like thyme, marjoram, savory, parsley, sage, basil, or chives. You certainly would not want a six-foot angelica plant on your windowsill! Help your herbs stay bushy by pinching off the terminal ends of the shoots.

Help your plants stay bushy by pinching off the terminal ends.

POTTING INDOOR HERBS

Pots made out of porous materials are desirable because they allow excess water to seep through. Most herbs cannot tolerate "wet feet." Whatever type of container you choose, *a drainage hole is a must.*

Use a suitable growing mixture. A sterilized potting soil is best. Bags of soil mixtures are available in most gardening stores.

Place a small piece of broken pottery or a few pebbles in the bottom of the container to keep the soil from spilling out of the drainage hole. Fill the container about halfway with the soil mix. Place the herb cutting or transplant in the pot and pack soil around it, leaving a one-inch headspace. Water well.

NURTURING INDOOR-GROWN HERBS

Light
Herbs are sun lovers. They should receive at least 5 to 6 hours of direct sunlight a day. Grow-lights can be used if you lack sufficient natural light. A combination of warm and cool white fluorescent tubes is recommended. The lights should be laced about 6 inches from the tops of the plants and should shine 8 to 10 hours a day if they are the only light source.

Temperature
Herbs prefer day temperatures of 65°F to 70°F (18°C to 21°C) night temperatures of about 10°F (6°C) cooler. Most houses tend to be dry in the winter. The more humidity you can put in the air, the better.

Water
Let your plants dry out between waterings. Too much water has probably killed more container-grown herbs than too little. Feel the soil and be sure it is dry about an inch down. Water thoroughly so that it flows out of the drainage hole. Plants are like people—they prefer a warm bath to a cold shower!

Fertilizer

Potted herbs thrive on small, regular doses of water-soluble fertilizer. Treat them with a *diluted* solution of liquid seaweed or fish emulsion once a week. (Halve the recommended dosage.)

POTENTIAL PROBLEMS
WITH INDOOR-GROWN HERBS

Although insects and diseases are rarely a problem with garden-grown herbs, you may occasionally encounter a pest or disease on indoor herbs. There are several common culprits.

Red spider mites. Cause a yellowish, mottled discoloration of the foliage. May be seen with a hand lens. Wash the plant with a soapy water solution.

White flies. Tiny, mothlike, white pests that suck the sap out of the leaves. They rise like a little cloud when the plant is disturbed. Wash with a soapy water solution. Pyrethrum insecticides successfully combat white flies.

Damping off. This disease is often a problem on overwatered herbs or newly started transplants. Be sure your potting mix is sterilized. Do not overwater. Thin plants to allow good air circulation.

GROWING ROSEMARY

Rosmarinus officinalis grows best outdoors where winters are mild. For those of us who harbor pet rosemaries indoors every winter, the secrets of success are coolness, sun, good drainage, and frequent misting.

Indoors, rosemary should be misted often, and it should be watered carefully—overwatering can kill rosemary very quickly. Proper drainage is essential as well. With potted rosemary, be sure that water never accumulates in the saucer beneath the pot. In fact, placing the pot in a large pebble-filled pan is ideal; it allows the water to drain out of the pot and collect beneath the pebbles, thus providing the plant with the dewy moisture it craves as the water evaporates from the pebbles.

When a sunny window is not available, try growing rosemary under horticultural grow-lights. (Actually, any cool fluorescent fixture will work.) Rosemary requires at least 6 hours of sunlight every day to flourish—an unheated sunroom is ideal.

Monthly feeding with a good houseplant fertilizer is recommended, as is occasional treatment with a dose of Epsom salt. Epsom salt kills bugs while also providing the rosemary with magnesium. Used in the ratio of 1 teaspoon per quart (5 ml per liter) of tepid water, it is the "secret ingredient" that encourages sturdier stems and stronger fragrance.

DRYING HERBS

Hang drying is the most popular method for drying herbs. Tie the freshly picked herbs in small bunches and hang them upside down in a warm, dark, airy place. You can place the herb bundles in paper bags with holes punched in them to reduce their exposure to light and dust. If you have a dark, airy attic or similar room, you may be successful without the bags.

The herbs should be thoroughly dry in about 2 weeks, or when they crumble to the touch. Strip the leaves off the stalks and crush them finely if they are to be used in cooking. Tea leaves should be kept whole. Seed heads can be stored whole or threshed to separate the seeds from the chaff.

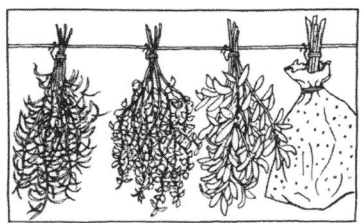

Screen drying works best with small quantities of herbs with leaves or seed heads that have been stripped off the stem. Spread a single layer of herbs evenly over fine mesh, and place it where air can circulate freely over the entire form. The herbs should dry in a week or two.

To oven dry, heat the oven to 150°F (65°C), scatter the herbs on a baking sheet, and place them in the oven with the door ajar. Stir every few minutes; remove the herbs when they are crisp.

Store dried herbs in dark, airtight containers.

STORING DRIED HERBS

Here are some simple but very important considerations when storing dried herbs.

- The type of container is vital, and glass or metal is best. Dark glass is especially good, as it prevents light from fading the herbs' vitality.
- Herbs must be completely dry or they will mold.
- Store immediately after drying to best preserve volatile oils, color, texture, and flavor.
- Use airtight containers to keep out dust and vermin.
- Package each herb separately and label every container carefully.
- Monitor containers regularly to make sure there is no condensation.
- Store in a cool, dry, dark place for best results.

Recycled glass jars are ideal for storing herbs. If the containers are clear glass, store them in a dark place, out of direct sunlight.

PLANNING A VEGETABLE GARDEN, PART 1 OF 2

Getting Started

Seed companies are well aware of the itchiness that gardeners develop as snow drifts deepen, and they time the delivery of their catalogs to coincide with the onset of cabin fever. A common reaction to the glossy pictures and glowing praises of each new variety is to overreact and order more seeds than the entire neighborhood could use. To avoid this, plan your garden carefully.

- Decide on the size garden you want.
- Determine what vegetables your family enjoys. If just one person enjoys rutabagas, does it make sense to plant an entire row of them?
- Consider the local climate. Eggplant may be a delicacy, but is the chance for success with this vegetable good in an area with a short growing season?

PLANNING A VEGETABLE GARDEN, PART 2 OF 2

Gardening on Paper

Draw up a plan for your garden on a piece of graph paper. Locate the tallest plants near the northern edge of the garden so that they will not shade shorter neighbors.

The table in tip 345 will help you determine how much space you need for particular vegetables.

The row spacing in the table is the minimum. If your garden soil is rich, the plants will probably be crowded, and it would be advisable to increase the distance between rows by 30 percent.

HOW MUCH ROOM DO PLANTS NEED?

This table indicates how much seed or how many plants of the most popular vegetables are needed to plant a 50-foot (15.24 m) row and to produce a season's supply of each vegetable for one person. Distances between rows are also suggested.

Vegetable	Seeds or plants for a 50' row	Distance between rows	Spacing between plants
Beans, dry	4 oz	18"	6–8"
Beans, shell	4 oz	18"	8–10"
Beans, snap	4 oz	18"	2–4"
Beets	1/2 oz	12"	2–4"
Broccoli	25 plants	24"	12–24"
Brussels sprouts	25 plants	24"	12–24"
Cabbage	25 plants	24"	12–18"
Carrots	25 plants	24"	14–24"
Cauliflower	1/8 oz	12"	1–3"
Corn	1 oz	24"	9–15"
Cucumbers	1/4 oz	48"	12"
Eggplant	25 plants	24"	18–36"
Endive	1/8 oz	18"	8–12"
Kale	1/8 oz	18"	18–24"
Kohlrabi	1/8 oz	18"	3–6"
Lettuce, head	1/8 oz	15"	10–15"
Lettuce, leaf	1/8 oz	12"	10–12"
Muskmelons	12 plants	48"	12"
Onion sets	1 lb	12"	2–4"
Parsnips	1/4 oz	18"	3–6"
Peas	8 oz	24"	1–3"
Peppers	33 plants	18"	12–24"
Potatoes	33 plants	30"	9–12"
Pumpkins	1/4 oz	60"	36–60"
Radishes	1/2 oz	12"	1–2"
Salsify	1/2 oz	18"	2–4"

Spinach	1/2 oz	15"	2–6"
Squash, summer	1/4 oz	60"	24–48"
Squash, winter	1/2 oz	60"	24–40"
Swiss chard	1/4 oz	18"	3–6"
Tomatoes	12–15 plants	30"	12–24"
Turnips	1/4 oz	15"	2–6"
Watermelon	30 plants	72"	72–96"
Zucchini	1/4 oz	60"	24–48"

CONSIDER YOUR TOOLS

When making out your garden plan, also consider what type of cultivating equipment you will use. If you plan to use a hoe, rows may be spaced irregularly. If you intend to use a rototiller, plan your rows so the machine will fit between them and won't disturb the plants once they have begun to grow.

WHY GROW PLANTS FROM SEED?

In today's busy world, many of us look for the easiest and quickest way to achieve a goal. Buying plants at the nursery is a fast and simple way to get a garden growing. But there are several reasons you might want to start your own plants from seed.

Each year, seed companies introduce new annuals with larger or more colorful flowers and vegetables with more luscious fruit. You may want to try new perennials from faraway places, or perhaps you have an "old-time" favorite. It's not always possible to find nursery plants of these varieties, and if you want them, you must grow them from seed.

Growing your own plants is more economical, a serious consideration if you have a large garden.

Some plants do well *only* when grown from seed. These include some annuals such as California poppy, sunflower, sweet pea, and nasturtium, and vegetables such as beets, carrots, radishes, and peas.

Children may be introduced to gardening by growing their own seedlings. Watching them witness the wonder of "creation" is a reward in itself.

And, finally, there is a certain satisfaction, come July, in looking around a thriving garden and knowing that you were responsible for starting those plants from the very beginning.

348

AVERAGE SEED STORAGE TIMES

The following chart shows how long you can hold on to any leftover seeds. In general, vegetable seeds should be stored in a cool, dry, dark location.

Dependable 1 Year	2 or 3 Years	4 or 5 Years
Onion	Asparagus	Beets
Parsley	Beans	Cabbage
Parsnips	Carrots	Cauliflower
Sweet corn	Peas	Cucumber
	Peppers	Eggplant
		Lettuce
		Muskmelon
		Pumpkin
		Spinach
		Squash
		Tomato
		Turnip
		Watermelon

START ONION SEEDS INDOORS

Where the growing season is short, start onion seeds indoors 10 to 12 weeks before the last expected frost. Onion seeds will germinate in 7 to 10 days if kept at 64°F to 77°F (16°C to 25°C). They can germinate at a temperature as low as 45°F (8°C) but it will take longer.

1. Fill a seed flat with sterile potting soil, and tap it down gently.
2. Shake seeds thinly over the soil so they're well spaced.
3. Cover seeds with 1/4 inch (6 mm) of fine soil. If some seeds show through the next day, sprinkle a little more soil over them, but never bury them deeply.
4. Stand the flat in a tray of water so the water rises 3/4 inch (19 mm) up the sides. Remove the flat from the water as the soil looks moist. Let the surplus water drain out of the flat. Keep the flat in a warm spot.
5. When the onions start to show, move to a bright spot.
6. Bottom-water seedlings when they start to look dry. Once the little plants are well up, water them with a fine spray from above. Thin to 4 seedlings per inch (2.5 cm).
7. When the onions are pencil thick, harden them off. Put the flat outside for periods of increasing length, beginning with the warmest time of day and eventually leaving them out all night. This should take 2 weeks.
8. Before transplanting onions, wash soil off roots, trim any extra-long roots, and trim green leaves to about 5 inches (12.7 cm).

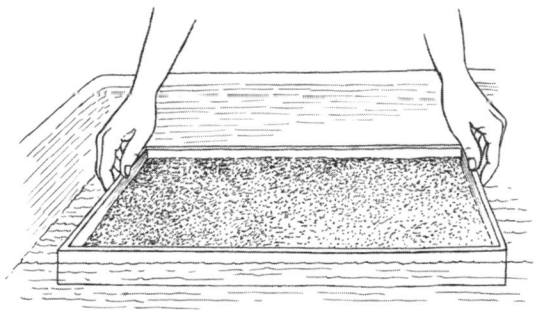

Bottom-watering keeps seedlings moist.

350

PLANNING AHEAD: TRANSPLANT TIMING

Plants started in the home or greenhouse offer a gardener a chance to harvest early, have a succession of ready crops, and harvest vegetables that could not usually be grown in his or her climate. Normally, transplants are started several weeks prior to outdoor planting. This table indicates the number of weeks needed to grow plants before setting them in the ground outside.

Vegetables Suitable for Transplanting and Methods of Sowing Seed

Number in parentheses is approximate time (weeks) from sowing seed to transplanting to garden.

Easy to transplant. Can be sown in flats in rows and transplanted bare root.	Must be started in individual containers and transplanted without disturbing roots.
Broccoli (5–7)	Cantaloupe, all muskmelons (3–4)
Brussels sprouts (5–7)	Cucumbers (3–4)
Cabbage (5–7)	Squash, summer and winter (3–4)
Cauliflower (5–7)	Watermelon (5–7)
Celeriac (7–12)	
Celery (7–12)	
Chinese cabbage (5–7)	
Collards (5–7)	
Eggplant* (6–8)	
Lettuce (5–7)	
Onion (8–10)	
Parsley (8–10)	
Peppers* (6–8)	
Sweet potato (3–4; start from tuber and not seed)	
Tomato* (6–8)	

*Sometimes sown in flats and then transplanted into individual containers before transplanting to garden.

351

CONSTRUCT A BARREL COMPOSTER

If you have limited space or just need a small, quickly made bin for composting, you can simply use a garbage can or a steel drum. This is a great system if you are concerned about rodents and if you don't generate large quantities of compostable materials. Either galvanized metal or heavy-duty polyethylene cans will work. The polyethylene ones with locking lids are best for this. Lids that don't lock will have to be secured using a rubber tie-down strap run from one can handle over the top to the other handle.

To make the composter, punch or drill 1/4-inch (6-mm) holes in the bottom, sides, and lid of the can for drainage and aeration. Set the can up on bricks or concrete blocks so that it will drain properly. As you fill this composter, cover each layer of waste materials with a layer of soil. This system holds water well, but may need additional water at times. To prevent odors, stir the material once in a while.

It usually takes at least a couple of months to get usable compost from a barrel composter. Fully composted material will settle toward the bottom, and the uncomposted top material will have to be removed to reach and use the finished stuff. It helps to have two barrels set up—when one barrel is full, begin filling the second barrel. The first barrel should be fully composted and ready to use when the second barrel is full.

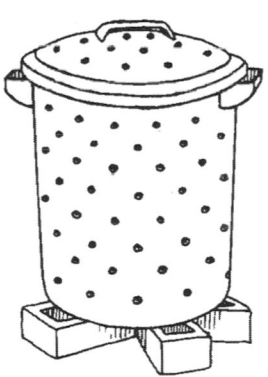

ACTIVATOR: THE KEY TO COMPOST

To get a compost pile working well, it's essential to have several layers of an activator throughout. An activator is a source of both nitrogen and protein—ingredients that help all the various microorganisms and bacteria break down compost material.

Alfalfa meal is one of the cheapest, quickest-acting activators. If you can't find it at your garden or feed stores, try Litter Green, a cat-litter product that's 100 percent alfalfa meal.

Other good activators include barnyard manure; natural products such as bonemeal, cottonseed meal, and blood meal; and good, rich garden soil.

Any time you add to your compost pile, dust it with a little activator.

RECIPE FOR COMPOST

In order for organic material to compost properly, you must mix materials so that the mixture is about 30 parts carbon to 1 part nitrogen. There is nothing precise about this, but be aware that a mixture with too much carbon, such as a pile of leaves, will not heat up, while a mixture with too much nitrogen will manufacture ammonia—and the nitrogen will be wasted. Also, be sure to thoroughly dust each new addition to the compost with some alfalfa meal, and then moisten the pile a little.

In the following list, the figure given is the amount of carbon per 1 part of nitrogen:

Straw	150–500	Grass clippings	25
Sawdust	150–500	Manure with bedding	25
Pine needles	60–110	Vegetable trimmings	25
Ground corn cobs	50–100	Animal droppings	15
Oak leaves	50	Leguminous plants	15
Young weeds	30		

Health and Wellness

GREAT GRAINS FACIAL

This mixture makes an excellent daily facial cleanser and scrub, and it keeps for a long time.

1 cup (3.5 oz/99 g) rolled oats
1/4 cup (1 oz/110 g) ground almonds
2 tablespoons (30 ml) lavender flowers
2 tablespoons (30 ml) chamomile flowers
1/4 cup (2.25 oz/64 g) clay
1 teaspoon (5 ml) goldenseal root powder
1 teaspoon (5 ml) slippery elm powder

Grind the oats, almonds, and flowers until the mixture is a fine consistency. Add the clay and powders, then store in a jar with a tight-fitting lid.

To use, mix a small amount of the blend with either water or yogurt to make a paste. Scrub your face gently with the mixture, then rinse with warm water.

355

RELAXING TEA FOR MOTHERS AND BABIES

Breast-feeding mothers can prepare this infusion, which always seems to settle nursing babies. We're not really sure if it calms the mother and thus calms the baby, or if it calms the baby via the breast milk.

2 teaspoons (10 ml) chamomile flowers
1 teaspoon (5 ml) fennel leaves
1 teaspoon (5 ml) catnip
2 cups (16 fl oz/473 ml) heated water

Infuse the herbal ingredients in the heated water. Drink the infusion as a tea with some honey.

STIMULATING ROSEMARY BATH

For a stimulating soak that will relieve a tired, achy body, add a rosemary infusion to your bath or footbath.

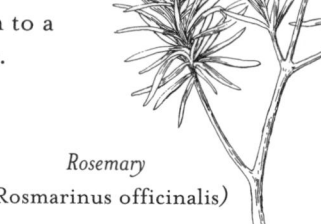

1 cup (237 ml) dried rosemary
2 quarts (3.33 pts/2 l) boiling water

In a bowl, pour the boiling water over the rosemary. Cover and let steep for 10 minutes, then strain. For a footbath, add the infusion to a basin of warm water. For a full bath, add the infusion to a tub filled with warm water.

Rosemary
(Rosmarinus officinalis)

ADDING ESSENTIAL OILS TO BATHS

Don't Add Oils While the Water Is Running

Essential oils should be added to a bath just before you enter the tub. If added to the water while the tub is filling, much of the oils' precious essences goes up in steam and very little is left to be absorbed by the skin.

Mix Well
Once you have added the oils, be sure to mix them into the water well. It is very important to avoid direct skin contact with undiluted essential oils that may irritate or cause skin sensitivity. You can also dilute the essential oils in a carrier oil before adding them to the bath or, as some people prefer, in 1/4 cup (62.5 ml) milk or cream.

Remember That Less Is Best
Adding more essential oils will not necessarily make you feel better than a small amount of oils will. These are very concentrated and should be used sparingly and well diluted. Generally, err on the side of too little rather than too much.

Watch Your Step
Caution: pure essential oils mixed in an oily base before being added to a bath may make the tub surface slippery. Watch your step when entering and leaving the tub!

CHILDREN AND ESSENTIAL OILS

When using essential oils with children at tub time, always exercise caution. Stick to mild oils and remember: less is best. Make sure the oils are well diluted in the water and that the water is the proper temperature. Improper dilution can result in skin irritation, especially with citrus oils, so resist the urge to use just a little more.

Children must always be supervised when using pure essential oils and should never be allowed to make their own bath without guidance.

EASING COLDS WITH ESSENTIAL OILS

Add oils directly to a tub full of warm water and mix well.

Cold Care Bath

This pungent blend opens the nose and soothes aching muscles. It is effective when a cold is coming on. Before using, apply it to a small patch of skin on the inside of the arm to test for sensitivity.

5 drops eucalyptus
2 drops peppermint
2 drops lavender

Chest Cold Care Bath

This blend is useful for that congested, tight feeling in the chest that often accompanies a cold or flu.

3 drops frankincense
3 drops hyssop
6 drops eucalyptus

If this blend smells too medicinal for you, add a drop or two of a favorite oil such as ylang-ylang, rose geranium, or jasmine absolute to sweeten it to your taste.

AROMATHERAPY BATHS

You can create your own spa experience with just a few essential oils and a tub of hot water. Experiment with 3 to 5 drops of complementary oils, adjusting the total amount to suit your individual taste. You can add the oils directly to the bath or, for added luxury, disperse them in a cup of milk first. Here are some excellent combinations:

Soothe Your Worries Away
Lavender, chamomile, and geranium

Floral Escape
Rose, bois de rose, and ylang-ylang

Pampered & Scented
Bois de rose, frankincense, clary sage, and geranium

Luxurious Soak
Roman chamomile, angelica, neroli, and clary sage

Deep Forest Pool
Pine, rosemary, and eucalyptus

Escape to the Woods
Sandalwood, neroli, and cedarwood

Vitality
Ravensara, thyme, and MQV

Very Calm Night Soak
Marjoram, cypress, and lavender

HOMEMADE DIAPER-RASH OINTMENT

First check with your health-care provider to diagnose any rash the baby may have. For a regular mild diaper rash, try this ointment. After application, let the baby go without a diaper for a while to let the air help heal the rash. Please do not use large amounts of any homemade ointment on your baby's skin until you are sure it will not cause irritation. (Test it on the inside of your elbow for a week, then in a minute amount on your baby's bottom.)

2 cups (473 ml) unscented petroleum jelly
1 tablespoon (15 ml) chamomile flowers
1 tablespoon (15 ml) calendula flowers
1/2 cup (118 ml) plantain leaves
1 tablespoon (15 ml) lemon balm
2 teaspoons (10 ml) comfrey

Heat the herbs in the petroleum jelly in the top part of a double boiler for 3 hours. Then strain the mixture through a cotton cloth and store in jars. Apply sparingly to the irritated area.

A SURE-FIRE WARM-UP

For colds and chills, place 1/4 to 1/2 teaspoon (1.3 to 2.5 ml) dried cayenne in 1 pint (473 ml) of tomato juice and warm the mixture, stirring until the cayenne is distributed. Sip 1/2 to 1 cup (118 to 237 ml) at a time for a heat-producing, sinus-clearing, vitamin-packed drink. Store the remainder in the refrigerator for later use and rewarm before drinking.

Cayenne pepper (Capsicum annuum)

JET LAG INHALATION

Traveling a lot over the holidays? Try this invigorating herbal inhalation.

5 drops geranium essential oil
5 drops bay laurel essential oil
5 drops lavender essential oil

Combine the oils in a small glass vial with a tight stopper.

To use: Carry a vial in your pocket or purse while traveling. Sniff periodically throughout the day to forestall the exhaustion and brain fog of jet lag.

364

NEW YEAR'S CIDER TONIC

This tonic is a popular, healthful drink that will help ease indigestion and nausea from overindulgence. Drink up and face the new year!

1 large glass water
1 teaspoon (5 ml) cider vinegar
1 teaspoon (5 ml) honey

Mix ingredients well and drink. You can substitute sparkling water or tonic for the water.

Home

365

WHAT IS A CORD?

A cord of wood is a stack 8 feet (2.4 m) long, 4 feet (1.2 m) deep, and 4 feet (1.2 m) high. Its volume is therefore 128 cubic feet (3.5 cubic meters). But because the stack is not solid wood, about 20 percent of that volume is air. Different kinds of wood weigh differently, of course, but the average cord weighs about 1 1/2 tons (1.4 tonnes). It contains about 35 logs that are 10 inches (25 cm) in diameter and 16 inches (40.6 cm) long, or about 10 trees measuring 8 inches (20 cm) in diameter at about chest height. (If you count the branches, though, a medium-size tree can produce half a cord.) An average cord produces the same heat energy as 166 gallons (628 l) of No. 2 oil, 3/4 ton (680 kg) of hard coal, or about 5,000 kilowatt hours of electricity.

366

APPROXIMATE WEIGHTS AND HEAT VALUES FOR DIFFERENT WOODS

	Weight/cord		Available heat Million BTU	
	Green	Air Dry	Green	Air Dry
Ash	3840	3440	16.5	20.0
Aspen	3440	2160	10.3	12.5
Beech, American	4320	3760	17.3	21.8
Birch, yellow	4560	3680	17.3	21.3

Elm, American	4320	2900	14.3	17.2
Hickory, shagbark	5040	4240	20.7	24.6
Maple, red	4000	3200	15.0	18.6
Maple, sugar	4480	3680	18.4	21.3
Oak, red	5120	3680	17.9	21.3
Oak, white	5040	3920	19.2	22.7
Pine, eastern white	2880	2080	12.1	13.3

DURABILITY OF UNTREATED HEARTWOOD

Decay Resistance	Tree Type	Life Expectancy
Excellent	Osage orange	20–30 years
	Western juniper	
Good	Cherry	10 years
	Red cedar	
	Sassafras	
	White oak	
Poor	Ash	2 years
	Birch	
	Beech	
	Elm	
	Hemlock	
	Hickory	
	Maple	
	Poplar	
	Red Oak	
	Willow	

HOW TO REPAIR A LEAKING FAUCET

What You Need
A box of assorted-size washers, unless you know the size you need
A screwdriver
An adjustable wrench

1. First turn off the water at the shutoff valve nearest to the faucet (*fig. 1*). Then turn on the faucet until the water stops flowing.

2. Loosen packing nut with wrench (*fig. 2*). (Most nuts loosen by turning counterclockwise.) Use the handle to pull out the valve unit (*fig. 3*).

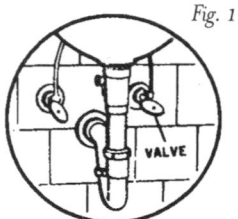
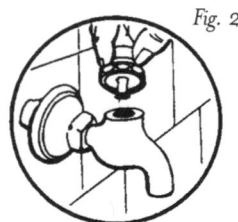
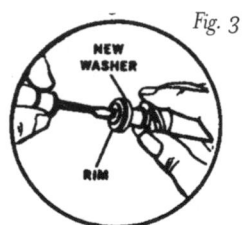

Fig. 1   Fig. 2   Fig. 3

3. Remove the screw holding the old washer at the bottom of the valve unit (*fig. 4*).

4. Put in new washer and replace screw (*fig. 5*).

5. Put valve unit back in faucet. Turn handle to the proper position.

6. Tighten the packing nut (*fig. 6*).

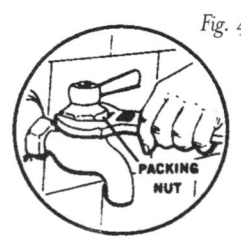
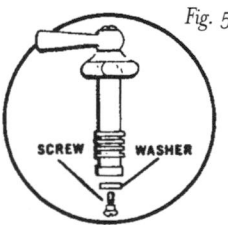
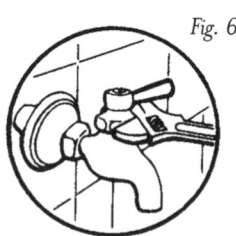

Fig. 4   Fig. 5   Fig. 6

7. Turn on the water at the shutoff valve.

Note: If the water is leaking around the packing nut, try tightening the nut or replacing the washer under it (if there is one). If there's no washer, wrap the spindle with "packing wicking" (*fig. 7*), replace the packing nut and handle, and turn the water back on at the shutoff valve.

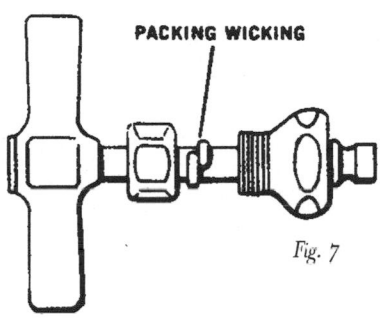

PACKING WICKING

Fig. 7

DRAINING YOUR HOT-WATER HEATER SYSTEM

In the event of an extended blackout, your hot-water heating system will need to be drained. Hot-water heating systems circulate hot water, heated in a boiler, through pipes and radiator units. For a time after a power failure, the water will still circulate without being pumped, but cold weather and a prolonged outage may endanger the pipes.

To drain, attach a hose to the drain valve that is in the lowest part of the system, generally at the base of the boiler. Open and drain water from all radiator bleeder valves. The expansion tank for the system must also be drained.

There will still be water in some of the pipes. Look for a vertical shutoff valve to drain the water stored in the pipes between the water meter and the vertical shutoff. With a hacksaw, saw this section of pipe in half. Bend the two parts of the pipe to drain both sections. Once the power has been restored, solder these pipes together before the water is turned back on.

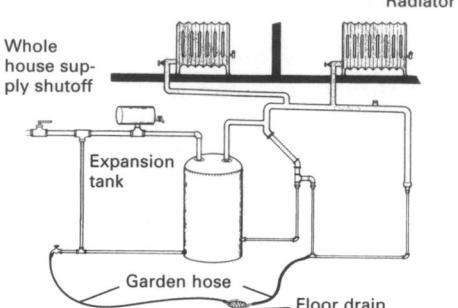

Radiator

Whole house supply shutoff

Expansion tank

Garden hose

Floor drain

THAWING FROZEN PIPES

Usually pipes do not freeze their entire length; they freeze at points where they are exposed to the cold, especially near sills, exterior walls, and uninsulated spaces. To locate the freeze-up, turn on the water faucets. Follow the frozen pipe back to a juncture. Then test water taps off this second pipe to determine whether the pipe has frozen farther downstream.

Once you have located the culprit section, you probably can pinpoint the location of the freeze-up by deciding where the pipe is coldest. Open the affected faucets to allow for the expansion of the frozen water.

To thaw pipes, try wrapping rags soaked in hot water around them (right), or try using a propane torch with safety shielding behind it (left).

If there is an outlet nearby, you can also try using a hair dryer (left) or applying an electric heating pad (right).

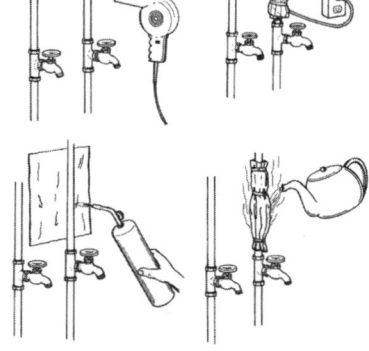

BUYING COUNTRY LAND

So you want to give it all up and move to the country? Good. Do it. But before you do, know what you are getting into.

First, you'll want to think about what kind of land you will need. This will be determined by what you intend to make of it. Do you want a vacation home with good fishing? Then buy land near a body of water. Are you a hunter? Then you will want to be near good woodland. If you want to homestead, you will need tillable land, a woodlot, and, probably, a pasture.

Consider how important neighbors are to you. It may be romantic to visualize yourself independently facing the elements, away from everyone, but these things have their harsh realities in times of emergency, especially for the elderly and those living alone. Also consider the distance to a general store and to a decent hospital— each is vital in its own way.

If you have children or are anticipating them, consider schools and facilities for child care. Don't just look at the quality, but also check out things like distance to travel, costs, and opportunities for outside activities for the kids.

Last but not least, think about transportation—rarely will you find any public form of it in the country. People who commute to work or transport marketable items must think about the effect of gasoline shortages. For the family depending on the farm income to live, the gasoline issue will be among the most important to consider.

HOW TO USE A HAMMER

Using a hammer seems self-explanatory: swing the hammer down and hit the nail. But there's always a *better* way—here it is.

Hold a hammer near the end of the handle for more hitting power. To start a nail, hold it in place and tap it gently a few times until it is firmly set. Hit it straight in (*fig. 1*).

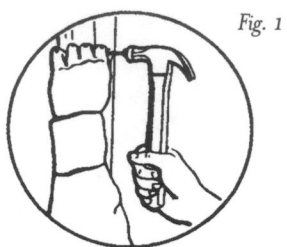
Fig. 1

To avoid hammer marks on wood, use a nail set (*fig. 2*) or another nail to drive a nail the last 1/8 inch (3 mm) into the wood.

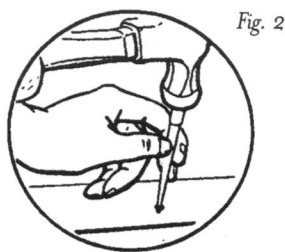
Fig. 2

To remove a nail, use the claw end of the hammer. Place a small block of wood under the head of the hammer to avoid marking the wood (*fig. 3*).

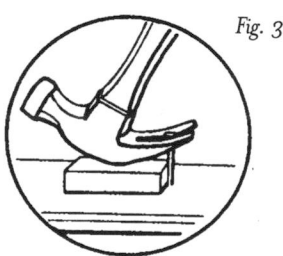
Fig. 3

373

PROPER USE OF A HANDSAW

A handsaw with about 10 teeth to the inch (2.5 cm) is good for most household work.

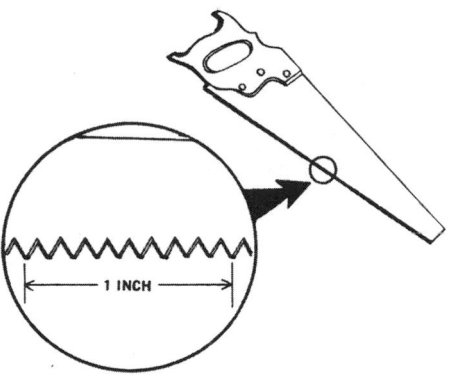

To use the handsaw properly, mark where you want to cut. Pull the saw back and forth several times to start a groove. Let the weight of the saw do the cutting at first. If you are sawing a board, it will be easier if you support it and hold it firmly near where you're cutting.

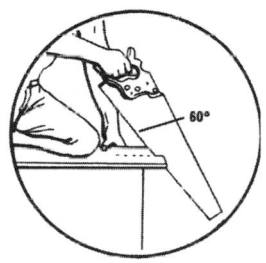

APPENDIX A

Typical Weather Across the United States
Average Daily Temperatures (°F)/Average Precipitation (inches)

Region	Jan.	Feb.	Mar.	Apr.	May	June	July	Aug.	Sept.	Oct.	Nov.	Dec.
Northeast												
Boston, MA	29/3.8	31/3.5	38/3.9	48/3.6	59/3.3	68/3.1	74/2.9	72/3.4	65/3.3	55/3.5	45/4.2	34/4.0
Buffalo, NY	25/3.0	26/2.4	34/2.9	45/3.0	57/3.1	66/3.5	71/3.1	69/4.0	62/3.6	51/3.1	41/3.9	30/3.7
Burlington, VT	18/2.0	19/1.7	31/2.3	44/2.8	56/3.2	65/3.4	71/3.8	68/4.0	59/3.5	48/3.0	37/3.1	24/2.3
New York, NY	32/3.5	34/3.2	43/4.1	53/4.1	63/4.4	71/3.6	77/4.4	76/4.1	68/4.1	58/3.5	48/4.3	37/3.8
Philadelphia, PA	32/3.3	34/2.8	42/3.7	53/3.5	64/3.8	72/3.5	77/4.3	76/3.8	68/3.5	57/2.7	47/3.3	36/3.3
Pittsburgh, PA	28/2.7	30/2.4	39/3.3	50/3.1	60/3.6	68/3.9	73/3.9	71/3.3	64/3.0	52/2.3	42/2.9	32/2.9
Washington, DC	35/3.0	38/2.6	46/3.5	56/2.9	65/3.9	74/3.3	79/3.5	77/3.7	70/3.6	58/3.1	49/3.0	39/3.1
Southeast												
Atlanta, GA	43/4.8	46/4.7	54/5.6	62/4.0	70/4.1	77/3.6	79/5.2	79/3.7	73/3.8	63/3.1	53/4.0	45/4.1
Birmingham, AL	43/5.2	47/4.6	54/6.1	62/4.8	69/4.7	76/3.8	80/5.2	79/3.6	74/4.0	63/3.0	53/4.4	46/4.8
Charleston, SC	48/3.5	51/3.0	58/4.2	65/2.6	73/3.6	78/5.8	82/6.5	81/6.9	76/5.5	67/3.0	58/2.4	51/3.1
Miami, FL	68/2.0	69/2.1	72/2.5	75/3.2	79/5.9	82/8.9	84/5.8	84/8.0	82/8.2	79/6.3	74/3.1	69/1.9
Mobile, AL	50/5.2	54/5.3	60/6.7	68/5.0	75/5.8	80/5.1	82/7.0	82/6.7	78/6.0	68/3.1	59/4.6	53/5.1
Orlando, FL	61/2.3	62/2.8	67/3.1	72/2.3	77/3.4	81/7.1	82/7.5	83/6.8	81/6.2	75/3.0	68/2.1	62/2.2
Raleigh, NC	39/3.8	43/3.6	51/3.9	60/2.8	67/4.0	75/3.6	79/4.4	77/4.2	71/3.6	60/3.2	51/3.1	44/3.2
Richmond, VA	37/3.4	39/3.1	48/3.8	57/3.1	66/3.8	74/3.6	78/5.2	77/4.5	70/3.5	58/3.4	50/3.1	40/3.2
South Central												
Dallas/Fort Worth, TX	44/1.8	48/2.3	57/2.9	66/3.4	72/5.0	80/3.4	85/2.3	84/2.1	77/3.0	71/3.7	56/2.5	47/2.1
Houston, TX	52/3.7	55/3.0	63/3.1	69/3.4	76/5.5	81/5.6	84/3.8	83/4.0	79/4.7	70/4.5	62/4.1	54/3.6
Jackson, MS	45/5.4	49/4.6	57/5.7	64/5.8	72/5.1	79/3.5	82/4.6	81/3.8	76/3.5	65/3.4	56/4.8	48/5.6
Kansas City, KS	28/1.2	34/1.1	45/2.7	56/3.4	66/5.0	75/5.3	79/3.9	77/3.8	70/4.9	58/3.5	45/2.3	32/1.6
Little Rock, AR	39/3.8	45/3.6	53/4.9	62/5.4	70/5.2	78/3.8	82/3.5	81/3.2	74/4.0	63/3.9	52/5.3	44/4.6

APPENDIX A CONT.

Region	Jan.	Feb.	Mar.	Apr.	May	June	July	Aug.	Sept.	Oct.	Nov.	Dec.
South Central cont.												
New Orleans, LA	52/5.5	55/5.7	62/5.1	68/4.8	75/4.8	81/6.1	82/6.3	82/6.1	79/5.5	69/3.0	61/4.7	55/5.4
Oklahoma City,OK	37/1.2	42/1.6	50/2.7	60/2.9	68/5.5	77/4.4	82/2.7	81/2.6	73/3.9	62/3.3	49/2.0	39/1.6
Central												
Charleston, WV	33/3.1	37/3.1	45/3.8	55/3.3	63/4.1	71/3.8	75/4.9	74/4.0	68/3.4	56/2.7	46/3.5	37/3.3
Chicago, IL	23/1.8	27/1.5	37/2.8	49/3.7	60/3.4	69/3.8	74/3.7	73/4.2	66/3.4	54/3.6	41/3.0	28/2.5
Columbus, OH	27/2.5	31/2.3	41/3.1	52/3.3	62/3.9	70/4.0	75/4.6	73/3.5	66/2.9	54/2.2	44/3.2	33/2.8
Indianapolis, IN	27/2.5	31/2.4	41/3.6	52/3.3	63/4.0	72/3.9	75/4.4	74/3.6	67/2.9	55/2.7	43/3.5	32/3.1
Louisville, KY	33/3.2	37/3.3	46/4.6	57/4.1	66/4.7	74/3.6	78/4.3	77/3.4	80/3.2	58/2.7	47/3.7	37/3.6
Nashville, TN	37/4.0	41/3.9	50/4.9	59/4.1	68/4.9	76/3.8	79/3.9	78/3.4	72/3.5	60/2.8	49/4.1	41/4.6
St. Louis, MO	29/2.0	35/2.2	45/3.5	57/3.6	66/4.0	75/3.8	80/3.9	78/3.0	70/3.0	58/2.8	45/3.4	34/2.9
East North Central												
Des Moines, IA	19/1.0	26/1.2	37/2.3	51/3.5	62/4.0	72/4.5	76/4.9	74/4.3	65/3.3	54/2.6	38/2.0	25/1.3
Detroit, MI	25/1.8	27/1.8	37/2.4	48/3.0	60/2.9	68/3.6	74/3.2	72/3.4	64/3.1	52/2.2	41/2.7	30/2.5
Duluth, MN	8/1.2	13/0.8	24/1.8	39/2.3	51/3.0	60/4.1	66/2.9	64/4.0	54/3.9	44/2.5	28/1.9	14/1.3
Madison, WI	17/1.1	22/1.1	33/2.3	46/3.1	58/3.1	67/3.9	72/3.4	69/3.1	61/3.1	49/2.3	36/2.1	33/1.7
Milwaukee, WI	20/1.7	24/1.5	34/2.6	45/3.6	56/2.9	66/3.4	72/3.6	70/3.5	62/3.1	51/2.4	38/2.5	26/2.2
Minneapolis/	14/1.0	20/0.9	32/1.9	47/2.4	59/3.3	68/4.4	74/3.6	71/3.9	62/3.0	50/2.1	34/1.6	19/1.1
St. Paul, MN												
West North Central												
Billings, MT	24/0.8	29/0.6	35/1.1	46/1.7	56/2.5	65/2.0	72/1.1	71/0.9	60/1.3	48/1.1	35/0.8	26/0.7
Bismarck, ND	9/0.5	16/0.4	28/0.8	43/1.5	56/2.2	65/2.7	70/2.4	69/1.9	58/1.5	46/0.9	28/0.6	15/0.5
Cheyenne, WY	27/0.4	29/0.4	34/1.0	42/1.4	52/2.5	62/2.1	68/2.1	66/1.7	57/1.3	47/0.7	35/0.6	28/0.4
Missoula, MT	24/1.2	28/0.8	36/1.0	45/1.0	53/1.8	60/1.8	67/1.0	66/1.3	56/1.1	44/0.8	32/0.9	24/1.2
Omaha, NE	21/0.8	27/0.8	38/2.0	52/2.8	62/4.4	72/4.0	77/3.8	75/3.3	65/3.4	54/2.2	38/1.5	26/0.9
Rapid City, SD	22/0.4	27/0.5	34/1.0	45/1.9	55/2.7	65/3.0	72/2.0	71/1.6	61/1.1	48/1.1	35/0.6	25/0.4
Sioux Falls, SD	14/0.5	20/0.6	33/1.6	47/2.5	58/3.3	68/3.5	74/2.9	71/2.9	61/2.8	48/1.8	33/1.1	18/0.7

Region	Jan.	Feb.	Mar.	Apr.	May	June	July	Aug.	Sept.	Oct.	Nov.	Dec.
Southwest												
Albuquerque, NM	35/0.4	41/0.4	47/0.5	56/0.5	65/0.6	75/c.6	79/1.3	76/1.6	69/1.0	57/0.9	44/0.5	36/0.5
Colorado Springs, CO	28/0.3	32/0.4	38/1.1	46/1.4	55/2.4	65/2.3	71/2.9	68/3.0	60/1.2	50/0.9	37/0.5	30/0.5
Denver, CO	30/0.5	34/0.6	39/1.3	48/1.8	57/2.4	68/1.7	73/1.9	72/1.5	62/1.1	51/1.0	38/0.9	31/0.6
Las Cruces, NM	42/0.5	46/0.4	52/0.3	60/0.3	68/0.3	75/c.5	79/1.6	80/1.8	75/1.5	62/1.1	50/0.5	42/0.7
Phoenix, AZ	54/0.8	58/0.7	62/0.9	70/0.3	79/0.1	88/0.1	94/0.8	92/1.0	86/0.8	75/0.7	62/0.7	54/0.9
Salt Lake City, UT	28/1.3	34/1.3	42/1.9	50/2.0	59/1.8	69/0.9	78/0.7	76/0.8	65/1.3	53/1.4	40/1.3	30/1.3
Tucson, AZ	52/1.0	55/0.7	59/0.7	66/0.3	74/0.2	84/0.2	87/2.3	85/2.3	81/1.5	71/1.1	59/0.7	52/1.0
West												
Las Vegas, NV	46/0.6	51/0.5	56/0.5	65/0.2	74/0.2	85/0.1	90/0.4	88/0.5	81/0.3	68/0.2	55/0.4	46/0.4
Los Angeles, CA	57/2.9	58/3.1	59/2.4	62/1.0	64/0.3	67/0.1	72/0.0	73/0.1	72/0.3	67/0.4	64/1.1	58/2.2
Reno, NV	34/1.1	38/1.0	43/0.8	48/0.4	56/0.7	65/0.5	74/0.3	70/0.3	61/0.4	51/0.4	40/0.8	34/1.0
Sacramento, CA	46/3.7	51/2.9	54/2.6	59/1.2	65/0.4	72/0.1	75/0.1	75/0.1	72/0.4	64/0.9	53/2.2	46/2.5
San Diego, CA	57/2.0	58/1.7	60/2.0	62/0.8	64/0.2	67/0.1	71/0.0	73/0.1	71/0.2	68/0.4	62/1.3	58/1.4
San Francisco, CA	50/4.4	53/3.5	55/3.1	56/1.4	58/0.4	61/0.1	62/0.0	62/0.1	64/0.2	62/1.1	56/2.9	49/3.3
Northwest												
Boise, ID	29/1.4	36/1.1	42/1.3	49/1.3	58/1.2	67/0.8	74/0.4	74/0.3	64/0.8	52/0.8	40/1.4	31/1.4
Coeur d'Alene, ID	25/3.3	31/2.5	40/2.3	47/1.3	55/2.1	62/2.0	68/0.9	68/1.1	60/1.0	49/1.7	37/3.1	30/3.4
Eugene, OR	40/7.9	43/6.0	46/5.5	50/3.1	56/2.3	61/1.4	67/0.5	67/1.0	62/1.5	53/3.4	45/8.0	41/8.3
Idaho Falls, ID	19/1.0	24/0.9	34/1.0	45/1.0	54/1.5	61/1.2	69/0.6	67/0.7	57/0.9	47/0.9	33/0.9	22/1.0
Portland, OR	40/5.4	43/4.1	47/3.7	51/2.5	57/2.2	63/1.6	68/0.6	68/0.9	64/1.7	55/2.9	46/5.5	43/6.1
Seattle, WA	41/5.2	44/3.9	46/3.5	50/3.4	56/1.7	61/1.5	65/0.8	66/1.1	61/1.6	54/3.2	45/5.3	41/5.9
Spokane, WA	27/2.0	33/1.5	39/1.5	46/1.3	54/1.5	62/1.3	69/0.7	68/0.7	59/0.8	47/1.1	35/2.2	28/2.3
Alaska												
Anchorage	15/0.8	18/0.8	26/0.7	36/0.6	47/0.7	55/1.1	58/1.7	56/2.4	48/2.7	35/2.0	22/1.1	16/1.1
Fairbanks	-10/0.6	-4/0.4	11/0.4	31/0.3	49/0.6	60/1.4	62/1.9	57/1.8	45/1.0	25/0.9	4/0.7	-6/0.8

APPENDIX A CONT.

Region	Jan.	Feb.	Mar.	Apr.	May	June	July	Aug.	Sept.	Oct.	Nov.	Dec.
Hawaii												
Honolulu	73/3.3	73/2.4	74/2.3	76/1.3	77/1.0	79/0.4	80/0.6	81/0.5	81/0.7	80/2.2	77/2.6	74/3.4

Typical Weather Across Canada
Average Daily Temperatures (°C/millimeters, top), (°F/inches, bottom)

City, Territory	Jan.	Feb.	Mar.	Apr.	May	June	July	Aug.	Sept.	Oct.	Nov.	Dec.
Edmonton, Alberta	-15/23	-11/15	-5/18	4/22	11/45	14/82	16/88	15/66	10/41	5/19	-5/17	-12/20
	11/0.9	14/0.6	25/0.7	40/0.9	52/2.0	58/3.5	62/3.5	59/3.6	50/1.5	41/.5	23/0.6	13/1.0
Halifax, Nova Scotia	-6/142	-5/115	-1/128	4/114	10/108	13/97	18/98	18/103	17/69	9/13	3/14	3/144
	23/5.5	23/4.3	30/4.9	40/4.5	49/4.3	59/4.1	65/4.0	65/4.0	59/3.9	48/5.2	39/5.6	28/5.9
Iqaluit, Nunavut	-26/21	-27/18	-23/21	-15/27	-4/26	4/35	7.8/58	7/63	2/52	-5/38	-13/31	-22/20
	-15/0.9	-17/0.7	-10/0.8	6/1.0	24/0.9	39/1.4	46/2.2	45/2.4	36/3.0	23/1.5	9/1.2	-7/0.8
Montreal, Quebec	-10/75	-9/64	-3/73	6/76	13/73	18/83	21/89	20/92	15/89	9/77	2/91	-6/85
	14/3.1	17/2.6	27/30	42/2.9	56/2.9	65/3.4	70/3.6	68/3.6	59/3.5	47/3.1	35/3.6	20/3.4
St. John's, Newfoundland	-5/142	-6/127	-2.7/123	2/112	6/96	11/94	16/88	16/101	12/113	7/145	3/149	-2/145
	24/5.6	23/5.1	27/4.8	35/4.5	43/3.8	52/3.7	60/3.4	60/4.1	54/4.6	45/5.8	37/5.9	29/5.8
Toronto, Ontario	-5/66	-4/57	-1/66	6/66	13/72	18/69	21/73	20/73	16/77	10/62	4/72	-2/68
	23/2.3	24/2.0	33/2.5	44/2.6	55/2.6	65/2.7	70/2.8	68/3.0	61/3.0	50/2.5	39/2.7	28/2.6
Vancouver, British Colombia	3/154	4/128	6/110	9/78	13/61	15/51	17/36	17/42	14/60	11/114	6/172	4/178
	38/5.8	41/4.8	43/4.1	49/2.9	54/2.4	59/2.0	63/1.3	64/1.5	58/2.2	50/4.5	43/6.4	39/6.8
Winnipeg, Manitoba	19/22	-16/19	-8/26	3/34	11/57	17/83	20/75	16/68	12/55	5/36	-6/25	-14/21
	0.2/0.8	6/0.7	20/0.9	39/1.3	63/2.2	62/3.3	68/2.8	65/2.7	54/2.1	42/1.4	23/1.0	7/0.8
Yellowknife, Northwest Territories	-27/14	-24/13	-18/12	-6/10	5/18	13/24	17/35	42/40	7/31	-2/38	-14/24	-24/17
	-16/0.5	-11/0.5	0/4.3	22/0.4	42/0.7	56/0.9	62/1.7	57/1.5	45/1.2	29/1.3	7/0.9	-10/0.7

APPENDIX B
Produce Prevalence by Season

Editor's Note: The following is a general list of which fruits and vegetables are in season when. Growing seasons differ across North America and affect when a particular type of produce is available and for how long. For example, tomatoes, a traditional summer crop in northern climates, are a winter crop in southern locales such as Florida, where summers are too hot for tender plants. Bananas are available all year round but can be grown only in areas with an average year-round temperature of 80°F (27°C).

This list presumes a growing season that begins with a cool, gradually warming spring followed by a hot but not scorching summer, a cool fall, and a cold winter when no outdoor growing can be done. When each season begins and ends varies by location. Seasonal produce in areas with year-round growing climates may differ.

Some of the crops are available all year, but are listed here under only the most popular varieties' peak seasons. Also, different varieties of particular crops thrive best at different times of the year; the Hass variety of avocado, for instance, peaks in summer, but other, less well-known avocado varieties are available throughout the year.

Finally, some crops are listed in more than one season because their growing season extends from one season into another.

Spring

Avocados‡	Asparagus	Lima beans
Bananas	Beans, green or wax	Mustard greens
Blood oranges	Bok choy (late spring)	Onions‡
Cherries (late spring)	Broccoli	Peas, green
Grapefruits	Cabbage	(English/shelling)
Kiwis	Cauliflower	Peas, sugar snap and snow
Lemons	Celeriac	Potatoes, new
Limes	Celery	Potatoes, white
Mangoes	Collard greens	Radishes
Oranges	Fava beans	Rhubarb (late spring)
Pineapples	Fennel (early spring)	Scallions‡
Strawberries (late spring)	Kale (early spring)	Spinach
	Kohlrabi	Squash, summer
Artichokes	Leeks (early spring)	(including zucchini)
Arugula	Lettuces	

‡ depends on variety

Summer

Apples‡ (late summer)
Apricots
Avocados‡ (Hass, the
  most popular variety,
  at peak)
Bananas
Blackberries
Blueberries
Boysenberries
Cherries
Figs (late summer)
Grapes
Lemons (peak)
Limes (peak)
Mangoes
Melons (musk/can-
  taloupe, casaba,
  Crenshaw, honeydew,
  Persian, watermelon)
Mulberries
Nectarines

Oranges
Passion fruit
Peaches
Pears (late summer)
Pineapples
Plums
Pluots
Raspberries (late-summer/
  early-fall peak)
Strawberries
Tomatoes (late-summer/
  early-fall peak)

Arugula
Beans, green or wax
Beets
Cabbage
Carrots
Celery
Corn
Cucumbers

Eggplants
Garlic
Kohlrabi (summer peak)
Lettuces (Belgian endive,
  radicchio)
Lima beans
Okra
Onions‡ (Vidalia, Walla
  Walla, and red at peak)
Peas, green
  (English/shelling)
Peppers, sweet/bell and
  hot/chile
Potatoes, white
Radishes
Rhubarb (early summer)
Summer squash (including
  zucchini)
Swiss chard

‡ depends on variety

Autumn

Apples (most North
  American varieties at peak)
Avocados‡
Bananas
Clementines
Coconuts
Cranberries
Grapefruits
Grapes (peak)
Huckleberries
Figs
Lemons
Limes (early-autumn peak)
Melons (casaba,
  Crenshaw, honeydew,
  Persian; early autumn)
Oranges
Pears
Persimmons (late autumn)
Plums
Pomegranates
Quince

Raspberries (late-
  summer/early-fall peak)
Tomatoes (late-
  summer/early-fall peak)

Artichokes
Beans, green or wax
Beets
Bok choy
Broccoli
Brussels sprouts
Cabbage
Carrots
Cauliflower
Celeriac
Celery
Chard
Collard greens
  (late autumn)
Cucumbers
Eggplants
Fennel (late autumn)

Garlic
Kale
Kohlrabi
Leeks (late autumn)
Lettuces
Okra
Onions‡
Parsnips (late autumn)
Peppers, sweet/bell and
  hot/chile
Potatoes, sweet
Potatoes, white
Pumpkins
Radishes
Rutabagas
Salsify (late autumn)
Scallions‡
Spinach
Squash, winter
Turnips (late autumn)
Yams

‡ depends on variety

Winter

Avocados‡	Quince	Kohlrabi
Bananas	Tangerines	Leeks
Clementines		Lettuces
Coconuts	Beets	Mustard greens
Cranberries	Broccoli	Onions‡
Grapefruits	Brussels sprouts	Parsnips
Kiwis	Cabbage	Potatoes, sweet
Lemons	Cauliflower	Potatoes, white
Limes	Celeriac	Rutabagas
Oranges (winter peak)	Celery	Salsify
Papayas	Collard greens	Squash, winter
Persimmons	Fennel	Turnips
Pomegranates	Kale	

‡ depends on variety

APPENDIX C

Phases of the Moon: 2008 to 2020
Universal Time (UT)

Year	New Moon	First Quarter	Full Moon	Last Quarter
2008	Jan 8 11:37	Jan 15 19:46	Jan 22 13:35	Jan 30 05:03
	Feb 7 03:44	Feb 14 03:34	Feb 21 03:31	Feb 29 02:18
	Mar 7 17:14	Mar 14 10:46	Mar 21 18:40	Mar 29 21:47
	Apr 6 03:55	Apr 12 18:32	Apr 20 10:25	Apr 28 14:12
	May 5 12:18	May 12 03:47	May 20 02:11	May 28 02:57
	Jun 3 19:23	Jun 10 15:04	Jun 18 17:30	Jun 26 12:10
	Jul 3 02:19	Jul 10 04:35	Jul 18 07:59	Jul 25 18:42
	Aug 1 10:13	Aug 8 20:20	Aug 16 21:16	Aug 23 23:50
	Aug 30 19:58	Sep 7 14:04	Sep 15 09:13	Sep 22 05:04
	Sep 29 08:12	Oct 7 09:04	Oct 14 20:03	Oct 21 11:55
	Oct 28 23:14	Nov 6 04:04	Nov 13 06:17	Nov 19 21:31
	Nov 27 16:55	Dec 5 21:26	Dec 12 16:37	Dec 19 10:29
	Dec 27 12:23			
2009		Jan 4 11:56	Jan 11 03:27	Jan 18 02:46
	Jan 26 07:55	Feb 2 23:13	Feb 9 14:49	Feb 16 21:37
	Feb 25 01:35	Mar 4 07:46	Mar 11 02:38	Mar 18 17:47
	Mar 26 16:06	Apr 2 14:34	Apr 9 14:56	Apr 17 13:36
	Apr 25 03:23	May 1 20:44	May 9 04:01	May 17 07.26
	May 24 12:11	May 31 03:22	Jun 7 18:12	Jun 15 22:15
	Jun 22 19:35	Jun 29 11:28	Jul 7 09:21	Jul 15 09:53
	Jul 22 02:35	Jul 28 22:00	Aug 6 00:55	Aug 13 18:55
	Aug 20 10:01	Aug 27 11:42	Sep 4 16:03	Sep 12 02:16
	Sep 18 18:44	Sep 26 04:50	Oct 4 06:10	Oct 11 08:56
	Oct 18 05:33	Oct 26 00:42	Nov 2 19:14	Nov 9 15:56
	Nov 16 19:14	Nov 24 21:39	Dec 2 07:30	Dec 9 00:13
	Dec 16 12:02	Dec 24 17:36	Dec 31 19:13	
2010				Jan 7 10:40
	Jan 15 07:11	Jan 23 10:53	Jan 30 06:18	Feb 5 23:49
	Feb 14 02:51	Feb 22 00:42	Feb 28 16:38	Mar 7 15:42
	Mar 15 21:01	Mar 23 11:00	Mar 30 02:25	Apr 6 09:37
	Apr 14 12:29	Apr 21 18:20	Apr 28 12:18	May 6 04:15
	May 14 01:04	May 20 23:43	May 27 23:07	Jun 4 22:13
	Jun 12 11:15	Jun 19 04:30	Jun 26 11:30	Jul 4 14:35
	Jul 11 19:40	Jul 18 10:11	Jul 26 01:37	Aug 3 04:59
	Aug 10 03:08	Aug 16 18:14	Aug 24 17:05	Sep 1 17:22
	Sep 8 10:30	Sep 15 05:50	Sep 23 09:17	Oct 1 03:52
	Oct 7 18:44	Oct 14 21:27	Oct 23 01:36	Oct 30 12:46
	Nov 6 04:52	Nov 13 16:39	Nov 21 17:27	Nov 28 20:36
	Dec 5 17:36	Dec 13 13:59	Dec 21 08:13	Dec 28 04:18

Year	New Moon	First Quarter	Full Moon	Last Quarter
2011	Jan 4 09:03	Jan 12 11:31	Jan 19 21:21	Jan 26 12:57
	Feb 3 02:31	Feb 11 07:18	Feb 18 08:36	Feb 24 23:26
	Mar 4 20:46	Mar 12 23:45	Mar 19 18:10	Mar 26 12:07
	Apr 3 14:32	Apr 11 12:05	Apr 18 02:44	Apr 25 02:47
	May 3 06:51	May 10 20:33	May 17 11:09	May 24 18:52
	Jun 1 21:03	Jun 9 02:11	Jun 15 20:13	Jun 23 11:48
	Jul 1 08:54	Jul 8 06:29	Jul 15 06:40	Jul 23 05:02
	Jul 30 18:40	Aug 6 11:08	Aug 13 18:58	Aug 21 21:55
	Aug 29 03:04	Sep 4 17:39	Sep 12 09:27	Sep 20 13:39
	Sep 27 11:09	Oct 4 03:15	Oct 12 02:06	Oct 20 03:30
	Oct 26 19:56	Nov 2 16:38	Nov 10 20:16	Nov 18 15:09
	Nov 25 06:10	Dec 2 09:52	Dec 10 14:36	Dec 18 00:48
	Dec 24 18:06			
2012		Jan 1 06:15	Jan 9 07:30	Jan 16 09:08
	Jan 23 07:39	Jan 31 04:10	Feb 7 21:54	Feb 14 17:04
	Feb 21 22:35	Mar 1 01:22	Mar 8 09:40	Mar 15 01:25
	Mar 22 14:37	Mar 30 19:41	Apr 6 19:19	Apr 13 10:50
	Apr 21 07:18	Apr 29 09:58	May 6 03:35	May 12 21:47
	May 20 23:47	May 28 20:16	Jun 4 11:12	Jun 11 10:41
	Jun 19 15:02	Jun 27 03:30	Jul 3 18:52	Jul 11 01:48
	Jul 19 04:24	Jul 26 08:56	Aug 2 03:27	Aug 9 18:55
	Aug 17 15:54	Aug 24 13:54	Aug 31 13:58	Sep 8 13:15
	Sep 16 02:11	Sep 22 19:41	Sep 30 03:19	Oct 8 07:33
	Oct 15 12:02	Oct 22 03:32	Oct 29 19:50	Nov 7 00:36
	Nov 13 22:08	Nov 20 14:31	Nov 28 14:46	Dec 6 15:32
	Dec 13 08:42	Dec 20 05:19	Dec 28 10:21	
2013				Jan 5 03:58
	Jan 11 19:44	Jan 18 23:45	Jan 27 04:38	Feb 3 13:56
	Feb 10 07:20	Feb 17 20:31	Feb 25 20:26	Mar 4 21:53
	Mar 11 19:51	Mar 19 17:27	Mar 27 09:27	Apr 3 04:37
	Apr 10 09:35	Apr 18 12:31	Apr 25 19:57	May 2 11:14
	May 10 00:29	May 18 04:35	May 25 04:25	May 31 18:58
	Jun 8 15:56	Jun 16 17:24	Jun 23 11:32	Jun 30 04:54
	Jul 8 07:14	Jul 16 03:18	Jul 22 18:15	Jul 29 17:43
	Aug 6 21:51	Aug 14 10:56	Aug 21 01:45	Aug 28 09:35
	Sep 5 11:36	Sep 12 17:08	Sep 19 11:13	Sep 27 03:56
	Oct 5 00:35	Oct 11 23:02	Oct 18 23:38	Oct 26 23:41
	Nov 3 12:50	Nov 10 05:57	Nov 17 15:16	Nov 25 19:28
	Dec 3 00:22	Dec 9 15:12	Dec 17 09:28	Dec 25 13:48
2014	Jan 1 11:14	Jan 8 03:39	Jan 16 04:52	Jan 24 05:19
	Jan 30 21:39	Feb 6 19:22	Feb 14 23:53	Feb 22 17:15
	Mar 1 08:00	Mar 8 13:27	Mar 16 17:09	Mar 24 01:46

Year	New Moon	First Quarter	Full Moon	Last Quarter
2014	Mar 30 18:45	Apr 7 08:31	Apr 15 07:42	Apr 22 07:52
Cont.	Apr 29 06:14	May 7 03:15	May 14 19:16	May 21 12:59
	May 28 18:40	Jun 5 20:39	Jun 13 04:11	Jun 19 18:39
	Jun 27 08:09	Jul 5 11:59	Jul 12 11:25	Jul 19 02:08
	Jul 26 22:42	Aug 4 00:50	Aug 10 18:09	Aug 17 12:26
	Aug 25 14:13	Sep 2 11:11	Sep 9 01:38	Sep 16 02:05
	Sep 24 06.14	Oct 1 19:33	Oct 8 10:51	Oct 15 19:12
	Oct 23 21:57	Oct 31 02:48	Nov 6 22:23	Nov 14 15:16
	Nov 22 12:32	Nov 29 10:06	Dec 6 12:27	Dec 14 12:51
	Dec 22 01:36	Dec 28 18:31		
2015			Jan 5 04:53	Jan 13 09:47
	Jan 20 13:14	Jan 27 04:48	Feb 3 23:09	Feb 12 03:50
	Feb 18 23:47	Feb 25 17:14	Mar 5 18:06	Mar 13 17:48
	Mar 20 09:36	Mar 27 07:43	Apr 4 12:06	Apr 12 03:44
	Apr 18 18:57	Apr 25 23:55	May 4 03:42	May 11 10:36
	May 18 04:13	May 25 17:19	Jun 2 16:19	Jun 9 15:42
	Jun 16 14:05	Jun 24 11:03	Jul 2 02:20	Jul 8 20:24
	Jul 16 01:24	Jul 24 04:04	Jul 31 10:43	Aug 7 02:03
	Aug 14 14:54	Aug 22 19:31	Aug 29 18:35	Sep 5 09:54
	Sep 13 06:41	Sep 21 08:59	Sep 28 02:50	Oct 4 21:06
	Oct 13 00:06	Oct 20 20:31	Oct 27 12:05	Nov 3 12:24
	Nov 11 17:47	Nov 19 06:27	Nov 25 22:44	Dec 3 07:40
	Dec 11 10:29	Dec 18 15:14	Dec 25 11:11	
2016				Jan 2 05:30
	Jan 10 01:30	Jan 16 23:26	Jan 24 01:46	Feb 1 3:28
	Feb 8 14:39	Feb 15 07:46	Feb 22 18:20	Mar 1 23:11
	Mar 9 01:54	Mar 15 17:03	Mar 23 12:01	Mar 31 15:17
	Apr 7 11:24	Apr 14 03:59	Apr 22 05:24	Apr 30 03:29
	May 6 19:30	May 13 17:02	May 21 21:15	May 29 12:12
	Jun 5 03:00	Jun 12 08:10	Jun 20 11:02	Jun 27 18:19
	Jul 4 11:01	Jul 12 00:52	Jul 19 22:57	Jul 26 23:00
	Aug 2 20:45	Aug 10 18:21	Aug 18 09:27	Aug 25 03:41
	Sep 1 09:03	Sep 9 11:49	Sep 16 19:05	Sep 23 09:56
	Oct 1 00:12	Oct 9 04:33	Oct 16 04:23	Oct 22 19:14
	Oct 30 17:38	Nov 7 19:51	Nov 14 13:52	Nov 21 08:33
	Nov 29 12:18	Dec 7 09:03	Dec 14 00:06	Dec 21 01:56
	Dec 29 06:53			
2017		Jan 5 19:47	Jan 12 11:34	Jan 19 22:14
	Jan 28 00:07	Feb 4 04:19	Feb 11 00:33	Feb 18 19:33
	Feb 26 14:58	Mar 5 11:32	Mar 12 14:54	Mar 20 15:58
	Mar 28 02:57	Apr 3 18:39	Apr 11 06:08	Apr 19 09:57
	Apr 26 12:16	May 3 02:47	May 10 21:43	May 19 00:33

Year	New Moon	First Quarter	Full Moon	Last Quarter
2017 Cont.	May 25 19:44	Jun 1 12:42	Jun 9 13:10	Jun 17 11:33
	Jun 24 02:31	Jul 1 00:51	Jul 9 04:07	Jul 16 19:26
	Jul 23 09:46	Jul 30 15:23	Aug 7 18:11	Aug 15 01:15
	Aug 21 18:30	Aug 29 08:13	Sep 6 07:03	Sep 13 06:25
	Sep 20 05:30	Sep 28 02:54	Oct 5 18:40	Oct 12 12:25
	Oct 19 19:12	Oct 27 22:22	Nov 4 05:23	Nov 10 20:37
	Nov 18 11:42	Nov 26 17:03	Dec 3 15:47	Dec 10 07:51
	Dec 18 06:31	Dec 26 09:20		
2018			Jan 2 02:24	Jan 8 22:25
	Jan 17 02:17	Jan 24 22:20	Jan 31 13:27	Feb 7 15:54
	Feb 15 21:05	Feb 23 08:09	Mar 2 00:51	Mar 9 11:20
	Mar 17 13:12	Mar 24 15:35	Mar 31 12:37	Apr 8 07:18
	Apr 16 01:57	Apr 22 21:46	Apr 30 00:58	May 8 02:09
	May 15 11:48	May 22 03:49	May 29 14:20	Jun 6 18:32
	Jun 13 19:43	Jun 20 10:51	Jun 28 04:53	Jul 6 07:51
	Jul 13 02:48	Jul 19 19:52	Jul 27 20:20	Aug 4 18:18
	Aug 11 09:58	Aug 18 07:49	Aug 26 11:56	Sep 3 02:37
	Sep 9 18:01	Sep 16 23:15	Sep 25 02:53	Oct 2 09:45
	Oct 9 03:47	Oct 16 18:02	Oct 24 16:45	Oct 31 16:40
	Nov 7 16:02	Nov 15 14:54	Nov 23 05:39	Nov 30 00:19
	Dec 7 07:20	Dec 15 11:49	Dec 22 17:49	Dec 29 09:34
2019	Jan 6 01:28	Jan 14 06:45	Jan 21 05:16	Jan 27 21:10
	Feb 4 21:04	Feb 12 22:26	Feb 19 15:53	Feb 26 11:28
	Mar 6 16:04	Mar 14 10:27	Mar 21 01:43	Mar 28 04:10
	Apr 5 08:50	Apr 12 19:06	Apr 19 11:12	Apr 26 22:18
	May 4 22:45	May 12 01:12	May 18 21:11	May 26 16:33
	Jun 3 10:02	Jun 10 05:59	Jun 17 08:31	Jun 25 09:46
	Jul 2 19:16	Jul 9 10:55	Jul 16 21:38	Jul 25 01:18
	Aug 1 03:12	Aug 7 17:31	Aug 15 12:29	Aug 23 14:56
	Aug 30 10:37	Sep 6 03:10	Sep 14 04:33	Sep 22 02:41
	Sep 28 18:26	Oct 5 16:47	Oct 13 21:08	Oct 21 12:39
	Oct 28 03:38	Nov 4 10:23	Nov 12 13:34	Nov 19 21:11
	Nov 26 15:06	Dec 4 06:58	Dec 12 05:12	Dec 19 04:57
	Dec 26 05:13			
2020		Jan 3 04:45	Jan 10 19:21	Jan 17 12:58
	Jan 24 21:42	Feb 2 01:42	Feb 9 07:33	Feb 15 22:17
	Feb 23 15:32	Mar 2 19:57	Mar 9 17:48	Mar 16 09:34
	Mar 24 09:28	Apr 1 10:21	Apr 8 02:35	Apr 14 22:56
	Apr 23 02:26	Apr 30 20:38	May 7 10:45	May 14 14:03
	May 22 17:39	May 30 03:30	Jun 5 19:12	Jun 13 06:24
	Jun 21 06:41	Jun 28 08:16	Jul 5 04:44	Jul 12 23:29
	Jul 20 17:33	Jul 27 12:32	Aug 3 15:59	Aug 11 16:45

Year	New Moon	First Quarter	Full Moon	Last Quarter
2020	Aug 19 02:41	Aug 25 17:58	Sep 2 05:22	Sep 10 09:26
Cont.	Sep 17 11:00	Sep 24 01:55	Oct 1 21:05	Oct 10 00:39
	Oct 16 19:31	Oct 23 13:23	Oct 31 14:49	Nov 8 13:46
	Nov 15 05:07	Nov 22 04:45	Nov 30 09:30	Dec 8 00:37
	Dec 14 16:17	Dec 21 23:41	Dec 30 03:28	

INDEX